Guide to the Museums of Tusc

GW01425083

Regione Toscana

Guide to the Museums of Tuscany

edited by Donatella Salvestrini

Giunta regionale toscana
Electa

Published by the
Dipartimento istruzione e cultura

Entries by:

Edi Campolmi
Sandra Cosma
Donatella Salvestrini

Assistants to the editor:
Chiara D'Afflitto (Museo Civico of Pistoia) for the historical and art museums
Orazio Paoletti (Cooperativa Co.Idra) for the archaeological museums

Photographs:
Scala

Translations:
Max Waldron

Many thanks are due to the officials of the Tuscan Authorities, the museums' owners and the museum employees for their practical and constant collaboration.
In particular valuable contributions were made by: *Giancarlo Gentilini, Anna Maria Guiducci, Lucy Hunter, Guido Moggi*.

Many thanks for permission to use photographs are also due to *Andrea Bazzechi, Aldo Mela*, the administration of the museums of Tuscany, *the Soprintendenza per i beni storico artistici di Pisa*, the *Soprintendenza per i beni storico artistici di Siena*, the *University of Florence*, for the scientific museums.

This book was produced with the contribution of:

© 1988 by Regione Toscana
Giunta Regionale

Introduction

This book which is the result of the extensive work carried out by the offices of the Tuscan Department of Education and Culture with the collaboration of numerous organizations, associations and individuals working in the cultural sphere is the first complete catalogue of Tuscan museums. Thanks to this effort over several years a precise survey has been born capable of giving an up-to-date overview of the museum situation in Tuscany. The compilation method has indeed always remained faithful to the desire to report all the facts: alongside the museums of international importance the reader will find micro-collections which, though wanting in the structural or organizational fields, are evidence of this region's extreme vitality.

The methodological choice has thus been one of an objective survey which does not take on the significance of an official recognition: the institutional policy of the Regione Toscana is indeed quite different and is to be found in other sources.

The Guide intends to be first and foremost a source of information on the huge and varied nature of the Tuscan museum panorama and an aid to the different categories of use. To this end it has been sought to point out concisely the existing educational services, providing addresses, opening times and definite points of reference.

Even the most absent-minded reader, glancing through the 275 entries collected here which refer to as many different museums and collections, will be struck by the magnificent wealth of this cultural heritage, a concentration unique in the world, the fruit of centuries of history but also of the local administrative policies of the last few decades: there are dozens and dozens of collections and exhibitions which are less than twenty years old. In this field it is up to the Regione Toscana, in full respect for the initiatives of the local organizations, to perform a decisive role of planning and direction in order to avoid the risk that such diversity and richness be transformed into incoherence and disintegration. It is therefore ever more necessary to rethink the organization of the network of Tuscan museums and this Guide to the Museums of Tuscany can provide a valid informational support for this complex task in which the Regione will take on the responsability which falls upon it. The introductory notes which accompany the book constitute an important first step in this direction.

La Giunta regionale Toscana

A Priceless Heritage

To begin with, as an appropriate introduction to a book which aims to give an account of the panorama of museums in Tuscany today, a few numbers. As far as is known the total number of institutions — state, municipal, ecclesiatical, private or semi-private — in the Region is 275, a truly outstanding number without comparison in Italy. Tuscany's pre-eminence emerges more clearly if we compare it with the data from other regions with a similar wealth of historical and cultural heritage and traditions. Thus the whole of Lazio contains 149 museums (including Rome, of course, with the numerous Vatican collections), Lombardy 150, Veneto 111 and Umbria, though a region very rich in art and history, just 61.

Even if we exclude from the total number of Tuscan museums the share accounted for by the city of Florence alone, the confirmation remains of an extraordinary diffusion and deep-rootedness of the museum institution in our Region. Of the Regions similar to our own in terms of history, traditions and economic level, Emilia Romagna is the only one whose total number reaches even near that of Tuscany. But from the discussion which follows I hope it will emerge clearly that at the basis of the diffusion of museums in the cities of Emilia Romagna lie cultural and historico-political motivations at least partly akin to those which have governed the situation in Tuscany. Whatever the case, this situation remains a happy anomaly in the overall national panorama. Let us try to understand why.

I do not believe that in explanation of the number and antiquity of the museums in this region (let us not forget that the Uffizi was, in 1582, the first «modern» museum in the world) it is possible to put forward reverential or eulogistic suggestions, alleging a presumed «uniqueness» or «superiority» of the Tuscan artistic civilization.

That which Giorgio Vasari was allowed to say is no longer permitted to us his heirs, imbued with historicism and relativism, nor would it have any sense today to establish hierarchies of importance and merit among the ancient cultural and artistic centres of Italy. And yet Vasari must be our starting point if we are to understand the singular nature of Tuscany's museum panorama. Indeed, without the Arentine's lucid and haughty historiographical plan, founded on the concept of Tuscan supremacy in the figurative arts, the equally old task we have taken on of collecting and preserving the evidence of that proclaimed supremacy would not have taken shape. The masters and the masterpieces celebrated in the *Lives* started long ago to be appreciated, protected, collected, providing opportunities and material for the future museums. And long ago the Accademia delle Arte del Disegno founded by Vasari started to perform the functions of a regional Superintendence for the protection and appreciation of antique Tuscan art. This is just to point out how much the authority of Vasari's words have contributed to the early formation of a firm and protective historical conscience in the towns and cities of the Grand Duchy, and how much all of this has favoured the growth of a cultural climate suited to the destiny of our museums. There is also another historical reason which cannot is ignored, and that is, as everyone knows, the enlightened policies of the Medicis and the Dukes of Lorraine; policies which have made Florence one of the greatest concentrations of museums in the world encouraging and favouring as a consequence similar aggregations (the original nuclei of the present-day public collections) in the provinces of pre-unification Italy, from Pisa to Siena to Lucca. There are Italian dynasties — sometimes well-deserving in other respects — which have indissolubly linked their memory to the disastrous squandering of extraordinary cultural patrimonies. Thus it is for the Este family of Modena who will never be forgiven for having sold to the Elector Augustus III of Saxony the masterpieces in the family's collections, today the pride of the Gemäldegalerie in Dresden; thus it is too for the Gonzaga family of Mantua on which weighs the shame of having passed to King Charles of England perhaps the most splendid collection of paintings in Europe packed with works by Mantegna, Giambellino, Correggio, Rubens and Caravaggio. To the Medici family of Florence, on the other hand, eternal gratitude is due by all not just for the quality and intelligence of their collecting, but above all for the famous Convention of 1743 by which Anna Maria Ludovica de' Medici, the last surviving member of a dynasty destined to die with her, ceded to the State and the city of Florence in perpetuity the entire Medici artistic patrimony; that is to say the greatest and most precious part which is today preserved in the State museums of Florence. In the same years in which another Italian sovereign, Duke Francesco III of Modena, was transferring abroad the cream of his family's art collection (1745), in Florence the political powers were formally undertaking to ensure that «... all the furniture, effects and treasures in the inheritance [...] such as galleries, paintings, statues, libr-

aries, jewels and other precious objects such as holy relics, reliquaries and their ornaments from the chapel of the royal palace...» should pass to the authority of the Grand Duke of Lorraine and his heirs, with the explicit clause that «it is for the ornament of the State, for use by the public and to stimulate the curiosity of travellers, and none of it shall be transferred and removed from the capital and the State».
Since in history everything follows from everything else, there is no doubt that museum culture and practice in Florence and Tuscany owe much to that providential decision. Not only because it has by law prevented transfers and the dispersals which would otherwise be more than likely, but also because it has contributed to the clear affirmation in Tuscany of certain concepts which have remained unchanged since then and which still today are the unrenounceable basis of our modern idea of the museum.
The concept, that is, of a prestigious site for the whole community (the «ornament of the State»), as an opportunity for spiritual growth and educational advancement (the «public use») and lastly as a valuable resource also from the economic point of view («to stimulate the curiosity of travellers»). If one adds the concept of the patrimony as inseparable from the geographical and cultural environment which has produced it and from the places which have sheltered it over the centuries (with the consequent normative – juridical principle that this patrimony cannot be moved physically), we can say that by half way through the 18th century and thanks principally to the Electress Palatine Anna Maria Ludiovica de' Medici, Florence and Tuscany were in the forefront in Italy, and in an altogether modern position in the field of museology.
Finally, a third and fundamental element which must be borne in mind in running through the history of the museum in Tuscany is represented by the decisive action performed in the 19th century by a civic culture which was by tradition active but was above all rekindled in that period by liberal and progressive influences.
The 19th century civic museum — the rich network of minor museums which still today is spread over the whole of central Northern Italy, a real and true supporting structure underpinning local conservation — was born and consolidated mainly by the breaking up of the ecclesiastical patrimony following the Siccardi laws of 1866, laws which the clerical community hurried to declare «subversive». This is all well known. And it is also known that the civic museum born in the

years following the unification of Italy, more than an instrument of mere preservation, wanted to be an agglomeration of memories, a didactic foundation, the proud affirmation of local character and in addition an unrenounceable starting point for the civilization of the new Italy, for the lay and progressive plan which supported and gave direction to the ideals of the *élites* of the Risorgimento. The studies carried out by Andrea Emiliani on the history of the Italian museum in the modern age clarify these aspects of the 19th century local museum and we would refer the reader to his works (see in particular A. Emiliani, *Il Museo laboratorio della storia*, in *Capire l'Italia. I Musei*, published by the Touring Club Italiano, Milan 1980, pp. 19 and seg.).

In this respect the history of the civic museum in Tuscany in the 19th century is comparable to what happened in the same period in regions with similar civil traditions and political situation, such as Lombardy and in particular Emilia Romagna. The works of art confiscated from suppressed religious orders, the relics which had survived the clearing and modernization of the historic town centres were placed in museums with the intention of providing reminders of past glories and an opportunity for stimulus and as an example for the future destiny of the local and national homeland. The phenomenon in Tuscany takes on, however, peculiar characteristics and the Romantic-Risorgimento ideals planted in the fertile ground of an older and more informed sensitivity to museums and preservation produced results of remarkable value. One example will tell. The museum of the Collegiate Church of St. Andrew in Empoli was founded in 1859 as an ecclesiastical museum, that is recognized as the property of and administered by the parish priest of Empoli, though having all the characteristics of a civic museum in that it collected and collects the historical and artistic treasures of the city and the surrounding area, whether they be of religious origin, coming from churches and chapels in the vicariate, or of lay origin, the storehouses of the important families of Empoli. And yet the museum was founded under the provisional government of Tuscany, and its promoter and financer was the lawyer Vincenzo Salvagnoli, at that time Minister for Religious Affairs, and member of an old Empoli family whose members lie in a chapel in the Collegiate Church. As students of the Risorgimento well know, Salvagnoli was anything but a bigot. A liberal of rigorous principles, an earnest supporter of the Church's autonomy from the State he had in fact the reputation of an intransigent anti-clerical. While he was Minister for Religious Affairs he risked a breach with the Archbishop of Florence for having wanted to support the right of worship and proselytism for Protestants in Florence, while his parliamentary bill for the abolition of the 1851 Concordat between Tuscany and the Holy See and the even more radical bill on the abolition of the feudal emphyteuses dominated by the ecclesiastical mortmain earned him the hostility of the moderate sections of the same provisional government. And yet this champion of the 19th century laity did not hesitate to accord to the local church the right to property and to the administration of the artistic heritage which had accumulated over the centuries around and for the church.

During a period in which the local museums were being fast set up with the artistic treasures confiscated from the ecclesiastical organizations — and hence at the price of damaging upheavals, often inappropriate transfers of works and serious and widespread dispersions — a similar result (that is the foundation of a local museum) was reached in Empoli in full agreement with the religious authorities and, above all, without removing the patrimony from its historical home.

Not that events have always proceeded in this way in Tuscany. What with the Lorraine suppressions of 1785, the Napoleonic suppressions of 1810 and finally the «subversive» law of 1866 the age of enligtenment and progress steam-rollered into the Tuscan artistic patrimony throwing it into confusion and scattering precious collections and unique treasures. The museum of Santa Maria Novella in Florence, opened in 1983, together with its accompanying catalogue clearly documents the damage which the 19th century suppressions caused to the heart of a conventual complex which was among the most illustrious and artisticaly endowed in Europe. Notwithstanding this, Tuscany boasts numerous examples of cases where the local museum of 19th century foundation succeeded in rescuing in time and in selecting with sensitivity the truly important evidence of the town's artistic history, organizing it along non-provincial scientific and didactic lines. It is enough to cite the municipal museum of San Gimignano, founded in 1852, whose picture-gallery packed with masterpieces from the most important periods of art history from works by Memmo di Filippuccio to those of Filippino Lippi can be considered among the most well-endowed public collections in the whole of Tuscany. Or the gallery of the Palazzo Pretorio in Prato founded in 1858, so rich in works of the highest quality that only comparison with the major state museums forces us to consider it as «minor». And one could mention still more examples, from the Museo Civico in Montepulciano (founded in 1861) to the Museo dell'Opera del Duomo in Siena (founded in 1870) to the Museo dell'Opera del Duomo in Florence opened in 1891 and already considered at that time by scholars the world over as an extraordinary collection of sculpture and the applied arts of the Tuscan Renaissance, worthy to stand beside the Bargello.

To speak about Tuscan museums naturally means being drawn into a predictable and inevitable discussion regarding the special position which Florence enjoys. With its 64 museum collections Florence is an admirable *monstruum* with few if any equals in the world. We are talking of a museum network spread throughout the city, involving the highest administrative costs, number of staff and pressures of visitors in the whole of Italy. It is enough to think that the Florentine state institutions alone (that is to say excluding such popular museums as Palazzo Vecchio or the Museo dell'Opera del Duomo which have a different legal status) had 3,017,168 visitors in 1985 (in 1965 the number was 1,246,935: an increase of almost 300 per cent in twenty years). This is not the place to talk about the costs and risks of mass tourism which has grown overwhelmingly in recent times, nor of the ever more pressing and sometimes dramatic problems which must be faced by those — guardians or politicians — who are called to combine the growth in demand with the rigidity of the unchangeable as well as extremely fragile museum structures. What is certain is that the Florentine institutions as a whole constitute the most demanding testing ground of modern museology, a science which the recent and unforeseen variable of enjoyment by a mass public forces us to rethink from first principles. Not for nothing when we talk in Italy of restrictive measures in the use or enjoyment of cultural treasures (the so-called «limited numbers») or of new technical and administrative solutions (the Soprintendenze appointed for the exclusive management of the great public collections) or again laws and special projects, one cannot but refer to Florence's museums, to their apparently insoluble problems and to the difficulty of administrating them. On the other hand what characterizes the Florentine museums is not just their size and administrative aspects. It is also a question of their extraordinary variety. What other city has transformed the refectories of former convents into a series of museums? And where else exists a collection comparable to the Opificio delle Pietre Dure, the former Medicean semi-precious gem workshop still alive and well today and active as a restoration workshop? A collection which is at once a document of industrial archaeology, a valuable mineralogy collection, a shining example of the art of the State in its most refined incarnation. In what other major town in Italy or Europe is brought together such an outstanding group of museums, both in terms of quality and quantity, linked to the names of famous collectors, antiquarians and art historians? And it is enough to list the names of Bardini, Horne, Stibbert, Davanzati, the Contini Bonacossi collections, Salvatore Romano, Alberto Della Ragione, the collections of the Bedrenson Foundation and the Longhi Foundation. Not to mention the monograph museums, those dedicated to the name and memory of one artist, for instance the Museum of San Marco or Casa Buonarroti, specialist museums (the Museo degli Argenti, delle Porcellane and delle Carrozze museum in the Palazzo Pitti complex, Gabinetto dei disegni e delle stampe in the Uffizi, the plaster casts in the Istituto Statale d'Arte, the antique musical instruments in the Cherubini Museum), not to mention the excellent and generally unknown world of the scientific museums. Not everyone knows, for example, that the public collections in zoology, paleontology, mineralogy and lithology which are preserved in Florence are altogether among the most outstanding and valuable in the world. Now, to say all of this (and whoever wants to know more about the fascinating history and difficult present of Florence's museum heritage can profitably turn to the beautiful catalogue *La Città degli Uffizi* published in 1982) means also to say that the administration of Florence's museums is such a complex problem, involves such numerous and varied capacities and demands such extensive resources that it far transcends the regional dimension. The museums of Florence, indipendent of their legal or ownership status, are a national concern, just as the cultural values which they preserve and protect are of national or rather supranational importance. It would nevertheless be a great mistake to create a break between the museums in Florence and those in the chief towns of the various provinces and the territory of the whole Region. Almost everywhere in Italy and above all in Tuscany the culture of the provincial centres has

grown in a harmonious even when dialectic osmotic relationship with the minor cities and the surrounding territory; and the museums — which are the memory and symbol of the town — have always sought to represent more the unity of a fundamentally common history than the diversity (even when critically acknowledged or rather consciously turned to advantage) of varied fates and intertwined destinies. On close study a fraternal appearance links the Tribuna of the Uffizi to the Museo Civico of Borgo San Sepolcro and both of them are in some way related to the famous basilica of Florence, the ancient rural church of the Mugello and of the Montagna Pistoiese.
The museum here in Florence (to our great good fortune) is also outside the museums. It is a useful piece of advice for whoever wants to use this guide to its best advantage but it is definitely a useful piece of advice also for whoever, like the authors of the guide, live and work within the museums.

ANTONIO PAOLUCCI

Soprintendente per i beni artistici e storici delle province di Firenze e Pistoia.

Museums in Tuscany: Problems and Hypotheses

The truly remarkable number of museums in Tuscany allows us, a least in theory, to relate them in terms of their content and access so as to shape — almost made to measure — cultural routes of great quality and importance. National museum and those run by local organizations, university museums, church-owned museums and those set up by foundations, institutes and private individuals possess a widely varying yet linked heritage comprising historical and artistic testimony of every sort and from every period. Prehistory and protohistory, archaeology and ethnography, the history of science and culture, the figurative and applied arts, the treasures of natural history, excavations and sites. What is missing from this almost perfect spread? And yet, for all this abundance, notwithstanding often very high standards of quality, among the finest in the world, and in spite of the additional educational importance which often accompanies them (and which once again is of exceptional value), their combined role is not up to what one would expect.

In Tuscany there are so many of the fixed sites decreed by the museum pilgrimage route as among the most important of the «things-to-be-seen», with a considerable total number of visitors which in itself can cause problems: there is certainly no shortage of visitors from abroad, indeed they arrive in such numbers that they often throw into crisis and sometimes endanger both the structures and the contents. But these are just particular cases, while dozens and dozens of other museums, some important, though not 'enjoying' the similar status of 'not-to-be-missed' sites, remain neglected or never achieve more than a very limited fame, in more than a few cases granted to guests from abroad. Thus there exists in Tuscany a diffuse and accessible collection of museums which is in no way organized into a network even on the level of affinities and specializations. I personally believe neither in union imposed from above nor dependent on choices which are perhaps more 'collegial' but vitiated by the abstraction of some philosophy of the moment, but I'am nevertheless convinced that the situation in Tuscany is such as to demand reflection and intervention in the short and medium term to bring it out of its occasionally 'historical' contradictions and limitations, and taking care to avoid starting from the top (as, in my humble opinion, it has been sought to do).

Looking through the lists of the diverse situations of the museums in the Region, what strikes one above all is their lack of scientific and management organization, not excluding that of the National museums. There are great museums with insufficient personnel, both on the management and the administrative levels; in the case of local museums this state of affairs is quite typical, and this consideration alone is enough to make clear the impossibility not of launching but even as much as simply guaranteeing the survival of the treasures currently in collections. The same state-level administration does not manage to find for research and intervention to preserve its own treasures and those for which it is responsible technical and practical methods and structures adequate to the often pressing needs of this immense heritage; the situation on local and private levels is, if possible, in an even worse state. It is thus of primary importance to ensure throughout an adequate and consistent level of preservation and management in our museums: suitable scientific and administrative structures, the search for and improvement of the existing collaboration, guarantees of involvement and the preparation and training of personnel.

It is clear that such a programme — and many of its tasks are already performed by various offices — can neither accept nor leave things as they are: cross-feeding, possible and necessary correlations, common projects, the same operational limitations will in some cases also bring about a rethinking of the appropriateness of retaining (if only on paper, as happens in some cases) some 'museum situations' which lack a suitable hinterland and concrete and permanent operational conditions. I am referring in the first instance to the somewhat ambiguously termed museums 'of local interest' to which the regional government of Tuscany must officially and with urgent priority address itself when it talks of its duty towards the museums in its territory. And moreover, given the all too well known financial difficulties, this criterion too will have to be refined with the progressive abolition of very many temporary posts. It is reasonable to accept that the major regional organization should give a decisive initial boost to a system of museum administration which it deems interesting, but it is unthinkable that this organization should then have to bear a burden which in some areas becomes exclusive.

Here too, value should be given to the role which the existing or new museum structure could play in a very well-defined area of the Region's own choice of cultural policy. Certainly, the first question could be

whether the Regional government as an institution should have a cultural policy, but I firmly believe that the answer is yes; it is enough to think of its responsibility in marking out the general lines of growth which need to be set up and reinforced within Tuscany, and thus of the directly cultural interrelations which this implies (permanent educational roles, research, professional training, to mention just a few). Museum organization, even the museums themselves, will have to be involved in these undertakings, some of which already form part of their task, and in return will have to be assisted in the fields of presentation, promotion and educational productivity in proportion to their ability if they are to be effective and proven. This book is directed above all at the general public, and many readers will perhaps consider these demands irrelevant to the subject of 'museums'. I believe, however, that no more than one visit to a few examples of actual Tuscan museums will lead the observer to realize — and will prove to him — that behind what he sees (or what is lacking) there are some complex reasons which he too as a citizen — not necessarily of Tuscany — must participate in clarifying, and difficulties which he too can help to solve. For instance, by using the museum in an original and different way without the usual limitations, or by reasonably requesting certain services, or by seeking contemporary standards of presentation (which does not necessarily mean experimental or sophisticated). A school group, a society, a research team, anyone interested in learning about or studying the historical and artistic testimony preserved there can trace, starting from the information provided in the pages of this book, their own route of visits and in a certain sense can create their own 'museum network' to follow in order to understand and elaborate their contents; examination on site will allow them to verify their premises or to react against them, and there is no doubt that by virtue of a conscious use of what is available the visitor will be able to stimulate a wider and more general awareness of museums.
It is not possible to provide here a 'prospectus' of specific museum routes to be then checked by adjusting them to fit one's own requirements, but it will certainly not be difficult to catch glimpses of various possibilities by referring to the general list. One can, however, certainly make some suggestions drawn from the less visited museums but which nevertheless deserve much greater attention. An archaeological itinerary, for instance, could link the

Pontremoli museums with their stelae-statues, the one in Fiesole containing Etruscan and Roman material, the Museo Archeologico Nazionale in Chiusi with its Greek exhibits, the Guarnacci museum in Volterra which has a notable Etruscan section, or the museum of the Accademia Etrusca in Cortona with its Etruscan, Roman and Egyptian material. Among the Natural History museums one can mention the university museums of Calci in the Province of Pisa, of the Accademia dei Fisiocritici in Siena and of the Liceo Macchiavelli in Lucca; the last is also important for its collection of scientific instruments, as are the Istituto Salvemini in Florence and the Cicognini in Prato. As for anthropology one should without doubt suggest the great Museo Nazionale di Antropologia ed Etnologia again in Florence, very little known by the general public outside the professional scholastic field, while of the ethnographical museums (in practice museums of peasant culture), at least those in Castiglione Garfagnana, in Villafranca Lunigiana and in Alberese (in preparation) should be seen. Of the museums under Church management, the most interesting are the Cathedral Museums of Arezzo and Pisa, as well as at least the museum in the Collegiate Church of St. Agatha in Asciano, the Cathedral Museum of St. Zeno in Pistoia and that of the Basilica of St. Mary in Impruneta. The 'multiple' museum are many and I will limit myself here to mentioning only three: the Museum of St. Matthew's in Pisa, the Stibbert museum in Florence and the Museo Civico in Pistoia; as for a Province with an overall well-organised series of 'local' museums, I believe that those in the Province of Arezzo can be justly highlighted.

The first key to the reading of a museum as a whole can be one which seeks to understand its history: its creation, exhibits and activities; and from this can spring an opinion on the suitability of the museum's structure. There are in fact museum sites which seem immediately incongrous, with contents whose standard is below the minimum level necessary: even with the best will that collection could never really be valuable. In some cases, reference is made to the opportunity of offering — for example to local school classes — at least a bit of material coming from their own area, as testimony of their own past. I am not personally convinced of the evocative value of the anonymous fragment (which while it may speak volumes to the specialist remains meaningless to the general observer), and I believe that this doubtful value contributes to the growth of 'false information' which is already too widespread. The fact that these exhibitions take place in good faith does not lessen their marginalising consequences. In these cases it would be more effective for the education department of a Council in possession of the objects to produce or to commission from a research group a good videocassette which could perform an historical and educational role and which could perhaps also better illuminate the objects preserved locally.

Another essential aspect of a museum is its exhibition format: the rooms and their lighting, the organisation of space, the types and techniques of display (the old glass cases, but possibly also dioramas, diagrams and working models). Above all it must be said that in the great majority of cases our museums, and not just those in Tuscany, are set up in buildings that were not designed as such, many of which have considerable in historical or artistic value, with the consequent demands of preservation also of the spatial proportions and the limitations which this imposes. In rare cases it is precisely their actual layout, their exhibition fittings, the relationship between the material preserved there and the classification of the spaces which constitutes the determining value: noone would think — I hope — to change them in the name of some mistaken concept of modernization, since they provide detailed and unique testimony of cultural periods which would otherwise be lost. In the great maiority, however, this initial unity has been lost over time, or is not such as to constitute a qualitative term of reference. It is thus necessary to intervene in order to encourage a contemporary rethinking of the museum's contents, an examination of their essential communication and the message which can be drawn from it, and of their systems of presentation which should not be static and ceremonial or, worse, pseudosacred.

Here, however, we are simultaneously touching on many delicate points, apart from that of the search for and distribution of finances. Above all are we sure that the material preserved by the museums is sufficiently well-known and researched? For without knowledge there can be no intervention. The enormous majority of our museums — even those of the highest level — possess only 'inventories' of their material, which do no more than give 'institutional' information on the various pieces: a number in a series, a more or less summary description, measurements (not always complete) and some supposition as to chronology and/or origin; attributions are rare, even for important objects. What is lacking is effective cataloguing, with the necessary scientific and comparative apparatus, and under these conditions it can only work if the rearrangement of the material can count on specialists in the particular fields, since they alone will be able to work out and present new proposals for the contents and the messages to be drawn from them. From this point of view, it really is a serious fault that in the past, and not just the distant past, while there has been broad and full recognition of these problems, neither the university structures (in general) nor those of the State (again in general) nor any others have posed themselves the problem of a complete cataloguing of our cultural treasure. What has been done is little in comparison to what needs to be done, and these deficiencies are to be attributed not to individual institutions but to the mistaken policy towards our cultural treasures, up to now undertaken centrally, and the closed nature of academic circles; nor, it is true to say, have other institutions or organizations been able to promote the specialist professional training which ought to be sought always, necessarily, supported by the available expert advice. I do not mean that without cataloguing we will never have anything more than an uncommunicative label; it is nevertheless certain that a system of flexible permanent education suited to various levels of approach and understanding clearly cannot be born in a vacuum or entrusted to museum staff who are not specialists in the particular field (not forgetting that in many cases we have 'general museums' displaying a whole range of material: from furniture to ivory, from a tapestry to an archaeological relic from religious treasures to costumes, from a detached fresco to a medieval manuscript). The shortcomings regarding preparation in the so-called 'minor arts' have distant roots, in large part the fruit of the old idealism and not even overcome by the more recent studies of 'material culture'; and yet this specialization (which can only follow basic historical-artistic training) must be pursued, and I ask myself if the time is not ripe to promote it with suitable means and in suitable forms; without this, apart from its general appropriateness, the various 'layering' operations cannot but miss their target.

Another problem is that of the display of material when the choice has been defined and the complex of fundamental interrelationships has been clarified. The idea that the museum should be 'created' by a technical office (or by the museum administration in collaboration with it) can only rarely lead to a satisfactory result: when the office is particularly sensitive and experienced in the theme, and works in conjunction with an administration with particular elaborative gifts. In general this is not the case, but the damage can be even greater when an administrator without experience of museums comes on the scene: he may be worthy, but will often tend to superimpose his solution onto the material. There is no shortage of examples both in Italy and abroad, whereas good museum design, just as a good suit, should stand out as little as possible, in the sense that it should appear only as a structural element in the museum's overall style, an element by virtue of which the material should be helped to stand out and not become a pretext for visual bantering which overwhelms it in wanting to exalt it. The relationship between the jobs of scientific preparation and museum organization is decisive, even though there is obviously a difference between setting up a small exhibition section and getting to grips with the restructuring of a large complex. In Tuscany there is no shortage of interesting examples under different headings: such as the redevelopment of the Uffizi Tribuna, the municipal and ecclesiastical system in Pistoia, the restoration of the Stibbert.

Collaboration between specialists and planners (and, if appropriate, experts in visual communications) is indispensable.

One of the problems of the relationship which exists between the public and the museum is caused by the different interests which draw eventual visitors, and by the different approach taken by each of them. It is impossible to imagine all the possibilities, just as it would be a mistake to try to homologize the possible answers on the basis of a presumed 'average request' by a just as non-existent 'average visitor'. I am starting here too from a given fact: the public is by no means anonymous, and is hungry for all the information which it is able to understand; and when I use the term 'public' I make no exceptions as regards age, social background, level of formal education or specialized preparation.

But if this is how things stand, then in perspective it is necessary to diversify widely the overall presentation and communication of museums, and perhaps to start to modify our habitual response to the museum. For example, often the 'didactic approach' (a term which I consider restrictive) consists in a visit which the teacher leads along a path traced by his own interpretation of the museum, sometimes, though not always, supported by material prepared by the museum itself. It seems to me that it would be better to work in advance with the teachers in a direct and very detailed way, pehaps arranged by theme if that is necessary, in such a way as to provide a comparison between the educational plan of the teacher and suitable answers and proposals which can spring from the museum's comprehensive knowledge. In other areas it will be necessary for the museum itself to organise an internal 'education department' (not 'didactic') which should produce above all more complex material (hence less filing-cards and more cassettes, less concern for the singular and more for elements of relation, less reduction to the trivial and more information) which should also express as many diverse references as possible.

Today this is done very little, even in those institutions which work well, whereas it is very important to propose a variety of possible approaches and interpretations of the material presented. This means, however, also modifying the museum's nature, projecting it externally to a greater degree in order to find suitable communication channels, or in order to create them (and in this respect, for example, I believe in the formation of 'networks' of interrelated museums with similar material and approach, or between their corresponding sections). In this perspective I believe that the use of computerised information banks, above all for specific scientific research purposes where it has methodological value and general correlation is to be recommended; here too thought should be given to the necessary integration between highly specialised activities and their 'educational' uses.

These considerations may seem out of place, but everyone by now is aware on the one side of the 'consumption' of the higher quality and more indispensable museums throughout the world and on the other the growing importance of 'targeted' communication.

The more the need for knowledge widens, the less can that knowledge be 'direct' and 'immediate', also because the demand for information will become more complex. In this case it will be necessary to have readily available a reserve of prepared or partly prepared material with which it will be possible to work even before the direct experience, as a personal approach (and the 'approach towards the museum' is today but a specific case of the 'approach towards knowledge' suited to the speed of contemporary

cultural processes). In other words, in order to express itself as fully as possible, the museum too will have to be able to project itself well to the outside world.
A final consideration, anything but technical, concerns the problems of the security of people and objects. The apparatus of the vast majority of Tuscan — and Italian — museums is to say the least inadequate. If the atmospheric control systems are to be looked at with great care, and the climatisation of the various spaces and/or cabinets is to be considered case by case, an element such as the lighting system is not to be ignored. Many of the control systems are not up to standard, and in some cases — where it is not provided — the museums should be closed at least temporarily.
The same goes for security and fire alarm systems, for it is no longer possible to conceive of a museum without them.
Here, however, a further question arises, since in many cases the fire protection demanded by law is very difficult to apply to the letter; for some time now practical regulations covering historically or architecturally valued buildings which house museums, archives and libraries have been awaited, but so far nothing has been forthcoming; and it is unthinkable that absurd solutions (such as sprinkler systems) should be imposed on artistic environments full of works of art, and just as unthinkable to close those museums for that reason. Given that it is clear that every effort should be made — including very extensive financial effort — to put right the various situations (as has already been done in some cases and is being done in others), when the museum is in an historic building they will doubtless be corrected only by establishing an hourly quota of visitors, as already occurs in many cases abroad. This will require — once again — the 'external' proposal already mentioned in another context, but above all the extension of the afternoon and evening opening hours, and hence an increase in administrative and custodial staff, and hence the financial burden carried by the sector (lighting, too, costs money). If we move towards solutions of this type, which are indispensable in certain cases, it will be necessary too for there to be a much closer relationship between the museum and the community outside, and for the setting up of an organization aside from the actual museum work to increase group visits, to reach more of the possible interested parties. In any case, the 'knock-on benefit'

can no longer restrict itself to the number of visitors, but must aim at quality in cultural production and in the widening of its influence on the developed system of 'permanent education'.

LIONELLO G. BOCCIA

Soprintendente Museo Stibbert

Editor's note

The research on Tuscan museums was completed in the winter of 1987-1988. It includes all the museums, both private and public collections, spread throughout the region, including some which, for various reasons, are temporarily closed and which will shortly open their doors. This study was made possible only thanks to the valuable collaboration offered by those who work in the sector. The guide offers a snapshot, the clearest and most up-to-date possible, of the panorama of museums in the region. Some facts may, however, have been missed or some information become outdated; it must be remembered that we have before us a continually alterring situation with sometimes unforeseen changes: such is the case, for example, with the opening hours. Under each entry the reader will find a set of essential pieces of information to understand the type and organization of the museum: historical outlines on the collection, information on the material, an indication of the «pieces» of greatest historical, artistic or scientific significance. To these notes is added information on the cultural activities and educational services, the archives and internal libraries with the respective conditions for consultation of the material held. For each museum a concise bibliography is provided with suggestions for further reading or study.
For clarity in the explanations the following symbols have been used:

Objects, works and collections of historical, artistic and scientific interest

Size: small from 0 to 2000 sq. ft., medium from 2000 sq. ft. to 5000 sq. ft., large over 5000 sq. ft.

Opening times

Entrance

Accessibility for handicapped people

Permission to take photographs

Guided visits and educational services

Library, photograph library, archive, workshops

Cultural activities

Periodicals published by the museum, bibliography

Museo dell'Alta Valle del Tevere

52031 Anghiari (AR)
Piazza Mameli, 16
Tel. 0575/788001

The museum, set up in 1975 by the Soprintendenza of Arezzo contains various works, architectural fragments, sculptures, detached frescoes, paintings and a group of objects connected with popular life and traditions in the Val Tiberina, from churches and other buildings in Anghiari. In the number and variety of the items exhibited it represents a very important istitution of great local and artistic interest. It is housed in the splendid Palazzo Taglieschi which has seen extensive restoration work over the last thirty years to restore it to its original design.

Large

Winter, from 1st October to 28th February: weekdays 9 a.m.-2 p.m.; Sundays and public holidays 9 a.m.-1,30 p.m.

Summer, from 1st March to 30th September: weekdays 9 a.m.-7 p.m.; Sundays and public holidays 9 a.m.-1.30 p.m.

Free

♿
No access

📷
By arrangement

Architectural fragments and objects in stone (12th-18th C.).

Sculpures in wood from the 13th-16th C. (*Madonna and Child* by I. della Quercia). Important works in glazed terracotta (Altar-piece with *Adoration of the Magi* from the studio of A. della Robbia and lunette with *Samaritan at the well* by B. Buglioni).

Collection of religious art and altar-hangings (17th-18th C.). Furniture (15th-16th C.). Paintings on wood and canvas from the 16th-17th C. by G.A. Sogliani, J. Vignali, M. Rosselli.

Museo della Confraternita di Misericordia

Via Francesco Nenci
52031 Anghiari (AR)
Tel. 0575/89516-789577

Opened in 1975, it contains a small collection of objects and documents relating to the history and activities of the Confraternity: archival documents, objects and vestments used by the Misericordia over the ages, relics, ex-votos and religious objects donated over the ages. It is housed in several rooms in the society's headquarters, the former Badia building in the historical centre of Anghiari. Visits are by arrangement.

Galleria Comunale d'Arte Contemporanea

52100 Arezzo
Corso Italia, 113
Tel. 0575/27712

Since its opening in 1965 it has formed an extensive collection of contemporary art; in 1976 a permanent exhibition of Italian art from the 1950's to the present day was opened. The gallery performs an important informative and educational role by virtue of numerous temporary exhibitions. It is housed in various rooms of the Palazzo Guillichini, though its transfer has been planned for some time.

Medium

Weekdays 9 a.m.-1 p.m.; closed on Sundays

Free

Contemporary paintings, sculptures, ceramics and prints; works by artists active between the wars: C. Levi, V. Ciardo, F. Menzio, C. Cagli, O. Tamburi, E. Paulucci, Q. Martini; works by post-war artists: S. Vacchi, U. Attardi, R. Vespignani, A. Gianquinto, E. Calabria, G. Nativi, A. De Stefano, G. De Gregorio, S. Loffredo, R. Margonari and others. Section dedicated to the sculptures and drawings of V. Venturi.

No access

Yes

Guided visits on request

Contemporary art exhibitions arranged annually

Sergio Vacchi: The sack of Rome

Museo Archeologico Statale Gaio Cilnio Mecenate

52100 Arezzo
Via Margaritone, 10
Tel. 0575/20882

Large

Weekdays 9 a.m.-2 p.m., Sundays and public holidays 9 a.m.-1 p.m.; closed on Mondays

Entrance fee

Partially accessible

By arrangement

Portrait of Agrippa (?)

Opened in 1934 and housed in the rooms of the former Olivetan convent of St. Bernardo (14th C.) the museum, which was damaged during the Second World War, was reopened in 1951 and came under state control in 1957. It was recently restored and modernized. Originally made up of the collections of the Lay Fraternity, it was enriched by various donations among which the notable collection of the archaeologist Gamurrini who was appointed to the post of museum administrator in 1892. It also contains a variety of archaeological material from excavations in the city and the surroundings. Today it contains a vast patrimony and constitutes an essential reference point for the archaeology of the territory of Arezzo.

Prehistoric material dating from the Paleolithic period to the Bronze Age (an interesting costume attributed to the period of Rinaldone, from the area of Cortona). Impasto pottery from the early Iron Age. Attic pottery (including a *black-figured amphora* by the painter Affettato, the famous *krater*, with spiral decoration by Euphronios with Amazzonomachia and an *amphora with Penelope and Ippodamia* from the school of the painter of Dinos); bucchero mainly from Chiusi; Etruscan red-figured pottery; black-glazed pottery; representative selection of the important Aretine production of *sealed pottery*. Chiusine sculptures from the 6th-5th C. B.C. (sphinx, cippus).

Architectural terracotta, including a sima from Piazza San Jacopo (second quarter of the 5th C. B.C.) and Hellenistic material from Via della Societa Operaia and from Castelsecco. Tools and small bronzes from the Etruscan and Roman periods, represented by numerous statues of divinities, religious objects, grotesque figures, animals etc. Roman sculptures (including a bust possibly portraying *Agrippa*, a bust of *Livia*, an altar with scenes from the foundation of Rome, fragments of sarcophagi).
Tessera and black and white floor mosaics with Neptune's chariot and geometrical designs. Grave-goods from Roman Arezzo and the territory (of particular note the material recovered from a tomb in Apulia).

Etruscan and Roman glass: worthy of particular attention is a rare example of *glass with a portrait of man* (3rd C. A.D.).

P. Bocci Pacini, S. Nocentini Sbolci, *Museo nazionale archeologico di Arezzo. Catalogo delle sculture romane*, Rome 1983.

Photocopies and printed information sheets on the museum available to schools on request

Occasional conferences and exhibitions

Il Museo archeologico nazionale G.C. Mecenate in Arezzo, by various authors, Florence 1987.

Cups in Aretine pottery

Museo di Casa Vasari

52100 Arezzo
Via XX Settembre, 55
Tel. 0575/20295

Medium

Weekdays 9 a.m.-7 p.m., Sundays and public holidays 9 a.m.-12.30 p.m.; ring the bell

Free

Accessible

By arrangement

The Vasari Archive can be consulted on microfilm at the State Archive of Arezzo

The museum is located in the house in Arezzo which the artist bought in 1540 while it was still under construction and on which he worked from 1540 to 1548, decorating it with frescoes and furnishing it. Following the death of the last Vasari (1687) and after passing through various owners and changes of fortune it was bought in 1911 by the State which opened the Museo e Archivio Vasariano. The subject of extensive restoration work the house was reopened to the public and re-inaugurated in 1955. In addition to the frescoes and paintings by Vasari it also contains a significant collection of Tuscan works from the 16th C. which are documentary evidence of the era in which the artist lived and worked.

Frescoes on the ceilings and walls of the various rooms of the building which are the work of G. Vasari, dating from 1542 to 1548 *(Fame and the Arts, Apollo and the Muses, Abraham and Peace, Concord, Virtue, Modesty, Allegorical Figures, the Seasons, Stories of the Artists from Antiquity).*
Paintings of the Tuscan Mannerist school with works by Vasari, F. Zuccari, Maso da San Friano, Il Poppi, G. Stradano, A. Allori, Santi di Tito, J. Ligozzi; paintings on wood by Fra'Bartolomeo and Fra Paolino da Pistoia in the Chapel. A model in wood of the Palazzo delle Logge in Arezzo by Vasari and a sculpture in glazed terracotta with *Head of the Emporer Galba* by A. Sansovino are also exhibited.

L. Berti, *La Casa Vasari e il suo museo*, Florence 1955.

Museum catalogue in preparation.

Giorgio Vasari: Christ carried to the Tomb

Museo del Duomo

52100 Arezzo
Piazzetta dietro il Duomo
Tel. 0575/23991

Small

Winter, from 1st October to Holy Week: weekdays 9 a.m.-12 p.m.; closed on Sunday, Monday, Tuesday and Wednesday

Summer, from Holy Week to 30 September: weekdays 9 a.m.-12 p.m.; closed on Sunday

Entrance fee

No access

By arrangement

Guided visits on request

First opened in 1950 it was re-inaugurated in 1985 after long and extensive restoration of the works and the museum rooms. It contains a very rich and valuable collection of material from the Duomo and several other churches in the diocese: numerous paintings on wood and canvas and sculptures from the Tuscan school, illuminated choirbooks, fabrics and a valuable group of delicate and original ecclesiastical goldsmiths' work. The museum is housed in the rooms above the Duomo's sacresty and is run by the Cathedral Chapter.

Important examples of Romanesque sculpture (three polychrome wood *Crucifixes* from the 12th and 13th C.). Sculptures in terracotta from the 15th and 16th C. *(Annunciation and Stories of the Virgin*, altar-piece — originally polychrome — attributed to B. Rossellino).

Paintings on wood and detached frescoes of various origins by A. di Nerio, S. Aretino, L. d'Andrea, Mariotto di Cristofano, B. della Gatta *(St. Jerome)*.

Paintings on wood from the second half of the 15 th C. and late 16th C. by L. Signorelli, B. della Gatta *(Madonna and Child with Saints)*, by Il Pacchiarotto, G. Vasari (processional banner with *Preaching of the Baptist and Baptism of Christ, Three Biblical Stories)*, Santi di Tito *(Jesus in the House of Lazarus)*.

Ecclestiastical goldsmiths' work from the 12th to the 19th C. *(Bust-reliquary of San Donato* from 1346; the *Pax of Siena*, a Flemish work of the 15th C., enclosed in a neo-classical reliquary). Collection of Renaissance illuminated choirbooks and altar-hangings (16th-19th C.).

A. Tafi, *Il Duomo di Arezzo*, Arezzo 1985.

Museo Statale di Arte Medioevale e Moderna

52100 Arezzo
Via San Lorentino, 8
Tel. 0575/23868

Large

Weekdays 9 a.m.-7 p.m.; Sundays and public holidays 9 a.m.-1.30 p.m.

Entrance fee

No access

By arrangement

One of the most important in Tuscany, the museum contains outstanding collections of masterpieces of the Aretine, Sienese and Florentine schools and examples of the minor arts from the Middle Ages to the present day, including a splendid collection of majolica from the major Italian factories. The historical core of this vast patrimony has its origin in the Museum of the Lay Fraternity, established in Arezzo in 1823, and a group of works belonging to religious organizations which were suppressed by Napoleon in 1810. It has been enriched over the years by numerous donations and substantial gifts from the Gallerie Fiorentine and from various Aretine organizations. Since 1858 it has had its seat in the Palazzo Bruno Ciocchi (15th-16th C.). Having passed from council to state management in 1972 it was partially rearranged in 1977. It is being continually modernized.

Paintings from the area of Arezzo and Florence from the 13th to 17th C., including works by Margaritone d'Arezzo *(St. Francis)*, Spinello Aretino, Parri di Spinello, B. della Gatta *(Vision of St. Bernard)*, L. Signorelli, Rosso Fiorentino *(Madonna)*, G. Vasari *(St. Rocco, Apollo and Marcia, Ahasuerus' Dinner)*, A. Allori, Santi di Tito, il Cigoli, J. Vignali; it also contains canvases by S. Rosa, il Grechetto and A. Magnasco. There is a notable collection of 19th C. Tuscan works, from Neoclassicism (B. Benvenuti, L. Ademollo) to the 'Macchiaioli' school (G. Fattori, T. Signorini, A. Cecioni), and also from France. Lapidary material and sculptures in stone, marble and terracotta

Educational service organized by the Soprintendenza per i beni storico artistici di Arezzo in preparation for 1988

A programme of varied cultural events in progress

from the Middle Ages to the 16th C. (bottega of A. della Robbia). Bronzes and plaques from the 15th and 16th C.; collection of majolica from the 13th to the 18th C. representing the major Italian makers (Faenza, Deruta, Casteldurante, Pesaro, Gubbio); *Basin* in porcelain from the 16th C. with the Medici coat-of-arms.
Collection of medals containing around 3600 pieces including seals, coins and medals from the Middle Ages to the present day.

L. Berti, *Il Museo di Arezzo*, Rome 1961

R. Francovich, *La ceramica medievale nelle raccolte del Museo medievale e moderno di Arezzo*, Florence 1983

Il Museo statale di arte medioevale e moderna in Arezzo, edited by A. M. Maetzke, Florence 1987.

Margaritone d'Arezzo: Madonna and Child

Museo Michelangelo e Museo all'Aperto

52033 Caprese Michelangelo (AR)
Via Capoluogo
Tel. 0575/793912 (Comune)

Medium

All week 9.30 a.m.-12.30 p.m. / 3.30 p.m.-6 p.m.

Free

No access

Yes

Inaugurated in 1958, the artist's birthplace or «Casa del Podestà» preserves relics, heirlooms, photographic reproductions of his works, a small Michelangelo library and the room furnished with period furniture where tradition holds that Michelangelo was born. Following the restoration work on the adjacent castle, formerly in ruins, three new rooms were opened in 1969 where plaster casts of the artist's works are exhibited. Outside on the lawn a section dedicated to 20th C. Italian sculptors has been set up.

Casa del Podestà: plaster casts, photographic reproductions of the works and on the life of the artist, library with printed books on Michelangelo, room with Renaissance furnishings.

Castle: plaster casts of works by Michelangelo, sculptures by modern artists.

Lawn next to the castle: sculptures in bronze by contemporary artists (including E. Greco, P. Fazzini, A. Berti, M. Tommasi, I. Vivarelli, M. Negri).

Pinacoteca Comunale

52043 Castiglion Fiorentino (AR)
Piazza del Municipio
Tel. 0575/658042-3-4 (Comune)

Small

Weekdays 8 a.m.-2 p.m.; Sundays and public holidays by arrangement

Free

No access

By arrangement

Opened in 1911, the gallery is presently housed in a large room on the second floor of the Town Hall, rebuilt in the first half of the 16th C. on the site of the existing Palazzo dei Priori. It contains an important collection of precious goldsmiths' work and paintings mainly from the Collegiata and the Church of San Francesco. The museum is soon to be transferred to the historic Cassero complex which is currently undergoing restoration work under the care of the Soprintendenza of Arezzo.

Ecclesiastical vestments and vessels and goldsmiths' work from the 12th-15th C. (15th C. *Holy Cross* and 15th C. Franco-Rhenish *Reliquary bust of St. Ursula*).

Paintings of the Umbrian and Tuscan schools of the 12th-18th C. including a 13th. C. *Crucifix* attributed to the Maestro di San Francesco and works by Margaritone d'Arezzo *(St. Francis)*, T. Gaddi *(Madonna and Child)*, Giovanni di Paolo, B. della Gatta *(The Stigmata of St. Francis)*, L. Signorelli (bottega), G. D. Ferretti (*St. Catherine of Siena and St. Teresa of Avila*, 1723).

Museo dell'Accademia Etrusca

52044 Cortona (AR)
Piazza Signorelli, 9
Tel. 0575/62767

Founded in 1727, the museum has since 1945 been situated on the piano nobile of the Palazzo Casali, a Medieval building with Renaissance alterations. In 1984 it underwent radical renovation above all in the medieval and modern sections. A direct issue of the Accademia the museum documents its intense cultural activity with a rich patrimony of Etruscan, Roman and Egyptian antiquities, paintings and examples of the minor arts formed principally by donations: from the Baldelli bequest, the original core, to the urns donated by Mario Guarnacci in 1770-71, to the gem stamps sent by the Stosch, to the Egyptian collection donated towards the end of the 19th C. by Monsignor Guido Corbelli, papal delegate in Arabia

Large

Winter, from 1st October to 31st March: all week 9 a.m.-1 p.m. / 3 p.m.-5 p.m.

Summer, from 1st April to 30th September: all week 10 a.m.-1 p.m. / 4 p.m.-7 p.m.

Entrance fee

No access

By arrangement

The local library and the library of the Accademia Etrusca housed in the same building are regularly open to the public. The photograph library and the archives are only open by written arrangement.

Various cultural events organized by the Accademia. Occasional exhitions arranged.

Bronze lamp

and Egypt. The museum recently purchased the collection of the works of the Cortona painter Gino Severini. In addition it exhibits archaeological finds from Cortona and surroundings. In its variety and richness it constitutes one of the most important museums in the territory of Arezzo.

Archaeological collection:
Bronze lamp with satires, sirens and central Gorgon (5th C. B.C.). Bronze statuettes of Etruscan production, of Umbro-Sabellian and Roman origin — notable *Zeus di Firenzuola*, end of the 6th-5th C. B.C., and two examples with dedicatory inscriptions respectively to *Culans* and *Selvans*. Cypriot, Greek and Etruscan painted pottery (an interesting series of black-figured fragments of local origin, one of which attributed to Lydos, which are among the most ancient Attic imports into Etruria). Urns produced in Volterra and Chiusi decorated with figures (farewell scenes, Philoctetes in Lemnos, Scilla, hero fighting with the plough). Statuettes and Hellenistic anatomical *ex-votos* in terracotta. In the coin section, Etruscan, Umbrian, Romano-Campanian coin series, Imperial coinage up to Theodosius. Latin funerary inscription. Egyptian collection: Sculptures in granite and basalt, sepulchral bas-relief in limestone, funerary papyri, human and animal mummies; anthropoid sarcophagi; amulets.

Medieval and modern collection:
Rich collection of medals (Pisanello). Furniture (16th C. stalls), utensils and furnishings (18th C.). Collection of ivory, miniatures, bronzes. *Tempietto* in porcelain donated in 1756 by the Marquis Carlo Ginori, founder of the Doccia works.
Niccolò di Pietro Gerini, Neri di Bicci, Mariotto di Nardo, L. Signorelli *(Nativity)*, Michele di Rodolfo del Ghirlandaio *(Annunciation)*, A. Romano *(Madonna and Child)*, A. Allori, C. Allori (*Double portrait* formerly attributed to Cigoli), B. Ciarpi, P. da Cortona (sketch of *Angel*), G. B. Piazzetta. Works by G. Severini (*Maternity*, 1916).

C. Bruschetti, *Le tavole in rame incise dell'Accademia Etrusca*, Cortona 1970

P. Pacini, *La «Sala Gino Severini» nel Museo dell'Accademia di Cortona*, Cortona 1972

P. Bruschetti, *Il lampadario di Cortona*, Cortona 1979

L'Accademia Etrusca, catalogue of the exhibition, edited by P. Barocchi, D. Gallo, Milan 1985

P. Bruschetti, *Cortona*, Rome 1985

P. Bruschetti, *Gemme del Museo dell'Accademia*, Cortona 1987.

Museo Diocesano

52044 Cortona (AR)
Piazza del Duomo, 1
Tel. 0575/62830

Contains a substantial and important collection of paintings of the Tuscan school, goldsmiths' work and church silver mainly coming from the Cathedral and from various churches in the diocese. Opened in 1946 in the former Chiesa del Gesù (15th-16th C.) the museum has undergone restoration throughout, organized by the Soprintendenza of Arezzo. It was reopened in 1986.

Medium

Winter, from 1st October to 31st March: all week 9 a.m.-1

Paintings on wood of the Sienese school from the 14th-15th C., including works from the bottega of Duccio, by P. Lorenzetti *(Madonna and Child* and two *Crucifixes)*, Il Sassetta *(Madonna and*

p.m. / 3 p.m.-5 p.m.

Summer, from 1st April to 30th September: weekdays 9 a.m.-1 p.m. / 3 p.m.-6.30 p.m.

Closed on Mondays

Entrance fee

Partly accessible

By arrangement

Child with Angels and Saints)*, by M. di Bartolomeo. Sculptures from the 14th and 15th C. (Ciuccio di Nuccio). There are also paintings by B. della Gatta, Fra' Angelico *(Annuncation* and *Madonna and Child with Saints)*, L. Signorelli *(Deposition* and *Madonna and Child with Saints)*. Canvases of the 17th and 18th C. (G.M. Crespi, F. Cappella). Religious vestments and vessels and goldsmiths' work from the 13th-16th C. (*Vannucci Reliquary* by Giusto da Firenze 1457; *Passerini Altar-hanging* embroidered in velvet and gold probably from a design by A. del Sarto and Raphael of 1515).

Museo Paleontologico

52042 Farneta-Cortona (AR)
Abbazia di Farneta
Tel. 0575/610010

The small collection opened in 1967 is housed in two rooms in a building adjoining the Farneta Abbey. It contains paleontological finds and a variety of archaeological material from different periods found in the area.

Small

By arrangement

Free

Accessible

By arrangement

Fossil remains of local Pliocene and Villafranchian fauna.
Pottery fragments from various periods.
Etruscan urns in travertine marble, smooth and decorated with bas-reliefs.

S. Felici, *L'abbazia di Farneta in Val di Chiana*, Arezzo 1978.

Museo Comunale

52046 Lucignano (AR)
Piazza del Tribunale, 22
Tel. 575/836129

The museum, arranged on the ground floor of the Town Hall was founded in 1924. Completely restored and rearranged it was reopened in 1984. The principal interest of the small collection

Small

Winter, from 1st October to 30th April: all week 9 a.m.-noon / 3 p.m.-6 p.m.; closed on Wednesdays

Summer, from 1st May to 30th September: all week 10 a.m.-1 p.m. / 4 p.m.-7 p.m.

Entrance fee

San Francesco's tree

Accessible

By arrangement

consists in the Tree of St. Francis, an outstanding masterpiece of ecclesiastical goldsmiths' work of the 14th-15th C. Paintings of the Senese school from the 13th-15th C. are also exhibited.

Paintings on wood from the Senese school 13th-15th C. by 13th C. Anon. *(Crucifixion)*, by the Maestro of the Madonna di Lucignano (*Madonna and Child with donor*, formerly attributed to Ugolino di Nerio), by Bartolo di Fredi, Luca di Tomme', Pietro di Giovanni; works by L. Signorelli *(Madonna and Child)*.

Coffin pediment of the Senese school from the 16th and 17th C.

Gold reliquary in the form of a tree known as the *Tree of St. Francis*, a remarkable example of Senese goldsmiths' work begun by Ugolino di Vieri in 1350 and completed by Gabriello di Antonio over a century later.

Museo di Arte Sacra

52025 Montevarchi (AR)
Collegiata di San Lorenzo
Via Isidoro del Lungo, 4
Tel. 055/980468

Small

By arrangement

Free

Accessible

By arrangement

This particularly valuable museum was set up in 1973 by the Soprintendenza in several rooms of the former sacristy of the Collegiata di San Lorenzo (13th C. rebuilt in the 18th C.). It exhibits the Collegiate Church's treasure including church gold, illuminated choirbooks, fragments of frescoes and a della Robbia tempietto removed from the Church during the 18th C. rebuilding and partly restored.

Bas-relief in stone from 1283 *(Martyrdom of St. Lawrence)*

Ecclesiastical goldsmiths' work of the 6th and 7th C. (including *Processional Cross*) in silver by P. Spigliati 1552). Parchment choirbooks with illuminated characters from the 14th-15th C. Partly painted wooden ciborium in the form of a small Temple from the 16th C.

Detached frescoes of a local school from the 16th C. from the Church of San Andrea at Cennano (fragments).

Tempietto formerly in the Collegiate Church of San Lorenzo in Michelozzi style with decorations in glazed terracotta with friezes, rose-ceiling and altar with *St. John the Baptist* and *St. Sebastian* by A. della Robbia (c. 1500); bas-relief by della Robbia *Count Guerra delivers the Reliquary of the Holy Milk* (early 16th C.).

Museo Paleontologico

Accademia Valdarnese del Poggio di Montevarchi
52025 Montevarchi (AR)
Via Poggio Bracciolini, 38
Tel. 055/981227

Medium

Weekdays 9 a.m.- noon / 4 p.m.-6 p.m.; Sundays and public holidays 10 a.m.-12 p.m.; closed on Mondays

Owned by the Accademia Valdarnese del Poggio, the museum contains a rich collection of plant and animal fossils from the Pliocene and post-Pliocene periods, among the oldest in Italy, found mainly in the upper Valdarno area. The original core which was established in the 19th C., was researched by the Frenchman George Couvier. In 1821 it was transferred to its present seat the former convent of St. Ludovic (15th C.). Between 1873 and 1880 the collection consisting in 732 items was catalogued by Profs. Marchi of Florence and Mayor of Glasgow; the work was completed a few decades later by the geologist and paleontologist Giovanni Cappellini. Today the museum contains over 1600 items and in addition has at its disposal an extensive library and historical archive. Among the exhibits of great interest are the *istrix etrusca*, the *elephas meridionalis* and the *canis etruscus*.

Entrance fee

No access

By arrangement

Guided tours on request. Meetings for teachers and lectures on the historical, geographical and artistic aspects of the Valdarno area for elementary and secondary schools.

Extensive library with antique, scientific and historical and literary material, open on Mondays and Wednesdays from 3.30 p.m. to 6.30 p.m.

Study days. Educational shows.

Fossilized plant remains (ferns, pine, cypress, sequoia, magnolia, alder, ash, birch, elm, willow, poplar, oak, maple, plane, beach, hornbeam, chestnut, walnut, fig, vine, laurel, holly, cherry and sassafras) of the Upper Pliocene period found in the lignite mine in Castelnuovo dei Sabbioni.

Fossilized animal remains (monkeys, hare, beaver, porcupine, leopard, linx, tigers, hyenas, wolves, bear, elephants, mastodons, wild boar, hippopotamus, oxen, gazzelle, deer, rhinoceros, horses, tapi, tortoise, tench, fresh-water molluscs) of the Lower Pleistocene period found in the lacustrine sediment in the Valdarno.

Collana Memoria Valdarnesi edited by the Accademia Valdarnese del Poggio

C.T. Gaudin, C. Strozzi, *Contributions à la flore fossile italienne*, Zurich 1859

C. Bosco, *I roditori pliocenici del Valdarno Superiore*, Rome 1899

F. Bartolini, *Guida al Museo paleontologico di Montevarchi*, in Memorie Valdarnesi, VI, 1977, pp. 195-212

Museo Carlo Siemoni

52010 Badia Prataglia — Poppi (AR)
Via Nazionale, 14
Tel. 0575/559002 (Comando stazione forestale Badia Prataglia)

Small

Winter, from 16th September to 14th June: open by arrangement, write to the Ufficio Amministrazione Gestione ex ASFD, 52015 Pratovecchio.

Summer, from 15th June to 15th September: all week 9 a.m.- noon / 4 p.m.-7 p.m.

Entrance fee

Accessible

Yes

The museum is dedicated to the Bohemian forestry engineer, author of important forestry innovations in Casentino during the second half of the 19th C. Founded principally with educational aims in mind, the museum contains a small natural history collection and a variety of documents on the Casentine forest environment.

Collection of the principal forest species either indigenous or introduced into Italy, with brief descriptions. Trunks of characteris-

Sasso Fratino Nature Reserve

By arrangement, guided visits for groups with slide show and trips into the forest.

trees, examples of woods damaged by insects, collection of samples of local forest wood species.
Documentation on the main aspects of the State forests and in particular on the Sasso Fratino Nature Reserve.

Museo Ornitologico Forestale

52010 Camaldoli — Poppi (AR)
Tel. 0575/556014 (Comando stazione forestale Camaldoli)

Small

Winter, from 1st October to 31st May: open by arrangement, write to the Ufficio Amministrazione Gestione ex ASFD, 52015 Pratovecchio
Summer, from 1st June to 30th September: all week 8 a.m.- noon / 2 p.m.-7 p.m.

Entrance fee

Accessible

Yes

By arrangement, guided tours for groups with slide show and trips into the forest.

It was founded in 1963 following the acquisition by the State Forestry Commission (Pratovecchio administrative office) of an ornithological collection belonging to the heirs of the ornithologist Gino Biggeri of Bibbiena. It was subsequently enlarged with specimens of animals from various Tuscan forests, with sections of tree trunks, wood damaged by insects, examples of plant deformations and, in 1976, with a collection of samples of the main indigenous or introduced forest grass species. The museum is completed by photographs and plans on aspects of the State-run forests and in particular on the Sasso Fratino Nature Reserve.

Birds and animals from all over the world with their natural habitat. Flora and fauna characteristic of the central-northern Appennine environment and in particular of the State forests of the Casentine area.

Show-room

Museo Maria SS. delle Grazie

52027 San Giovanni Valdarno (AR)
Piazza Masaccio
Tel. 055/92445

Owned by the Church, the museum is presently closed for redevelopment work being undertaken by the Soprintendenza of Arezzo. Founded in 1864 and reorganized in 1959 it contains works by Tuscan artists of the 16th-18th C., goldsmiths' work and various religious vessels and vestments. The *Annunciation* by Fra' Angelico, returned after restoration, can presently be seen in a chapel of the Basilica.

Il Museo della Basilica a San Giovanni Valdarno, edited by L. Berti, Florence 1959.

Museo Civico

52037 Sansepolcro (AR)
Via Aggiunti, 65
Tel. 0575/76465

The Sansepolcro museum, one of the most renowned and valuable municipal collections in Tuscany was founded in 1975. It is housed in the Palazzo dei Conservatori (14th C.), specially redeveloped as a museum. The collection contains famous masterpieces by Piero della Francesca and important paintings from churches in the town and surroundings. The Cathedral treasure is also exhibited, rich in

Large

All week: 9.30 a.m.-1 p.m. / 2.30 p.m.-6 p.m.

Entrance fee

Partly accessible

By arrangement

Educational service with audiovisual material for schools or groups.

Exhibitions and conferences organized annually

precious goldsmiths' work, as is a collection of sculpture in stone and a collection of prehistoric material from the Val Tiberina. It has at its disposal an efficient educational apparatus.
At Monterchi, a few kilometres from Sansepolcro, the famous fresco by Piero della Francesca *La Madonna del Parto* can be visited by appointment (tel. 0575/70092), inside the Cappella del Cimitero.

Frescoes of the local school from the 14th C. Frescoes and paintings on wood by Piero della Francesca (including *The Resurrection* and *Polyptych "della Misericordia"*).

Paintings on wood and canvas of the Tuscan and Umbrian school from the 16th C. by Pontormo, L. Signorelli, Gerino da Pistoia, Raffaellino del Colle, Giovanni de' Vecchi, Santi di Tito; 17th C. Canvases by A. Ciampelli, D. Passignano, L. Bassano, L. Cigoli, J. da Empoli.

Piero della Francesca: Polyptych 'della Misericordia', central section

Robbian terracottas (A. della Robbia, *Madonna and Child*; G. della Robbia, *Crib*); wooden choir inlaid with perspective scenes, from the early 16th C.

Ecclesiastical objects and goldsmiths' work from the 13th-19th C. Collection of 17th C. copper and moulds by various local artists (C. Alberti, R. Cantagallina, R. Schiaminossi).
Collection of objects in stone, including a *large frieze* from the Romanesque period depicting warriors and animals.

Stone objects from the Paleolithic to Neolithic periods from sites in the Upper Val Tiberina; the Neolithic collection includes a display of clay fragments.

E. Agnoletti, *Il Museo civico di Sansepolcro*, Città di Castello 1977

M. Apa, *La Resurrezione di Cristo, itinerario sull'affresco di Piero della Francesca a Sansepolcro*, Città di Castello 1980

A.M. Maetzke, D. Galoppi Nappini, *Il Museo civico di Sansepolcro*, Florence 1988.

Antiquarium Nazionale

52038 Sestino (AR)
Via Marche, 12
Tel. 0575/772642
0575/772615

Small

Weekdays 3 p.m.-6 p.m.; closed on Saturdays and Sundays

Free

Accessible

By arrangement

Guided tours on request to the Council

Periodic conferences and exhibitions

Contains an important collection of archaeological material from the ancient Roman municipium of Sestinum made up by donations and from excavations in the area: sculptures, architectural fragments, grave-goods and inscriptions from the Augustan period. The original core of the collection was formed between 1930 and 1933 on the site of the ancient Forum, adjacent to the Romanesque parish church of San Pancrazio. In 1983 it was transferred to a building which was previously an elementary school and converted by the council for cultural use. A total redevelopment is planned, envisaging a substantial enlargement of the exhibition space and an enhancement of the collection.

Pottery; oil-lamps; Roman facing tiles found in Sestino and the surrounding territory. Outstanding *remains of a funeral monument* from the Republican period including heads of men and of a veiled woman, in addition to architectural fragments. Torsoes of statues of Diana, Venus, Eros, figures in togas, *head from giant statue* (possibly Augustus); reliefs depicting circus games. Funerary inscriptions; inscriptions from the base of statued and cippi dedicated to divinities, emperors and local personalities, including members of the Voluseni family.

La Raccolta epigrafica sestinate, edited by F. Galli, in Collana di studi e testi, 7, 1978

A. Minto, *Sestinum*, Rome 1983

Museo del Castello di Porciano

52017 Porciano — Stia (AR)
Tel. 0575/582635

Situated near the 10th C. Castle of the Guidi family, restored by its present owners the Conti Goretti-Specht, the museum was opened to the public in 1970. It consists in a display of agricultural and domestic tools and utensils, a collection of objects discovered during the restoration work and a small collection of North American Indian crafts. A permanent exhibition on the history of the

Small

Winter, from 15th October to 15th May: open to schools and groups by arrangement

Summer, from 16th May to 14th October: weekdays open to schools and groups by arrangement, Sundays and public holidays 10 a.m.- noon / 4 p.m.-7 p.m.

Free

No access

By arrangement

Guided tours on request

Historical-archaeological exhibitions; exhibitions on traditional life and Casentine art. Annual series of cultural conferences on historical, artistic, archaeological and literary themes.

castle and the family is under preparation.

Domestic utensils, agricultural tools relating to the peasant culture in the Casentine over the last two centuries.
Group of 19th C. pioneer and Sioux Indian implements and crafts from North Dakota (U.S.A.). Archaeological collection documenting the last period of power of the Earls Guidi; crockery from the late 13th C. to the second half of the 14th C. Also 15th-18th C. ceramic, glass, metal objects.

Il Castello di Porciano in Casentino. Storia e archeologia, edited by G. Vannini, Florence 1987

The Castle

Museo della Civiltà Contadina di Casa d'Erci

50030 Grezzano
Borgo San Lorenzo (FI)
Tel. 055/8401457
055/8457197 (Library)

Medium

Weekdays 2 p.m.-7 p.m.; Thursday and Saturday morning by arrangement

Free

Partly accessible

Yes

Founded in 1983 by a private company, the Erci group, in collaboration with the Council, the museum is housed in a former farmhouse on the bank of the Erci stream in the State-run «La Colla» complex. It is made up of about a thousand domestic implements and objects collected mainly from farms in the territory of Borgo San Lorenzo. Documentary and bibliographical material on the history, material culture and traditions of the Mugello area is also available. A mushroom exhibition is held annually and country festivals take place from Spring onwards.

Domestic implements and tools (19th-20th C.) grouped according to use and exhibited in keeping with daily use: reconstruction of a kitchen, bathroom, stable, cellar, barn, craftsman's workshop, spinning-mill.
Of note: a series of ploughs, antique wooden press, fodder-cutter and machine for cleaning grain, woodcutters', carpenters', shoemakers', and blacksmitsh' tools, hand grinders, spinning-wheels and looms, spits and various kitchen implements, steam-driven threshing machines.

Guided tour

Small book and photograph library and audiovisual material

Museo del Soldatino e della Figurina Storica

50041 Calenzano (FI)
Via Giotto, 5
Tel. 055/8879441 (Library)

Small

Monday, Tuesday, Wednesday and Friday 3 p.m.-7 p.m.; Thursday and Saturday 10 a.m.-1 p.m.; closed on Sundays

Free

No access

Yes

Opened in 1981 the Council-owned museum is housed in one room adjacent to the Municipal Library. It contains about six thousand model soldiers and historical figures, models, dioramas and explanatory panels.

Models of soldiers and historical figures in lead, kaolin, papier mache and plastic.
Among the exhibits: Model depicting Castruccio Castracani's siege of Calenzano castle (1325); «Lanzichenecco» (16th C.); various pieces in 59 mm (18th C.); «Carabinieri» made completely by hand; hand-made "16th C. sculptor in his studio"; Savoia Cavalry Officer (1692); Soldier in Bavarian armour (15th C.); 90 mm models «Bond Bosse» from the Cantons of Berne and Uri. Of particular note the section dedicated to *Nuremburg*.

Museo Archeologico Comunale

50042 Artimino
Carmignano (FI)
Via Papa Giovanni
Tel. 055/8718124
055/8712002 (Comune)

Small

All week 9 a.m.-12.30 p.m., Saturday 9 a.m.-12.30 p.m. / 3 p.m.-6.30 p.m.; closed on Wednesdays

Entrance fee

No access

By arrangement

Housed in the Medici villa «La Ferdinanda» and opened in 1983, the museum contains an interesting collection of pieces found during excavations in the area over the last two decades. It also houses temporarily a group of items found previously in the same area and formerly exhibited in the Museum of Archaeology in Florence.

Material from the Etruscan settlement at Artimino and from the territory's necropolises, dating from the 7th-1st C. B.C. Of consid-

Etruscan red-figured krater

Guided tours on request. The exhibition is introduced by an audiovisual show «Artimino. Un insediamento etrusco nella media valle dell'Arno».

erable interest is a *bucchero incense-burner* of the Oriental period with one of the most ancient Etruscan inscriptions of northern Etruria, and a large *krater from the Clusium-Volaterrae group* with figures from Dionysus' retinue. Also of note is the series of *ivory and bone objects* decorated with bas-reliefs and inscriptions from the monumental tombs of Comeana, the 4th C. bronze treasures including the aforementioned krater, a stele and some *«Fiesolan» cippae* sculpted in sandstone.

Pinacoteca di Santa Verdiana

50051 Castelfiorentino (FI)
Via Timignano, 1
Tel. 0571/64096

Presently housed in the parish building, the collection is soon to be transferred to rooms adjoining the Santa Verdiana Sanctuary presently undergoing restoration work. It consists of a remarkable group of works of art from the parish and other churches in the territory: paintings of the Tuscan school from the 13th-18th C. (Duccio, T. Gaddi, B. Gozzoli, Iacopo del Casentino, J. da Empoli), illuminated codices and ecclesiastical goldsmiths' work. It can presently be visited by appointment.

Villa Medicea di Cerreto Guidi

50050 Cerreto Guidi (FI)
Via Ponti Medicei, 7
Tel. 0571/55707

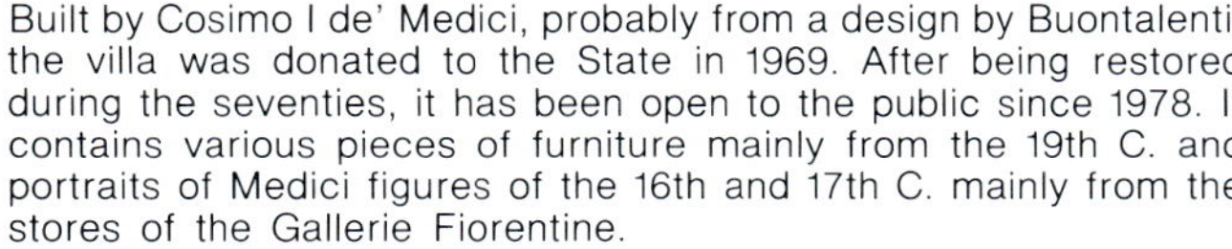

Built by Cosimo I de' Medici, probably from a design by Buontalenti, the villa was donated to the State in 1969. After being restored during the seventies, it has been open to the public since 1978. It contains various pieces of furniture mainly from the 19th C. and portraits of Medici figures of the 16th and 17th C. mainly from the stores of the Gallerie Fiorentine.

Large

Winter, from 1st October to 30th April: weekdays 9 a.m.-5 p.m., Sundays and public holidays 9 a.m.-1 p.m.

Summer, from 1st May to 30th September: weekdays 9 a.m.-6.30 p.m., Sundays and public holidays 9 a.m.-1 p.m.

Closed on Mondays

Free

Partially accessible

By arrangement

Anon.: Portrait of Don Giovanni De' Medici

Casa del Boccaccio

50052 Certaldo (FI)
Via Boccaccio
Tel. 0571/664208

Traditionally held to be the house where Boccaccio lived and died, the house was completely restored following damage suffered during the last war. Owned by the State it has been the seat of the national Giovanni Boccaccio Society since 1958 and houses an important specialized library which can be consulted by request.

Small

Weekdays 9 a.m.-12 p.m.;
3 p.m -6 p.m.;
closed on Sundays

Free

♿
No access

📷
By arrangement

Museo di Palazzo Pretorio

50052 Certaldo (FI)
Piazzetta del Vicariato, 3
Tel. 0571/668270

Purchased by the Council in 1889 the 12th-13th C. Palazzo was opened to the public in 1903. It consists of a series of monumental rooms (Camera delle Sentenze, Sala delle Udienze, Sala del Consiglio, Sala Grande) with remains of detached frescoes. It also houses a small group of archaeological exhibits from excavations in the territory; a collection of drawings by contemporary artists is temporarily not on exhibition due to restoration work in progress.

Large

Winter, from 1st October to 31st March: all week 9 a.m.- noon / 3 p.m.-6 p.m.

Summer, from 1st April to 30th September: all week 9 a.m.- noon / 4 p.m.-7 p.m.

Closed on Mondays

Entrance fee

No access

📷
Yes

Remains of detached frescoes from the 15th-16th C.

Contemporary art section with drawings illustrating the *Decameron*.

Archaeological section: remains from a late Etruscan tomb desecrated in ancient times and subsequently damaged by late 19th C. excavations, dating from the second half of the 2nd to the first half of the 1st C. B.C.; Roman amphora from the Imperial period; material from a Late Medieval farming settlement.

Museo Casa di Ferruccio Busoni

50053 Empoli (FI)
Piazza della Vittoria, 16
Tel. 0571/7070 (Comune)

Dedicated to Ferruccio Busoni (1866-1924) the museum contains documents, relics and a permanent exhibition on the artist's life. It is situated at his birthplace, seat of the Associazione Centro Studi Musicali Ferruccio Busoni.

Epistolario Busoniano, edited by S. Sablich, Milan 1988

Small

By prior arrangement with the Council

Free

No access

By arrangement

Library, archive and tape library open by prior arrangement

Concerts, conferences and publications

Ferruccio Busoni

Museo della Collegiata di Sant'Andrea

50053 Empoli (FI)
Piazza Propositura, 3
Tel. 0571/72220

Medium

All week 10 a.m.-12 p.m.; closed on Mondays

Entrance fee

Partially accessible

By arrangement

Founded in 1861 the museum which suffered extensive damage during the last war was totally restored and reopened in 1956. It contains a rich and important collection of paintings, sculptures and illuminated manuscripts from the 15th-18th C. mainly from the Collegiate Church, from other churches in the territory, from donations and acquisitions. A total redevelopment is planned shortly.

Paintings on wood and canvas of the Tuscan school from the 14th-19th C., works by the 'Maestro' from 1336, Niccolò di Pietro Gerini, A. Gaddi, Lorenzo di Bicci, L. Monaco, Filippo Lippi *(Enthroned Madonna with Angels and Saints)*, F. Botticini *(Angels and predella in the tabernacle of San Sebastiano)*, I. del Sellaio, Pontormo *(Saint Michael Archangel and St. John the Evangelist)*, G.A. Sogliani, Fra' Paolino, J. da Empoli *(St. Thomas' disbelief)*.

Detached frescoes by G. Starnina, Masolino *(Christ's Compassion)*.

Sculptures in marble, wood and terracotta by T. da Camaino, S. di Valdambrino *(St. Stephen)*, B. Rossellino *(Annunciation and Baptismal Font)*, A. Rossellino *(St. Sebastian)*, Mino da Fiesole, A. della Robbia, B. and S. Buglioni.

Escutcheons in marble and stone.

U. Baldini, *Guida alla visita del Museo della Collegiata di Empoli*, Empoli 1964

A. Paolucci, *Il Museo della Collegiata di Sant'Andrea in Empoli*, Florence 1985

Fondazione Museo Primo Conti

Centro di documentazione e ricerche sulle avanguardie storiche
50014 Fiesole (FI)
Via Giovanni Dupré, 18
Tel. 055/597095

Opened in 1987 the museum exhibits the rich Primo Conti collection, made up of a vast anthological survey of his work as a painter from 1911 to the present day. It is housed in the building of the Foundation, founded in 1980, according to the artist's wishes, with the aim of promoting study and research on the artistic and literary movements of the early 19th C. It also has at its disposal an interesting collection of archives concerning the avant-garde and a well-stocked library.

Medium

Winter, from 1st October to 31st March; weekdays 10 a.m.-1 p.m.

Summer, from 1st April to 30th September: weekdays 10 a.m.-1 p.m. / 3 p.m.-6 p.m. Closed on Sundays and Mondays

Entrance fee

Accessible

By arrangement

Archives and library open by prior arrangement on weekdays from 9 a.m. to 1 p.m.

Exhibition, conferences and debates on modern and contemporary artistic and literary themes.

Sixty three paintings from 1911 to the present day; one hundred and sixty three drawings and six engravings by Primo Conti. Among the most important works are: *Greengrocer, Nude of young boy, The coconut-seller, Simultaneity of environment, Acrobat, Still-life: pear, pine cone and egg, Eros, Cousin Pia, Head of cross-eyed peasant, Portrait of the artist's mother, Portrait of Maddalena, Reawakening, The plumb-line*.

Quaderni della Fondazione Primo Conti, edited by the Foundation.

Il Museo Primo Conti, presentation by M. Calvesi, edited by G. Dalla Chiesa, Milan 1987

Primo Conti: Demetrius happy

Museo Bandini

50014 Fiesole (FI)
Via Giovanni Dupré, 1
Tel. 055/59061

Founded in 1913, the museum, which is owned by the Chapter of Fiesole Cathedral, consists in an initial group of works from the bequest of the Canon Angiolo Maria Bandini, noted scholar and librarian of the Biblioteca Laurenziana in Florence. It has grown over the years through the addition of various works by local artists, substantially altering the original arrangement. Today it contains paintings and sculptures mainly of the Tuscan school from the 13th-17th C. and a valuable group of works in the minor arts. It is presently closed to the public for restoration.

Paintings of the Tuscan school from the 13th-16th C., including works by the Maestro della Maddalena, B. Daddi, T. Gaddi, L. Monaco, Giovanni del Biondo, Mariotto di Nardo, J. del Sellaio (*Triumph of Religion, Triumph of Love and Chastity, Triumph of Time* inspired by Petrarch's *Triumphs*). Sculptures in ivory, wood and terracotta (various works by Andrea and Giovanni della Robbia and B. Buglioni) from the 14th-16th C. Inlaid furniture from the 15th C.

Museo Civico — Zona Archeologica

50014 Fiesole (FI)
Via Portigiani, 1
Tel. 055/59477

Medium

Winter: all week 10 a.m.-4 p.m.

Summer: all week 9 a.m.-7 p.m.

Entrance fee

Partially accessible

By arrangement

Introductory archaeology courses for local schools

Occasional exhibitions

Opened in 1878 at the Palazzo Pretorio, the museum was transferred in 1914 to a Neo-classical building built inside the archaeological site from which most of the exhibits come. It contains excavated prehistoric, Etruscan, Roman and Medieval material from the territory of Fiesole and other items from various sources donated by private collectors.
Completely rearranged in 1981, it has been laid out with new didactic aims in mind. An Antiquarium will be opened soon in a building adjoining the museum, with Etruscan and Roman monuments discovered during the restoration work: the Costantini collection will be on display (Greek, Etruscan and Italian pottery) and a group of frescoes and other material from the late ancient period. The enclosed area in which the museum is situated represents the most important archaeological complex in the area of Florence, with remains of an Etruscan-Roman temple, the theatre and Roman Baths.

Examples of pottery from local sources, dating from the Neolithic period to the 6th C. A.D. Decorative objects in bronze and bronzes from various periods — outstanding late Archaic examples from Villa Marchi, from the Sanctuary and a Heracles of Cyprus-style statuette. Stelae ascribed to the «Pietre Fiesolane» and an urn-lid in «pietra serena»; cippus with inscribed border. Terracotta and other material mainly in clay from the temple. Etruscan red-figured and painted, black-glazed and achromatic pottery; glass unguentaries; Italian presealed and sealed pottery; oil-lamps; objects in metal

View of the Roman Theatre

from the Roman period. Bas-reliefs and full tondi, including portraits of members of the Emperor's family and other subjects, part of the theatre's decoration. Marble statues of Isis and Osiris; fragment of a sculpture in bronze, possibly a copy of the Capitoline Wolf. Lead cista with relief decoration, 2nd-3rd C. A.D. Jugs, objects in glass and precious metals found in tombs of the Longobard period.
Among the exhibits discovered at other sites in Etruria or from private collections: *sors* engraved with the name of Servio Tullio; bucchero vases; red — and black-figured Attic pottery; Apulian and Etruscan red-figured pottery; Etruscan urns with decorative illustrations; marble urns from the Imperial period; version of the Chigi Apollo, torsos of the pouring satyr by Praxiteles and of the Dresden-Capitoline Aphrodite.

M. De Marco, *Fiesole. Museo archeologico. Scavi*, Fiesole 1981

F. Bellini delle Stelle, A. Mannari, R. Sabelli, *Le terme romane di Fiesole*, Fiesole 1984

La collezione Costantini, by various authors, Florence 1985

M. Fuchs, *Le sculture del teatro di Fiesole*, Rome 1986

Museo Dupré

50014 Fiesole (FI)
Via Dupré, 19
Tel. 055/59171

This privately owned collection consists of a large group of models and casts by the sculptor Giovanni Dupré (1817-1882) and is housed in the former conservatory of the villa in which his heirs live. The small museum is open only to students and scholars by previous arrangement with the owners.

Museo Missionario Francescano

50014 Fiesole (FI)
Convento di San Francesco
Tel. 055/59175

Situated inside the Convent of San Francesco, the museum contains a group of archaeological exhibits found between 1906 and 1910 during local excavations as well as Egyptian antiquities and Chinese material brought back from missionary areas of the Franciscan Fathers. A complete redevelopment is planned.

Small

Winter, from 1st October to 30th April: all week 10 a.m.-noon / 3 p.m.-6 p.m.

Free

No access

By arrangement

Egyptian antiquities from Luxor and various funeral sites: fragments of sculptures in granite and alabaster; sarcophagus lid in painted wood; statuettes of gods; amulets in faience; pottery and oil-lamps; mummies; fragments of Coptic cloth. A variety of material dating from the Classical to the Roman periods and the early Middle Ages mostly of local origin. Etruscan bronze helmet. Architectural and marble statue fragments. Coins.

Section of Chinese exhibits comprising clothes, musical instruments, prototypes of printing dies, jade, porcelain and ivory statuettes.

Antica Spezieria Spedale Serristori

50063 Figline Valdarno (FI)
Piazza XXV Aprile
Tel. 055/953534 (Comune)

This is the old apothecary of the Ospedale di Figline, founded in 1399 by Ser Ristoro di Jacopo Serristori. It contains a rich collection of officinal glass from various sources and Tuscan majolica from the 16th-19th C. The studies and researches carried out on the whole hospital complex were the subject of an exhibition organized by the Council in 1982.

Small

By prior arrangement with the cultural office of the Council

Free

Accessible

By arrangement

Guided tour on request

Lo Spedale Serristori di Figline. Documenti e arredi, exhibition catalogue, by various authors, Figline Valdarno 1982

Show-room

Raccolta d'Arte Sacra

50063 Figline Valdarno (FI)
Collegiata S. Maria Assunta
Via Marsilio Ficino, 43
Tel. 055/958518

Small

By request

Free

Accessible

By arrangement

Opened in 1983 the collection comprises religious works and fittings mainly from the Collegiata. It is run directly by the parish priest.

Religious vessels and vestments, mainly 17th C. (Good Friday *standards* with symbols of the Passion).
Paintings on wood and canvas from the 15th-18th C. (*Two Angels* by D. Ghirlandaio 1480, side panels of the *altar-piece* by the 'Maestro di Figline' preserved in the Collegiata).
15th C. illuinated manuscripts from the Chapter.

Antica Spezieria di Santa Maria Novella

50123 Firenze
Via della Scala, 16
Tel. 055/216276 (Officina profumo farmaceutica di Santa Maria Novella)

Medium

By prior arrangement on weekdays: 8.30 a.m.-12.25 p.m. / 3 p.m.-6.55 p.m.;

The pharmacy's history is closely linked to the Santa Maria Novella conventual complex and more exactly to the pharmacological activities of the Dominican friars stretching back to 1221, the year of their settlement in Florence. The convent's chronicles hold Fra' Angiolo Marchissi (1592-1659) to be the founder of the 17th C. pharmacy and his successors, all expert pharmacists, to have been responsible for enlarging it and bringing it fame. Confiscated by the State along with the conventual complex following the 1866 suppressions it was bought by the Council in 1871. In 1879 the running of the pharmacy and its property passed into private hands, confirming the separation of the pharmacy from the convent administration. It still preserves today its original appearance and comprises a series of rooms with valuable furnishings and fittings.

Selling area restored in 1848 with period fittings (sales counter and

Saturday 3 p.m.-6.30 p.m.; closed on Monday morning

From June to September: closed on Saturdays

Free

No access

By arrangement

cupboards in walnut with precious 19th C. bottles). Room adjoining the garden with late 18th C. furniture, *Portraits of Friars*, and *Allegorical figures*, group of precious 17th C. pharmacists' jars from Montelupo.
Antique pharmacy with rich plaster decoration in the vaulted ceiling and glass-fronted cabinets with the antique pharmacists' equipment: jars from Montelupo (17th C.) and Richard Ginori (19th C.) alambics, room thermometers, mortars and various utensils.
San Niccolò Sacristy with frescoes of *Stories from the life of Christ* by Mariotto di Nardo (mid 14th C.).

S. Giovannini, G. Mancini, *La Farmacia di Santa Maria Novella*, Florence 1987

Antique Apothercary's Shop

Cappelle Medicee

50122 Firenze
Piazza Madonna degli Aldobrandini, 6
Tel. 055/213206

Medium

Weekdays 9 a.m.-2 p.m., Sundays and public holidays 9 a.m.-1 p.m.; closed on Mondays

Entrance fee

No access

By arrangement

The education section of the Uffizi Gallery (Via della Ninna 5, Firenze, tel.: 055/218341-

These comprise a series of rooms of great historical and architectural interest: the crypt with the tombs of members of the Medici family, the Chapel of the Princes Don Giovanni de' Medici with the grand-dukes' memorials and the outstanding craftsmanship of the decoration in pietre dure, the architectural-sculptural complex of the New Sacristy begun by Michelangelo with the Medici Tombs of Lorenzo, Duke of Urbino and Giuliano, Duke of Nemours. Having passed in 1896 from management by the Genio Civile to that of the State Galleries along with the Laurenzian complex, they were opened to the public in 1913. Since 1937 part of the treasure of the adjacent Basilica has been exhibited there, including a remarkable number of reliquaries in precious metals and pietre dure which in turn include antique vases belonging to Lorenzo the Magnificent. In the apse and the underground rooms of the New Sacristy one can see the recently discovered and restored architectural graffiti and drawings by Michelangelo.

Chapel of the Princes: facings in marble and pietre dure: frieze with coats-of-arms of the towns of Tuscany; statues in gilded bronze of the grand-dukes *Ferdinando I and Cosimo II* by P. and F. Tacca; altar (rebuilt in 1933) with 16th, 17th and 19th C. panels. The cupola is decorated with paintings by Pietro Benvenuti (1st half of the 19th C.) with biblical and New Testament scenes.
The treasure of San Lorenzo: Reliquaries and religious objects donated by popes (Leo X, Clement VII) and grand-dukes by various artists and from various periods (15th-18th C.); some in rock crystal previously the property of Lorenzo the Magnificent.

284272) organizes educational activities in the museum for schools at every level

New Sacristy: Statues of Giuliano de' Medici, Night and Day; of Lorenzo de' Medici, of *Dawn and Dusk* (works by Michelangelo Buonarroti), the *Madonna and Child* and *St. Cosma and Damiano* by Michelangelo and collaborators.
Wall drawings by Michelangelo and his pupils.

E. Marchionni, *Guida per i visitatori delle R. R. Cappelle Medicee e R. Opificio delle Pietre dure in Firenze*, Florence 1891

L. Berti, *Michelangelo: le Tombe Medicee*, Florence 1965

R. Chiarelli, *San Lorenzo e le Cappelle Medicee*, Florence 1971

U. Baldini, A.M. Giusti, A. Martelli Pampaloni, *La Cappella dei Principi e le Pietre dure*, Milan 1979

Michelangelo: Night, detail of the Tomb of Giuliano Duke of Nemours

Casa Buonarroti

50122 Firenze
Via Ghibellina, 70
Tel. 055/241752

Medium

Winter, from 1st November to 28th February: all week 10 a.m.-1 p.m. by appointment

Summer, from 1st March to 31st October: all week 9.30 a.m.-1.30 p.m.; closed on Tuesdays

Entrance fee

ꕔ
Accessible

By arrangement

Guided tour on request

Book and photograph libraries open to consultation by prior arrangement on weekdays 10 a.m.-1 p.m.

Annual exhibitions with accompanying catalogue

As well as exhibiting important masterpieces by Michelangelo, the museum documents the history of the family from 1508, the year in which the house was bought, until the death of Cosimo Buonarroti in 1858. Initially made up of three adjoining buildings, during the second half of the 16th C. it was converted into a single building by Leonardo, the artist's nephew. The house was subsequently re-developed by Michelangelo the Younger (1568-1647), a distinguished literary and intellectual figure: the monumental rooms on the first floor, decorated by Florentine and Tuscan artists, date from this period. The house was enriched with precious art collections including the outstanding archaeological collection formed by Filippo (1661-1733). Having no direct heirs, Cosimo Buonarroti (1790-1858) donated the house to the public and Pietro Leopoldo decreed its institution as an «Ente morale» in 1859. From the magnificent Michelangelo celebrations in 1875 to the temporary housing of the Museo Storico Topografico di Firenze at the beginning of the century, the building has alternated between periods of decline and renaissance. In 1964, the 400th anniversary of Michelangelo's death saw the opportunity for comprehensive restoration and conversion to museum use. After gaining in 1965 the new title of Ente Casa

Michelangelo: Madonna of the Steps

Buonarroti the museum was entrusted to the management of the noted Michelangelo scholar Charles de Tolnay. It today comprises a single museum entity which in addition to housing masterpieces by the artist also exhibits several groups of works in a series of twenty-one rooms: paintings, sculptures, majolica, archaeological material. It also preserves the most important collection in the world of autograph drawings by Michelangelo.

Archaeological collection of F. Buonarroti, with Roman sculptures and Etruscan works (urns, stelae, bronzes).
Paintings, sculptures, objects and furnishings from the collection of Michelangelo the Younger (15th-17th C.), including *Predella with Stories of St. Nicholas* by Giovanni di Francesco, *Epiphany* by A. Condivi, *Allegorical figure* by Fra' Mattia della Robbia, *Putto playing music* by G. della Robbia, sketch of *The Blessed Manetto dell'Antella* by C. Allori; majolica from Pesaro, Urbino and Cafaggiolo.

Early works by Michelangelo: *Madonna of the Steps*, c. 1490-92; *Battle of the Centaurs*, before 1492; wooden *Crucifix* from Santo Spirito. Also bozzetti in terracotta and wax by Michelangelo *(Torso of Hermaphrodite, Hercules and Cacus)* and by other 16th C. artists. Iconographic collection of 16th C. paintings depicting Michelangelo by G. Bugiardini, M. Venusti and others. Paintings and drawings derived from Michelangelo from the 16th-19th C., by B. Franco, Bronzino, G. Clovio, A. Allori, E. Delacroix.
In the 17th C. rooms on the first floor (Galleria, Room of the Night and Day, Room of the Angels, Library) oil paintings arranged on the walls and ceilings and frescoes produced between 1612 and 1638 by the major Florentine and Tuscan painters of the period. A Fontebuoni, D. Passignano, F. Boschi, J. da Empoli, M. Rosselli, F. Tarchiani, F. Curradi, S. Coccapani, G. Bilivert, A. Gentileschi, G. da San Giovanni, F. Furini, J. Vignali, P. da Cortona, B. del Bianco, Cecco Bravo.

Sculptures by D. Pieratti, A. Novelli, G. Finelli (*Bust of Michelangelo Buonarroti the Younger*, 1630).

P. Barocchi, *Michelangelo e la sua scuola. I disegni di Casa Buonarroti e degli Uffizi*, Florence 1962

U. Procacci, *La Casa Buonarroti a Firenze*, Milan 1965

A.W. Vliegenthart, *La Galleria Buonarroti. Michelangelo e Michelangelo il Giovane*, Florence 1976

Michelangelo. *I disegni di Casa Buonarroti*, edited by L. Berti, A. Cecchi, A. Natali, Florence 1985

G. Ragionieri, V.E. Vasarri, *Casa Buonarroti*, Florence 1987

Casa e Museo di Dante

50122 Firenze
Via Santa Margherita, 1
Tel. 055/283343

Medium

Traditionally held to be Dante's birthplace, the house which was opened to the public in 1911 has also been the seat of a small museum since 1965. It preserves documents on the life of Dante in Florence and in exile and various editions of the Divine Comedy.

Weekdays 9.30 a.m.-12.30 p.m. / 3 p.m.-6.30 p.m.; , Sundays and public holidays 9 a.m.-12.30 p.m.; closed on Mondays

Free

No access

By arrangement

Cenacolo di Andrea del Sarto a San Salvi

50135 Firenze
Via di San Salvi, 16
Tel. 055/677570

Medium

Weekdays 9 a.m.-2 p.m., Sundays and public holidays 9 a.m.-1 p.m.; closed on Mondays

Entrance fee

Accessible

By arrangement

The education section of the Uffizi Gallery (Via della Ninna 5, Firenze, tel.: 055/218341-284272) organizes educational activities in the museum for schools at every level

Frescoed by Andrea del Sarto between 1511 and 1527 the cenacolo was originally the refectory of the Vallombrosan Abbey of San Salvi (beginning of the 16th C.) subsequently a strictly cloistered convent of the nuns of the Blessed Humility until the early years of the 19th C. Having passed into State ownership after the suppressions it was converted into a storeroom and opened to visits during the second half of the 19th C. Badly damaged in the 1966 flood and the subject of a long process of restoration organized by the Soprintendenza of Florence, it was reopened in 1982. Three works by Andrea del Sarto, a selection of paintings on wood from the early 16th C. and large altar-pieces from Florentine churches and suppressed convents are exhibited in the magnificent 16th C. rooms («corridor», «refectory», «washroom», «kitchen») which preserve intact the memory of the ancient convent.

Large fresco with *The Last Supper* and *Noli me tangere, Annunciation* and *Pietà* by Andrea del Sarto. 16th C. Florentine frescoes and paintings on wood by Pontormo *(Madonna and Child with St. John)*, by Franciabigio *(Adoration of the shepherds, Holy Conversation, Noli me tangere)*, Ridolfo del Ghirlandaio *(St. Zanobi revives a young boy, Transporting of the body of St. Zanobi)*, G. A. Sogliani, G. Bugiardini, G. Vasari, C. Portelli, Poppi, Santi di Tito.

Marble fragments of the funeral monument to St. John Gualberto founder of the Vallombrosan order, a work by B. da Rovezzano (1507-1516).

Andrea del Sarto: Last Supper

S. Meloni Trkulja, S. Padovani, *Il Cenacolo di Andrea del Sarto a San Salvi. Guida al Museo*, Florence 1982

Cenacolo di Foligno
50123 Firenze
Via Faenza, 42

Former refectory of the Monastery of St. Onofrio di Foligno (15th C.), the museum contains *The Last Supper*, an important fresco by Perugino, at one time mistakenly attributed to Raphael. The refectory was purchased by the grand-duke Pietro Leopoldo in 1846. The convent which had been suppressed since 1800 and abandoned by the nuns was at the time the seat of a boarding-school for poor girls. Thus removed from the conventual complex the refectory housed during the 19th C. the Egyptian and Etruscan museum (subsequently transferred to the Crocetta). More recently it housed temporarily the Galleria Feroni (collection of various pictures from the 15th-18th C.) donated to the State by the Marchese Feroni.
It is presently closed to the public.

Cenacolo del Ghirlandaio
50123 Firenze
Borgo Ognissanti, 42
Tel. 055/296802

Medium

Weekdays 9 a.m.-12.30 p.m.

Free

Accessible

By arrangement

Situated in the convent complex of Ognissanti the refectory was frescoed by Ghirlandaio in 1480. Completely restored following the serious damage caused by the flood in 1966 it preserves, besides the *Last Supper*, frescoes and sinopias coming partly from the Church.
In the former capitular room (entered from the cloister) a small museum set up in 1973 by the Franciascan Fathers with various works from the convent can also be visited.

Refectory: *Last Supper* (with sinopia) by D. Ghirlandaio (1480), *St. Augustine studying* by S. Botticelli and *St. Jerome studying* by D. Ghirlandaio, frescoes from the choir of Ognissanti, further sinopias by D. Ghirlandaio *(Deposition)* and by A. Gaddi *(Resurrection)*. The museum contains church silver, ecclesiastical vestments, illuminated manuscripts, sculptures in polychrome terracotta (*Madonna and Child* attributed to N. Ungaro) from the 14th-16th C.

Cenacolo di Sant'Apollonia
50129 Firenze
Via XXVII Aprile, 1
Tel. 055/287074

Small

Weekdays 9 a.m.-2 p.m.; Sundays and public holidays 9 a.m.-1 p.m.; closed on Mondays

The old refectory of the cloistered convent of the Benedictine nuns, founded in 1339 and with fresco decoration added probably around 1445 it has been owned by the State since 1866 and the Museo di Andrea del Castagno has been housed here since 1891. The subject of a comprehensive restoration programme undertaken by the Florence Soprintendenza after the 1966 flood, it was reopened to the public in 1986 after alterations both to its architectural structure (six windows in the cloister were reopened) and in the arrangement of the works exhibited: the frescoes and sinopias by A. del Castagno are situated in the refectory and some 14th C. paintings originally belonging to the Church of St. Apollonia in the adjoining room.

Refectory: *Last Supper* and three *Stories from the Passion* (*Crucifixion, Deposition* and *Resurrection* and the respective sinopias) by Andrea del Castagno (c. 1450); in the same room, also by A. del

Free

Accessible

By arrangement

Castagno, *Pietà* with sinopia from the Monastery of St. Apollonia and *Crucifix with the Madonna, St. John and Saints Benedict and Romualdo* from the cloister of the former Degli Angioli convent. In the following room *Pietà* and *Crucifixion* (with sinopia) by P. Schiavo from the St. Apollonia monastery; *Madonna and Child with Saints* by Neri di Bicci from the Church of St. Apollonia; further paintings on wood and frescoes of the Florentine school from the 14th and 15th C.

Andrea del Castagno: Last Supper, detail

Chiostro dello Scalzo

50129 Firenze
Via Cavour, 69
Tel. 055/472907

Small

Weekdays 9 a.m.-2 p.m., Sundays and public holidays 9 a.m.-1 p.m.; closed on Mondays

Free

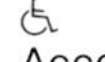
Accessible

By arrangement

The cloister was decorated with frescoes by Andrea del Sarto between c. 1507 and 1526. Two scenes were executed by Franciabigio in 1518-19 while the artist was in Paris. The work was carried out on behalf of the Brotherhood of Flagellants of St. John the Baptist known as the Barefooted Frairs, suppressed in 1785. Run today by the Soprintendenza per i beni artistici e storici of the Provinces of Florence and Pistoia it underwent comprehensive restoration work of which the most substantial took place in 1960. On the occasion of the celebrations to commemorate the 500th anniversary of the birth of Andrea del Sarto the cloister was opened to the public with fixed opening hours.

Cycle of frescoes by A. del Sarto: *Faith* (c. 1523); *The Angel appears to St. Zacharias* (1523); *The Visitation* (1524); *Naming of the Baptist* (1526); *The Benediction of St. John the Baptist leaving for the desert* (Franciabigio 1518-19); *The Meeting between Christ and St. John the Baptist* (Franciabigio 1518-19); *The Baptism of Christ* (c. 1507-8); *Charity* (c. 1513); *Justice* (1515); *The Preaching of St. John the Baptist* (1515); *The Baptism of the Multitude* (1517); *The Capture of the Baptist* (1517); *Salome's Dance* (1521); *The Beheading of the Baptist* (1523); *Herod's Feast* (1523); *Hope* (1526).

J. Shearman, *Andrea del Sarto*, Oxford 1965
S. Padovani, *Andrea del Sarto*, Florence 1986

Collezione del Collegio alla Querce

50133 Firenze
Via della Piazzola, 44
Tel. 055/573621

The collection's origins date back to 1868, the year of the College's foundation. Subsequently enlarged mainly through donations, it today comprises natural history and scientific collections and a group of archaeological material.

By prior arrangement

Free

Accessible
By arrangement

Etruscan archaeological collection, containing material mainly from Orvieto. Italian pottery from the area of Montesarchio (Benevento). Collection of scientific instruments (electromagnetic, seismological and astronomical) including a prototype of the tromometer by Padre Timoteo Bertelli, a mercury *coherer* and an 1870 telescope.

Natural history collection of animals from Italy, Europe and beyond.

Collection of fossils, minerals and rocks.

G. Camporeale, *La collezione alla Querce. Materiale archeologici orvietani*, Florence 1970.

Collezione Tecnologico Forestale

50145 Firenze
Istituto di selvicoltura
Facoltà di Agraria
Via S. Bonaventura, 13
Tel. 055/375147-311198

Small

Open to scholars and students by prior arrangement

Free

No access

By arrangement

Photograph library open on request

The collection, founded in 1969 at the seat of the State Forestry Institute of Vallombrosa, passed to the Agriculture Faculty in 1936 following the setting up of a degree course in Forestry Science. In 1978, after decades of neglect and in view of the creation of a Faculty forestry museum, the collection of material recommenced. The collection contains today three hundred and ninety models and forestry tools of which one hundred and ten belong to the old Vallombrosa Institute and two hundred and eighty have been acquired during recent years to document the forestry in the forests of the Alps and the Tuscan woods. Alongside the collection is an historical photolibrary concerning reafforestation and hydrogeological operations, set up by the State Forestry Corporation, as well as photographs and slides produced by the Faculty's students for educational uses.

Ordinamento dell'Istituto forestale di Vallombrosa e indicazioni del materiale scientifico di cui l'Istituto stesso è provveduto, in *Annali di Agricoltura*, 29, Roma 1980.

P. Piussi, A. Zonzi Sulli, *Idee e materiali per un Museo forestale, Atti del Convegno ICOM*, in *Selvicoltura*, Trento 1983

Collezioni Scientifiche dell'Istituto Tecnico «Gaetano Salvemini»

50121 Firenze
Via Giusti, 27
Tel. 055/2476941-2

Medium

By prior arrangement for scholars and students

The creation of the collections goes back to the first half of the last century under the auspices of the Scuole d'Arte e Mestieri and the Scuole Tecniche dell'Accademia di Belle Arti in Florence. In 1850 with the founding of the Imperiale e Regio Istituto Tecnico Toscano the collection was greatly increased on the initiative of Filippo Corridi, lecturer in mathematics at the University of Pisa who ran the collections until 1859. The original sections which have survived almost intact until the present day grew throughout the 19th C. to create a large and comprehensive collection in the various branches of the sciences, technology and their applications. Besides the instruments, models of machines and natural history and technological exhibits the museum's treasure includes bibliographical and archival material, a unique group of tools and instruments among the most important in Europe. The collection which has until now been under the care of the Istituto tecnico

Free

♿
No access

By arrangement

Extensive book and photograph library can be consulted on request. A workshop for the restoration and cataloguing of scientific instruments operates at the Gabinetto di Fisica.

Publication of catalogues of the historical collections on the initiative of the Provincia di Firenze. Occasional exhibitions. Research on the history of scientific instruments.

«Gaetano Salvemini» will form the basis for the activities of the Fondazione scienza e tecnica recently founded for cultural purposes on the initiative of local organizations and the major Florentine scientific institutions. The installation of a planetarium is also planned.

Physics laboratory: c. 3000 pieces of physics apparatus produced mainly in the last half of the 19th C. and the early 20th C. which systematically document all the discipline's sectors: mechanics, optics, acoustics, thermology, electrology and magnetism. The fully restored and catalogued collection permits the performance of the fundamental experiments of classical physics.

Natural history collection: large botanical, zoological, mineralogical and paleontological collections formed during the second half of the last century mainly for didactic purposes. Among these of particular note are some herbaria, crystalographic models, glass models of marine invertebrates, anatomical models in wax and anatomical diagrams.

La biblioteca dell'Istituto Tecnico Toscano, 1. Libri antichi: Catalogo (1482-1799), edited by G. Gori and M. Misiti, Florence 1986

Catalogo degli strumenti del Gabinetto di fisica dell'Istituto Tecnico Toscano, 1. Acustica, edited by P. Brenni, Florence 1986

Donazione Contini Bonacossi

50125 Firenze
Palazzina della Meridiana
Piazza Pitti
Tel. 055/218341
(Soprintendenza beni artistici e storici di Firenze)

Medium

By arrangement with the Uffizi Gallery

Free

♿
No access

By arrangement

Presented to the State (the Uffizi Gallery) in 1969 through an agreement with the heirs of the collector Alessandro Contini-Bonacossi, the collection comprises one hundred and forty-four pieces (paintings, sculptures, majolica, Robbian escutcheons) including important Italian and Spanish works. Opened in 1974 it is housed in several rooms of the Palazzina della Meridiana in Piazza Pitti.

Paintings on wood and canvas from the 13th-17th C. from Italy (Sienese, Florentine, Lombard and Venetian schools) and Spain: works by D. di Boninsegna *(Madonna and Child)*, Sassetta *(Altarpiece with Madonna 'della neve')*, A. del Castagno, B. Zenale, G. Savoldo *(Mary Magdalen)*, Bramantino, P. Veneziano *(Birth of St. Nicholas* and *St. Nicholas' Charity)*, Cima da Conegliano *(St. Jerome)*, P. Veronese *(Portrait of Count Jerome of Porto and his son)*, Zurbaran *(St. Antony the Abbot)*, Velasquez *(El Aguador de Sevilla)*, Goya *(Torero)*.
Numerous sculptures in wood and marble including *The Martyrdom of St. Lawrence*, by G.L. Bernini, Robbian terracottas, collection of majolica from Tuscany, the Marches, Umbria, Moorish Spain; antique furniture.

Inaugurazione della Donazione Contini-Bonacossi. Itinerario. Presentation by L. Berti, Florence 1974

Catalogo generale degli Uffizi, by various authors, Florence 1983

Fondazione Romano nel Cenacolo di Santo Spirito

50125 Firenze
Piazza Santo Spirito, 29
Tel. 055/287043

Large

Weekdays 9 a.m.-2 p.m., Sundays and public holidays 8 a.m.-1 p.m.; closed on Mondays

Entrance fee

The old refectory of the Augustinian friars of Santo Spirito, with a fresco by A. Orcagna, has housed the collection donated to the Council by the antiquarian Salvatore Romano since 1946. It contains important sculptures, architectural fragments, furniture and carved stone.

Architectural material and sculptures from the pre-Romanesque period to the end of the 15th C.: works by T. di Camaino *(Angel* and *Caryatid)*, Donatello, J. della Quercia (attrib.).
Frescoes *(Crucifixion* and *Last Supper)* by Orcagna and Marco di Cione (2nd half 14th C.).

L. Becherucci, *Fondazione Salvatore Romano e Cenacolo di Santo Spirito. Catalogo delle opere d'arte*, Florence 1946 L. Becherucci, *I Musei di Santa Croce e di Santo Spirito a Firenze*, Milan 1983

Fondazione di Studi di Storia dell'Arte Roberto Longhi

50135 Firenze
Via Benedetto Fortini, 30
Tel. 055/688794

Medium

Monday, Wednesday and Friday 4 p.m.-6.30 p.m., open only by appointment

Free

♿
Partially accessible

📷
By arrangement

Conferences, lectures, seminars

This is the valuable private collection of the historian Roberto Longhi (1890-1970) established as a foundation in 1971 and arranged in the rooms of the villa «Il Tasso» in the manner of a domestic interior. The collection which is strongly characterized by the presence of 17th and 18th C. and naturalistic paintings follows the direction taken by the critic's studies — sometimes very new and unconventional. The Foundation has a remarkable library at its disposal (including manuscripts) and a photo-library.

♔

The collection comprises over 200 paintings from the 13th-20th C., some sculptures from the 14th-19th C., medieval miniatures, more than 800 drawings (some drawn as study notes by R. Longhi). Paintings of the Bolognese and Emilian schools from the 14th-18th C., of the Lombard school from the 15th-18th C. and from the Genoese and Venetian schools; there is a notable group of Italian and foreign Caravaggioesque works. 20th C. works.

Annali of studies and research published by the Foundation.

A. Boschetto, *La Collezione Roberto Longhi*, Florence 1971

La Fondazione Roberto Longhi a Firenze, by various authors, Milan 1980.

Gabinetto Disegni e Stampe degli Uffizi

50122 Firenze
Via della Ninna, 5
Tel. 055/218341

Medium

The Institute has a very fine collection of drawings and prints started by the Medicis in the 16th C. and expanded greatly during the 17th C., above all due to the work of Cardinal Leopoldo de' Medici (1617-165). Ordered for Cosimo III by the scholar Filippo Baldinucci it was subsequently expanded by donations and acquisitions including those by Emilio Santarelli in 1866. It is located at the Uffizi in rooms which were originally part of the famous «Teatro Mediceo» built by Buontalenti in 1585. The Institute has no permanent exhibition but periodically organizes temporary exhibitions of part of its material. It also has study rooms at its disposal

Weekdays: study room 9 a.m.-1 p.m., exhibition room 9 a.m.-7 p.m.
Sundays and public holidays: study room closed, exhibition room 9 a.m.-1 p.m.
Exhibition room closed on Monday

Free

Accessible

By arrangement

Book and photograph library and archive open by prior arrangement

Temporary exhibitions on the works preserved in the Prints and Drawings Room.
Publication of the accompanying catalogues, in the series Gabinetto Disegni e Stampe degli Uffizi (since 1951).

for the consultation of its rich collection, a very fine library and a photographic library which can be visited by scholars.

C. 130,000 drawings and prints dating from the 14th-20th C. with the majority being examples of the Florentine 16th and 17th C. (Michelangelo, Pontormo, A. del Sarto, Raphael, G. Vasari, A. Allori, C. Allori, Cigoli, Santi di Tito, J. da Empoli, J. Ligozzi, F. Furini).

Graphic works from the Museo Horne and the Palazzo Pitti Galleria d'arte moderna are also stored at the Institute.

E. Santarelli, E. Burci, F. Rondoni, *Catalogo della raccolta dei disegni autografi antichi e moderni donati dal professore Emilio Santarelli*, Florence 1870

P.N. Ferri, *Indice geografico analitico dei disegni di architettura civile e militare esistenti nella Galleria degli Uffizi in Firenze*, Rome 1885

P.N. Ferri, *Catalogo riassuntivo della raccolta di disegni antichi e moderni posseduti dalla R. Galleria degli Uffizi*, Florence 1890

A. De Witt, *La collezione delle stampe*, Rome 1938

I grandi disegni italiani degli Uffizi di Firenze, introduction by A. Forlani Tempesti, notes by A.M. Petrioli Tofani, Milan 1972

Inventario disegni esposti, I and II, edited by A.M. Petrioli Tofani, Florence 1986-1987

Galleria dell'Accademia

50122 Firenze
Via Ricasoli, 60
Tel. 055/214375

Large

Weekdays 9 a.m.-2 p.m., Sundays and public holidays 9 a.m.-1 p.m.; closed on Mondays

Entrance fee

Partially accessible

By arrangement

In addition to housing *David* and other important masterpieces by Michelangelo which bring it world-wide fame, the Galleria dell'Accademia possesses one of the richest collection of paintings in Florence (mainly of the Florentine school from the 13th-16th C.) whose history has been attached many times over the centuries with that of other major State museums in the city: such as the Uffizi which several times drew on its rich collections, or the Galleria d'arte moderna set up at the Accademia and subsequently transferred to Palazzo Pitti. It was founded in 1784 by the grand-duke Pietro Leopoldo with the aim of providing the Florentine Academy of the Arts with a picture gallery of old masters to be used by the students as models for study. The gallery was substantially enlarged following the religious suppressions of 1786 and 1808-1810; since 1873 the *David* has been housed here, subsequently followed by other works by Michelangelo (in the «salone» and the specially built Tribune). The collection of plaster models by Bartolini was recently arranged here and restoration and organization of other important groups of works has taken place.

Sculptures by Michelangelo *(The Prisoners, St. Matthew, David)* and by Giambologna (*Rape of the Sabines*, original model).
Florentine paintings of the 13th and 14th C. by Pacino di Buonaguida, Maestro della Maddalena *(St. Mary Magdalen and*

stories from her life), T. Gaddi (panels with *Stories from the lives of Christ and St. Francis)*, B. Daddi, Giovanni da Milano *(Pietà)*, A. Orcagna; numerous paintings by L. Monaco. 15th C. Florentine works by A. Baldovinetti, Maestro del Cassone Adimari (*Wedding party*, frontal of a 'cassone' or marriage-chest), Maestro della Natività di Castello *(Nativity)*, S. Botticelli *(Madonna and Child with the Infant St. John and Angels)*, L. di Credi, C. Rossellini, Jacopo del Sellaio, Raffaellino del Garbo, Filippino Lippi, Perugino *(Assumption)*. Paintings on wood from the 16th C. by Pontormo, Fra' Bartolomeo *(Mystic wedding of St. Catherine, Isaiah, Job)*, M. Albertinelli *(Trinity, Annunciation, Madonna and Saints)* F. Granacci, Franciabigio *(Holy family with the Infant St. John)*, Bronzino *(Deposition of the Cross)*, A. Allori *(Annunciation, Coronation of the Virgin, Madonna with Saints)*, Santi di Tito.

Plaster models by L. Bartolini and L. Pampaloni.

U. Procacci, *La Galleria dell'Accademia di Firenze*, Rome 1951

R. Chiarelli, *La Galleria dell'Accademia e il Museo di San Marco*, Florence 1968

G. Bonsanti, *La Galleria dell'Accademia*, Florence 1987

The education section of the Uffizi Gallery (Via della Ninna 5, Firenze, tel: 055/218341-284272) organizes educational activities in the museum for schools at every level

Organization of exhibitions

Michelangelo: Prisoner

Galleria d'Arte Moderna di Palazzo Pitti

50125 Firenze
Piazza Pitti
Tel. 055/287096

Large

Weekdays 9 a.m.-2 p.m., Sundays and public holidays 9 a.m.-1 p.m.; closed on Mondays

Entrance fee

No access

By arrangement

Founded in 1914 on the basis of an agreement set up between the State and Florence Council the Galleria d'Arte Moderna was opened in 1924. Comprising a rich collection of over two thousand works it is particularly representative of Tuscan art of the 19th and 20th C. and also contains important examples of other Italian schools and some works by foreign artists. The oldest part of the collection comes from the Accademia di Belle Arti and from the Lorraine and then Savoy palace of Pitti. It was subsequently enlarged with donations and numerous bequests (including that of Diego Martelli and Cristiano Banti of works of the 'Macchiaioli' school, the bequests of Giacomo Conti and Domenico Trentacoste, the donations by Leone Ambron, Elisabeth Chaplin, Alberto Magnelli and others). It is situated on the top floor of Palazzo Pitti in the monumental rooms partly restored by Poccianti during the early years of the last century; the arrangement of the works, displayed in thirty magnificent rooms, is mainly the result of a total rearrangement undertaken between '70 and '79 by Sandra Pinto. The collection of 20th C. works is awaiting arrangement and the redecoration of the Appartamenti Monumentali, particularly the 'Meridiana' suite, is to be continued.

Works mainly of the Tuscan school from the late 18th C. on, by neoclassical painters such as P. Benvenuti *(The Saxons' oath, Portrait of the Contessa Mastiani Brunacci)* and G. Bezzuoli *(Charles VIII enters Florence, Portrait of the grand-duchess Maria Antonietta)* and by sculptors such as A. Canova *(Bust of Napoleon)* and L. Bartolini *(Carlo Ludovico di Borbone, Model for the Demidoff Monument)*. Historical and Romantic painting is represented by works by F. Hayez *(The two Foscaris)*, G. Sabatelli *(Uberti Farinata)*,

Giovanni Fattori: Caught in the stirrup

The education section of the Uffizi Gallery (Via della Ninna 5, Firenze, tel: 055/218341-284272) organizes educational activities in the museum for schools at every level.
Library and archives open to consultation by prior arrangement

Organization of exhibitions

F. Sabatelli *(Ajax of Olileo)*, E. Pollastrini *(The flooding of the Serchio)*, M. d'Azeglio *(Arab Cavalry)*. Sculptures from the same period by G. Dupre' *(Cain and Abel)*, P. Tenerani *(Psyche)*, O. Fantacchiotti. Paintings of the Tuscan «purists», by L. Mussini, A. Ciseri, S. Ussi.

Major works of the Tuscan 'Macchiaioli' school: G. Fattori *(The Italian Battlefield after the Battle of Magenta, The Battle of Custoza, Cavalry charge, The Palmieri Rotunda, Market in Maremma)*, S. Lega *(Bersaglieri leading Austrian prisoners)*, T. Signorini *(Garden at Careggi)*, R. Sernesi *(Florentine hills)*, G. Abbati *(Cloister, The song of the starling)*, C. Banti, A. Cecioni.

Also works by G. Boldini, G. De Nittis, F. Zandomeneghi, G. Previati, F. Palizzi, D. Morelli, Piccio, A. Fontanesi, 20th C. works by P. Nomellini, G. Chini, G. Severini, A. Soffici *(Tuscan hill)*, G. De Chirico, F. Casorati, F. Carena, O. Rosai, O. Ghiglia; sculptures by M. Rosso, L. Andreotti, L. Viani, R. Romanelli, M. Mariani, A. Magnelli.

A.J. Rusconi, *La Galleria d'arte moderna a Firenze*, Rome 1934

Collezioni della Galleria d'arte moderna di Palazzo Pitti: Ottocento parte I. Cultura neoclassica e romantica nella Toscana granducale. Collezioni lorenesi. Acquisizioni posteriori. Depositi, by various authors, Florence 1972

Galleria d'arte moderna in Palazzo Pitti. Guida alle Sale, Florence 1980

La collezione del Novecento 1915-1945, catalogue of the exhibition, edited by E. Spalletti, Florence 1986

K. Aschengreen Piacenti, M. Chiarini, E. Spalletti, *Palazzo Pitti*, Florence 1988

Galleria Corsini

50123 Firenze
Via del Parione, 11

The Gallery contains works by Italian artists, above all of the Florentine and Tuscan schools from the 17th C. It is housed in Palazzo Corsini on the Lungarno built at the end of the 17th C. by the architects Pier Francesco Silvani and Antonio Ferri. It is open to scholars by previous arrangement with the owners.

U. Medici, *Catalogo della Galleria dei Principi Corsini*, compiled by the sculptor U. Medici, Florence 1880

Galleria del Costume

50125 Firenze
Palazzo Pitti
Tel. 055/294279

Large

Weekdays 9 a.m.-2 p.m., Sundays and public holidays 9 a.m.-1 p.m.; closed on Mondays

Opened in 1983 the museum has a rich collection of antique costumes from the 18th-20th C. made up of donations (among the most important that by Umberto Tirelli) and acquisitions made by the museum itself. It is housed in the Palazzina della Meridiana, begun in 1776 by Gaspare M. Paoletti and completed by P. Poccianti under the grand-duke Leopoldo II, which was the favourite residence of Vittorio Emanuele II during Florence's period as capital of Italy. The exhibits are rotated every two years. It is part of the State Museums of Palazzo Pitti, administrated by the Florence Soprintendenza dei beni artistici e storici.

A selection of clothing illustrates the evolution of fashion in Italy and Europe from the 18th C. to the early decades of this century, in

Entrance fee

Accessible

By arrangement

The education section of the Uffizi Gallery (Via della Ninna 5, Firenze, tel: 055/218341-284272) organizes educational activities for schools at every level

Fabric restoration workshop open to scholars

Periodic exhibitions

conjunction with a varied display of accessories. Periodic exhibitions are organized on particular themes in the history of fashion.

La Galleria del Costume, Palazzo Pitti. 1, edited by K. Aschengreen Piacenti, Florence 1983

La Galleria del Costume. Palazzo Pitti. 2, edited by K. Aschengreen Piacenti, Florence 1986

La Galleria del Costume. Palazzo Pitti. 3, edited by K. Aschengrenn Piacenti, Florence 1988

K. Aschengreen Piacenti, M. Chiarini, E. Spalletti, *Palazzo Pitti*, Florence 1988

Galleria Palatina e Appartamenti

50125 Firenze
Palazzo Pitti
Piazza Pitti, 1
Tel. 055/210323

Large

Weekdays 9 a.m.-2 p.m., Sundays and public holidays 9 a.m.-1 p.m.; closed on Mondays

Entrance fee

No access

By arrangement

The education section of the Uffizi Gallery (Via della Ninna 5, Firenze, tel: 055/218341-284272) organizes educational activities in the museum for the schools at every level

Organization of exhibitions

Containing famous Italian and foreign masterpieces from the 15th-18th C. (including Titian, Raphael, Caravaggio, Rubens, Van Dyck) and housed in the magnificent rooms on the piano nobile of Palazzo Pitti, the Galleria Palatina is one of Florence's richest and most celebrated museums. Both the arrangement of the works, faithful to aesthetic criteria rather than systematic placing of the paintings according to school or period, and their display among the magnificent decoration and furnishings of the rooms preserves the character of a private royal collection unchanged over the years. The collections of works of art that the various members of the Medici family had formed at Palazzo Pitti and at their other residences were united in the second half of the 18th C. by Pietro Leopoldo in the wing of the Palazzo decorated with frescoes by Pietro da Cortona and Ciro Ferri (1637-65). The Galleria Palatina was officially created and opened to the public by Leopoldo II in 1828; it was presented to the State in 1911. Not long after the rooms of the so-called 'Quartiere del Volterrano', previously used as a private residence by the reigning family, were added to the Galleria.
Next to the Galleria, the Appartamenti Monumentali (temporarily closed for restoration) take up the other half of the piano nobile of Palazzo Pitti. The lavish rooms, formerly the residence of the Medici family and the Dukes of Lorraine and the Official residence of the Dukes of Savoy during Florence's period as capital of Italy, preserve precious 18th and 19th C. tapestries and hangings and original furnishings and fittings partially rearranged before the second world war.

Galleria Palatina

Important works by Raphael *(Portrait of a Lady ['La Velata'], Portrait of Maddalena and Agnolo Doni, Madonna 'del Granduca', Madonna 'della Seggiola', Portrait of Fedra Inghirami, Madonna 'del Baldacchino', Portrait of a woman expecting a child, Madonna 'dell'impannata')*, by Titian *(Portrait of a Lady ['La Bella'], Concert, Portrait of Ippolito de' Medici)*, by Rubens *(Return from the hayfields, Ulysses*

in the Phaecian Isle, The Four Philosophers, Consequences of War, Holy Family 'della cesta'). Paintings of the Umbro-Tuscan school from the 15th and 16th C.: Filippo Lippi *(Madonna and Child)*, Filippino Lippi *(Death of Lucrezia)*, S. Botticelli *(Portrait of lady in profile)*, Perugino *(Deposition, Mary Magdalen)*, A. del Sarto *(Deposition, Annunciation, St. John the Baptist, Assumption)*, Fra' Bartolomeo *(Deposition)*, Pontormo *(Martyrdom of the eleven thousand, Adoration of the Magi)*, Rosso Fiorentino *(Holy Conversation)*, B. Peruzzi, Bronzino *(Portrait of Guidobaldo della Rovere, Portrait of Don Garzia de' Medici)*. Venetian and Lombard works from the 16th C.: Giorgione (?) *(Three Ages of Man)*, Veronese *(Portrait of a gentleman, Baptism of Christ)*, S. del Piombo, Tintoretto, G.B. Moroni. Italian and foreign paintings from the 17th C. Caravaggio *(The Sleeping Cupid)*, Guido Reni, D. Fetti, A. Gentileschi, Guercino, S. Rosa *(Port at sunset, Port with boats, The Lie)*, Ribera *(Martyrdom of St. Bartholemew)*, A. Van Dyck (*Portrait of Cardinal Bentivoglio*), B.E. Murillo *(Madonna and Child)*, G. Dughet, C. van Poelenburg, B. Breenbergh.

Florentine paintings of the 17th C.: Santi di Tito, G. Pagani, Cigoli *(Sacrifice of Isaac, Martyrdom of St. Stephen, St. Francis, Deposition)*, Giovanni da San Giovanni *(The Wedding of St. Catherine, Painting)*, C. Allori *(St. Julian's hospitality, Judith)*, F. Furini *(Ila and*

Raphael: *Portrait of a lady ('La Velata')*

the nymphs), G. Bilivert, L. Lippi, C. Dolci *(The infant St. John asleep, Portrait of Claudia Felicita, St. John in Patnos, The Madonna appears to St. Lewis)*, Volterrano *(Trick of the parish priest Arlotto)*.

19th C. sculptures: *Venus Italica* by A. Canova, *Charity* by L. Bartolini.

Ceilings with 17th C. frescoes by P. da Cortona and Ciro Ferri, M. Rosselli and F. Tarchiani, Volterrano and from the neo-classical period by L. Sabatelli, G. Martellini, A. Fedi, A. Marini, L. Ademollo, P. Benvenuti.

Appartamenti Monumentali

Medicean furnishings from the 17th C. (ebony *Cabinet* by Vittorio della Rovere, *Cabinet* in ebony and ivory from a design by G.B. Foggini, *Priedieu*, with *Annunciation* by C. Dolci and *holy water stoup* by G.B. Foggini); Florentine and French 18th C. tapestries (series of *Louis XV hunting*, series with *Stories of Esther)*; 17th C. paintings (above all *Portraits* of Medicis and historical figures by J. Sustermans and F. Pourbus the Younger). Neo-classical furniture and ornaments (porcelain). 19th C. furnishings from the Savoy period, when Florence was the capital city (1861-1870), in the state rooms (Sala del Trono, Salotto Rosso, Toletta della Regina Margherita and others). Late 16th C. furniture in the Sala di Bona and Baroque furniture in the Chapel (once the bed-chamber of the Grand Prince Ferdinando de' Medici).
17th C. frescoes by A. Allori, B. Poccetti, C. Allori, M. Rosselli, D. Passignano; stucco and monochrome decorations in the Neo-classical style by G. Albertolli, G. Castagnoli, G.M. Terreni.

A.M. Francini Ciaranfi, *La Galleria Pitti. Galleria Palatina, guida e catalogo dei dipinti*, Florence 1964

La Galleria Palatina. Storia della quadreria granducale di Palazzo Pitti, catalogue of the exhibition, edited by M. Mosco, Florence 1982

K. Aschengreen Piacenti, M. Chiarini, E. Spalletti, *Palazzo Pitti*, Florence 1988.

Galleria Rinaldo Carnielo

50132 Firenze
Piazza Savonarola, 18
Tel. 055/298483 (Comune)

Medium

Weekdays: Saturday 9 a.m.-1 p.m.

Free

Accessible

By arrangement

Owned by the Council, the collection comprises works by the sculptor Rinaldo Carnielo (1853-1910) donated by his son in 1957 and is housed in his old studio.

Sculptures and sketches by R. Carnielo: small Liberty-style fittings in terracotta and bronze *(door knockers, fire-place pieces)*; Busts and portraits in plaster and in marble, plaster sketches of funerary monuments.

Esposizioni e vendita delle opere provenienti dalla raccolta del defunto scultore Prof. Rinaldo Carnielo. Dipinti, disegni e acqueforti dell'Ottocento italiano e straniero, Milan 1929

Galleria degli Uffizi

50122 Firenze
Loggiato degli Uffizi
Tel. 055/218341

Large

Weekdays 9 a.m.-7 p.m., Sundays and public holidays 9 a.m.-1 p.m.; closed on Mondays

Corridoio Vasariano and stores on the first floor: open by prior arrangement

Entrance fee

Accessible

By arrangement

The Uffizi houses, in an area of c. 8,000 sq.m., one of the most important art collections of all time, including antique sculpture and masterpieces on wood and canvas of Italian and foreign schools from the 13th-18th C. The building begun by Vasari (1560) and completed by Buontalenti was commissioned by Cosimo I to serve as government offices. The origins of the collection go back to Francesco I who in 1581 collected and exhibited on the top floor of the building the grand-ducal collections of antique sculptures, coins and medals, jewels, arms, paintings and scientific instruments. Untiring collectors, the Medicis expanded the collection constantly with acquisitions, bequests, dowries and donations: among the most important that of Vittoria della Rovere (an outstanding group of paintings including works by Piero della Francesca, Raphael and Titian) and of Cardinal Leopoldo de' Medici (jewels, medals and a famous collection of drawings and self-portraits). On the death of Gian Gastone, his sister Anna Maria the last descendant of the dynasty managed through the famous family pact (1737) to per-

Piero della Francesca: Federico da Montefeltro

Giotto: Maestà

The education section of the Uffizi Gallery organizes educational activities for schools consisting in visits and annual preparatory courses for teachers. Documentary material available

The Uffizi library is open to consultation by students and scholars by prior arrangement

Occasional organization of conferences and exhibitions concerning the most important restoration work

suade the Dukes of Lorraine to allow her to leave to Florence the collections formed by her ancestors over three centuries. The Dukes of Lorraine and Pietro Leopoldo, continuing in the Medici tradition, subtantially expanded the collection and organized it according to museum criteria. During the 19th C. much of the archaeological, sculptural and scientific material was transferred, going to create the core of other important Florentine museums. Thus the Uffizi has emphasized its character as a collection of paintings on wood and canvas, antique sculptures and tapestries. Some important changes have taken place during this century: the creation of the 'Sale dei Primitivi' by Scarpa, Michelucci and Gardella in the early post-war years, the inclusion of the Church of San Pier Scheraggio into the museum (1971), the reorganization of the rooms containing works by Lippi (1973-'74), by Botticelli (1978) and by Leonardo (1979), the preparation of the storerooms on the first floor. In 1973 the Corridoio Vasariano was reopened, linking the Uffizi with the Palazzo Pitti. Built on the occasion of the marriage of Francesco, the son of Cosimo, with Joan of Austria, the Corrodoio contains paintings from the 17th and 18th C. of Italian and foreign schools and an important collection of self-portraits from various periods. An integral part of the exhibition space, it can be visited by appointment. The «Grandi Uffizi» project, providing more space both for exhibits and for services is to be completed soon.

Agnolo Bronzino: Lucrezia Panciatichi

Sienese and Florentine paintings from the 13th C.: three *Madonna in Maestà* by Cimabue, D. di Buoninsegna and Giotto. 14th C. Sienese and Florentine works: S. Martini *(Annunciation)*, A. and P. Lorenzetti, T. Gaddi, B. Daddi; 15th C. works: G. da Fabriano *(Adoration of the Magi)*, Beato Angelico, P. Uccello *(Battle of San Romano)*, P. della Francesca *(Diptych)*, Masolino, Masaccio, Filippo and Filippino Lippi, A. del Pollaiolo *(Portrait of a lady, Hercules and Antaeus, Hercules and the Hydra)*, S. Botticelli *(Primavera, Birth of Venus, Madonna of the Magnificat)*, D. del Ghirlandaio, A. del Verrocchio, Leonardo da Vinci *(Annunciation, Adoration of the Magi)*, P. Perugino, L. Signorelli. The *Buontalenti Tribuna*: Sculptures from classical originals; *Portraits* by A. Bronzino and Pontormo. Works by German and Flemish masters from the 15th and 16th C.: *Portinari Triptych* by H. Van der Goes, *Deposition* by R. Van der Weiden, *Portrait of Martin Luther* by L. Cranach, *Adoration of the Magi* and *Portrait of the artist's father* by A. Dürer. Paintings of the Venetian school from the 15th-18th C.: G. Bellini *(Sacred Allegory, Pity)*, Giorgione *(Judgement of Solomon)*, Cima da Conegliano, Titian *(Venus of Urbino, Flora, Portrait of Francesco della Rovere)*, L. Lotto, S. del Piombo, P. Veronese, Tintoretto, Canaletto, F. Guardi, G.B. Tiepolo. Also works by A. Mantegna *(Madonna 'delle cave', Triptych of the Epiphany)*, Correggio *(Rest in Egypt, Virgin and Child)*, A. del Sarto *(Madonna 'delle Arpie')*, Fra' Bartolomeo, Rosso Fiorentino, Raphael *(Madonna 'del Cardellino')*, Michelangelo Buonarroti *(Tondo Doni)*, Pontormo *(Dinner at Emmaeus)*, Parmigianino *(Madonna 'dal collo lungo', Madonna di S. Zaccaria)*, D. Dossi, F. Barocci, A. Carracci, Caravaggio *(Young Bacchus, Sacrifice of Isaac, Medusa)*, P.P. Rubens, A. Van Dyck, Rembrandt, F. Goya, S.G. Simeon Chardin.

As for the antique sculpture, worthy of particular note are the copies — in marble and basalt — of the Policletean Doriforo, the replica of the *Ares* by Alcamene, the statues by Asclepio and Demetra, the *Medici Venus*, the Farnesean Heracles, the two statues by Marsia, the *Niobeans*, Boy with a thorn, the bust of the dying Alexander, the portraits of Octavian, Agrippa the Younger, Trajan, Antoninus Pius, Lucius Verus, Marcus Aurelius, Caracalla, Severus Alessandro; among the reliefs, the famous Neo-Attic *krater* with illustrated frieze and the sarcophagi with the Rape of Proserpine and with the story of Phaedra and Hippolytus.

Research notebooks *Gli Uffizi studi e ricerche*. Periodical published by the museum.
Pelli, G. Bencivenni, *Saggio istorico della R. Galleria di Firenze*, 2 vols., Florence 1799

A. Gatti, *Le Gallerie di Firenze*, Florence 1872

G. Poggi, *R. Galleria degli Uffizi. Elenco dei dipinti*, Florence 1923

G.A. Mansuelli, *Galleria degli Uffizi. Le sculture*, 2 vols., Rome 1958

L. Berti, *Gli Uffizi*, Florence 1971

W. Prinz, *Die Sammlung der Selbstbildnisse in den Uffizien, Band 1, Geschichte der Sammlung*, Berlin 1971

Catalogo generale. Gli Uffizi, by various authors, Florence 1979

Gli Uffizi, 2 vols., by various authors, Florence 1982

V. Saladino, Gli Uffizi. *Sculture antiche*, Florence 1983

Gli Uffizi. Storia e collezioni, by various authors, Florence 1983

C. Caneva, A. Cecchi, A. Natali, *Gli Uffizi*, Florence 1986

Giardino di Boboli

50125 Firenze
Piazza Pitti, 1
Tel. 055/218741

Large

November, December, January and February: all week 9 a.m.-4.30 p.m.; March, April, September and October: all week 9 a.m.-5.30 p.m.; May, June, July and August: all week 9 a.m.-7.30 p.m.

Free

♿
Accessible

By arrangement

Guided tours on request. Slide projections

Meetings, exhibitions and conferences

Over an area of about 30 hectares (75 acres) between Palazzo Pitti, Forte Belvedere and Porta Romana stretches the Giardino di Boboli, one of the most magnificent Italian style gardens in existence. Of great botanical and historical interest, rich in sculptures, architecture and delightful settings, its history is closely linked with the birth and development of Palazzo Pitti. Commissioned by Eleonora of Toledo (the very wealthy daughter of the Viceroy of Naples and wife of Cosimo I de' Medici) from Niccolò di Raffaello, known as Tribolo, in 1549 it was continued by Ammannati who also directed the work of extending the Palazzo. In 1569, after some work by other architects, Buontalenti took over and was responsible for some of the most celebrated parts of the garden (above all the Grotta Grande or del Buontalenti). Subject to further important work during the early decades of the 17th C. undertaken by the architect Giulio Parigi and his son Alfonso it was amply enriched with statues and other works during the rule of the Dukes of Lorraine. It had a new period of splendour under Pietro Leopoldo who decreed its partial opening to the public in 1766. The last substantial alteration to the garden occured during the period of French rule. Ferdinand III of Hapsburg-Lorraine subsequently undertook a comprehensive restoration programme which was completed by his son Leopoldo II. Its subsequent history is of little importance. Today it constitutes a real and true open-air museum much visited by Florentines and an essential stop on any tourist itinerary.

Gate of the Piazzale dell'Isolotto

Distributed around the garden are: the statue known as the *Morgante Dwarf* by V. Cioli, the *Grotta del Buontalenti* (with decorations of rock and stalactites, *Apollo* and *Ceres* by B. Bandinelli, murals by B. Poccetti, *Paris and Helen* by V. de' Rossi, copies of the *Prisoners* by Michelangelo, *Venus emerging from her bath* by Giambologna); *Grotta di Madama* attributed to B. Bandinelli and C. Fancelli (with *Goats* by C. Fancelli); *Amphitheatre* by G. and A. Parigi; the *Neptune Fountain* by S. Lorenzi; *Abundance* by Giambologna and P. Tacca; *Isolotto* and the *Ocean Fountain* (copy by the sculptor Romanelli) by Giambologna and his pupils. Also, situated along the main avenue (the *Viottolone*), and in the clearings groups in marble and stone from various periods, from Classical and Roman (copies and restored works) to the 16th C. (works by D. Poggini, M. Naccherino, V. Cioli, G.B. Caccini, V. Danti), and 17th-18th C. (works by C. Fancelli, S. Cioli, R. Curradi, D. and G.B. Pieratti, G. Silvani, G.B. Capezzuoli).

Catalogo delle piante esistenti nell'I. e R. Giardino di Boboli, Florence, 2 ed., 1841

Catalogo delle statue del R. Giardino di Boboli con la notizia dei loro autori, catalogo delle statue del R. Palazzo Pitti e della Galleria, Florence 1880

C. Caneva, *Il Giardino di Boboli*, Florence 1982

Gipsoteca dell'Istituto Statale d'Arte

50125 Firenze
Piazzale di Porta Romana, 9
Tel. 055/220521

Large

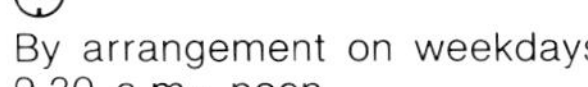

By arrangement on weekdays 9.30 a.m.- noon.

Free

Accessible

By arrangement

Guided tours by appointment

Comprising the abundant fund of casts from the Lelli makers (acquired in 1922), the plaster casts of the old Santa Croce art school and enriched by further donations, the gipsoteca today constitutes one of the most important collections in the world. It is attached to the Istituto Statale D'Arte and situated in the former royal stables of the Boboli Gardens. It contains copies from life of famous works of art, statues, architectural details from important monuments and buildings, portraits, coins and medals and antique works from the Greek, Roman, Byzantine, Gothic, Renaissance (the largest group) and neo-classical periods. To it is connected the still active cast workshop, of great historical, artistic and educational interest. The rearrangement of the exhibits, started in 1985, will be completed by the end of 1988.

Catalogo della Gipsoteca, by various authors, Florence 1979

Per un rinnovato uso del gesso, edited by R. Monticolo, Florence 1977

Donatello, edited by L. Bernardini, A. Capuco Colloud, M. Mastrorocco, Florence 1985

Istituto e Museo di Storia della Scienza

50122 Firenze
Piazza dei Giudici, 1
Tel. 055/293493-298876

Large

Weekdays: 9.30 a.m.-1 p.m.; Monday, Wednesday and Thursday 9.30 a.m.-1 p.m. / 2 p.m.-5 p.m.; closed on Sundays

Entrance fee

Accessible

One of the most important in the world, the museum preserves valuable collections of scientific instruments and objects. The oldest and most valuable group of exhibits comes from the grand-ducal collections of the Uffizi Gallery and the Imperiale e Regio Museo di Fisica e Storia Naturale. To these were subsequently added the extensive natural sciences collections of the celebrated Florentine scholar Giovanni Targioni Tozzetti, surgical instruments, apothecary's jars and collections of anatomical and obstetrical wax models. In addition to exhibiting and preserving this unique heritage the Institute undertakes extensive educational activities and promotes study and research on an international scale. Situated in Palazzo Castellani, the museum, which suffered extensive damage in the 1966 flood, has been the subject of restoration work and the collections have been reorganized.

Medici collection: quadrants, astrolabes, sun-dials and night-clocks, compasses, armillary spheres. Instruments belonging to Galileo Galilei (1564-1642) including two original telescopes, "objective lens", lodestones, geometrical and military compasses. Valuable instruments in blown glass from the Accademia del Cimento (1657-1667): long-stemmed and spiral thermometers, clinical 'frog' thermometers and numerous artistic glass objects produced in the

glass factory in the Boboli Gardens. Collection of globes from the 17th and 18th C. Binoculars, microscopes, telescopes and optical instruments from the 17th, 18th and 19th C.
Mechanical air-pumps both from abroad and manufactured by the workshop of the Imperiale e Regio Museo di Fisica e Storia Naturale, instruments concerning electrostatics and electromagnetics. Section dedicated to medicine with anatomical models in wax and terracotta, surgical instruments from the 18th C. Chemistry section with a laboratory bench and chemical preparations of Pietro Leopoldo. Display of weights and measures and mechanical clocks including a mechanical writing machine and 'perpetual motion instrument'.
Rich collection of minerals belonging to Giovanni Targioni Tozzetti (1712-1783).

Nuncius. Annali di Storia della Scienza, a periodical published by the museum twice a year

M.L. Righini Bonelli, *Il Museo di storia della scienza a Firenze*, Milan 1968

L'Istituto e Museo di storia della scienza a Firenze, by various authors, Florence 1978

M.C. Cantù, M.L. Righini Bonelli, *Gli strumenti antichi al Museo di storia della scienza di Firenze*, Florence 1980

L'età di Galileo. Il secolo d'oro della scienza toscana, exhibition catalogue, edited by Mara Miniati, Florence 1987

No

Extensive library open to the public on weekdays from 9.30 a.m. to 1 p.m. Photograph library and archives open for specific study purposes.

Astronomy lectures in the planetarium. Preparatory courses for teachers. School visits by prior arrangement.

Temporary thematic exhibitions with accompanying catalogue; seminars, conferences, visiting professors. Permanent research programmes: annual Bibliography of the Studi italiani di Storia della Scienza; Archive containing correspondence of Italian scientists. File of the scientific instruments preserved in Italy.

16th C. Astrolabe used by Galileo Galilei

Mostra Permanente della Comunità Israelitica

50121 Firenze
Via Farini, 4
Tel. 055/245252

Small

By arrangement

Free

No access

No

Guided tours on request

Opened in 1980 the museum contains material concerning Jewish life and culture in Florence and important and delicate examples of goldsmith's work and textiles which make up the Community's artistic heritage: cerimonial objects used at important moments in family life or for the celebration of the important Jewish festivals, silver and rare cloths used to decorate the Sepher. It is housed on the first floor of the Synagogue (1884), built in the Moorish style with frescoes throughout and rich mosaic decorations.

Fabric, silver and wood fittings, and other documents on Jewish life and culture, from 1581 to the 20th C.

Museo Agrario Tropicale dell'Istituto Agronomico d'Oltremare

50132 Firenze
Via A. Cocchi, 4
Tel. 055/573201

Large

9 a.m.-1 p.m. by previous arrangement for adults only

Free

No access

By arrangement

Guided tour on request

Library open for consultation on weekdays from 9 a.m.-2 p.m. by prior arrangement

Founded at the beginning of the century it contains agricultural produce and craft objects from tropical countries acquired mainly in the course of missions abroad undertaken by experts from the Istituto Agronomico d'Oltremare and outside researchers. There is an adjacent botanical garden with tropical and sub-tropical plants.

The produce is grouped by market criteria.

Nervine products, spices, cereals, fruit, cotton.

Tobacco, dyes and tannins, rubber and resins, india-rubber.

Medicinal plants, animal products, fibrous plants, essences and scents, vegetable ivory, starch- and sugar- yielding plants, oil-yielding plants.

Typical products from the following countries: Venezuela, Columbia, Ecuador, Brazil, Peru, Bolivia, Paraguay, Uruguay, Chile, Argentina, Libya, Ethiopia, Eritrea, Congo, Madagascar.

In the glass-houses: coffee, tea, cacao, mate, chat, karkade, pepper, cloves, teff, date, banana, pineapple, papaya, mango, cotton, tamarind, coca, palms, kapok, manioca, sugar-cane, oil-palm.

Collection of the Associazione Botanica «Bromelia».

A. Rosania, *Museo agrario tropicale dell'Istituto Agronomico per l'Oltremare*, Florence 1982

A. Rosania, *Inventario delle piante esistenti nelle serre calde e fredde e nel giardino botanico dell'Istituto Agronomico per l'Oltremare di Firenze*, in *Rivista di Agricoltura subtropicale*, LXXII, 3, 1983

Museo di Antropologia ed Etnologia

Sezione del Museo di storia naturale dell'Università di Firenze
50122 Firenze
Palazzo Nonfinito
Via del Proconsolo, 12
Tel. 055/296449

Large

Weekdays: Saturday 9 a.m.-1 p.m. 1st and 3rd Sunday of the month

Free

Partially accessible

By arrangement

Guided visits for schools and groups on Thursday, Friday and Saturday on request. Individual meetings for teachers by prior arrangement.

Anthropology and Ethnology library open to consultation by prior arrangement.

Series of conferences, occasional exhibitions and study meetings organized by the Museum of Natural History of the University of Florence.

Founded in 1869 by Paolo Mantegazza who was called in that same year to take up the first chair in Anthropology in Italy, at the University of Florence, the museum has had its seat since 1924 in the Palazzo Nonfinito. Through its long history it has been enriched with many valuable and antique collections, both in the fields of anatomy-osteology and in that of ethnography, until it now contains material on the civilizations of the whole world. Of particular interest is the material brought back by the first Italian and foreign explorers, the precious pre-columbian relics (formerly in the Medici collections) and the material from Captain Cook's third expedition, the extremely rare collection on the Kaffirs in Pakistan (donated in 1960 by Paolo Graziosi) and the collection of clothes and objects from the Ainu from Hokkaido (Japan). It also contains valuable osteological material (over six thousand human skulls from various origins), face models taken from life (Malays, Ethiopians, Pygmies, Somalians, Tebus, Libyans, Mongols etc.) and fossilized human remains. Connected to the osteological collections and developed precisely for the study of somatic anthropology are the scientific instruments of the anthropometric laboratory «Paolo Mantegazza», founded in 1901 and enlarged over the following years.

Ethnographical collections on the present-day «writing-less» peoples of Asia, Africa, America, Lapland, Samoa, Papua, Indonesia, Oceania, Somalia, Central Southern Africa, Ainu, Kaffir, the African and Asian nomads etc.
Osteological relics; stone objects from the non-European continents; mummified remains from ancient Peru. Hindu collection from the Indian museum. Several hundred human face-masks from various parts of the world.

Archivio per l'Antropologia e l'Etnologia, annual publication produced by the University Department.

A. Berzi, C. Cipriani,, M. Poggesi, *Florentine Scientific Museums*, in J. Soc. Bibl. nat. Hist. (1980) 9(4), pp. 413-425

S. Ciruzzi, *Il Museo Nazionale di antropologia e etnologia dell'Università di Firenze*, in *Notiziario*, VI, 3, March 1983

S. Ciruzzi, *Le Istituzioni scientifiche del Palazzo Nonfinito a Firenze (1869-1986)*, in *Archivio per l'Antropologia e l'Etnologia*, VCXVI, 1986

Il Museo di storia naturale dell'Università di Firenze, by various authors, Florence 1987

Museo Archeologico

50121 Firenze
Via della Colonna, 38
Tel. 055/2478641

Large

The museum boasts valuable treasures comprising a large collection of Etruscan antiquities, Greek and Roman material and an Egyptian collection among the most important in Italy. The origins of the museum go back to the celebrated collections of the Medicis and the Dukes of Lorraine which were originally held in the Uffizi, transferring subsequently to the Monastery of St. Catherine and partly to the Cenacolo di Foligno in Via Faenza; in 1880 it was transferred to Palazzo della Crocetta (the present seat), officially opened as the Regio Museo Archeologico. Of the subsequent important changes it is worth noting the institution of a new section, the Museo Storico Topografico dell'Etruria, the work of L. Milani

Weekdays 9 a.m.-2 p.m., Sundays and public holidays 9 a.m.-1 p.m.; closed on Mondays

Entrance fee

No access

By arrangement

Material available for teacher-led visits from the Education section of the Soprintendenza Archeologica (Via della Pergola 65, Firenze, tel. 055/ 2478642).

Occasional exhibitions

(1897) and the opening of the Regio Galleria di Pittura Etrusca (1832). The museum has since received by donation or through acquisition many valuable groups of material from various sources. Altered and reopened in 1950, the museum was badly damaged in the 1966 flood which devastated the ground floor and caused the closure of the Topographical Museum. Since that date the Soprintendenza of archaeology has set under way an extensive programme of restoration and redevelopment covering the museum's structure as a whole which is still in progress.

The museum is in the process of being rearranged and therefore only a few of the rooms are open to the public. Egyptian collection, one of the most important in Italy: statues and fragments of statues depicting pharoahs or dignitaries and officials, stelae, sarcophagi in stone and wood, statuettes of gods, amulets, scarabs, pottery, wooden chariot from a tomb in Thebes.
Ancient statues in marble (the *«Milani» kouroi*). The *François Vase*, an Attic black-figured krater made by Ergotimos and painted by Kleitias, one of the masterpieces of ancient painting. Cinerary statues from Chiusi. Hellenistic urns decorated with bas-reliefs with mythical scenes. Painted sarcophagus of the Amazzoni, from Tarquinia (4th C. B.C.). Of the numerous Etruscan bronzes: sheets of embossed bronze, one of which depicts the handing of arms to Achilles; fragments of a statue from Acqua Santa (Chianciano); statue of *Chimera* discovered in Arezzo in the 16th C.; statue known as the *Arringatore* or *Orator* from the end of the 2nd C. B.C.; crockery and utensils. A Horse's Head in gilded bronze probably of the Late Hellenistic period. Bronze statue of a young athlete from the Augustan period, known as the *Idolino*.

L. A. Milani, *Museo topografico dell'Etruria*, Florence 1898

Statue known as the Arringatore or Orator
Chimera

L. A. Milani, *Il Regio Museo archeologico di Firenze*, Florence 1923

A. De Agostino, *Il Museo archeologico di Firenze*, Florence 1968

Luigi Adriano Milani - *Origini e sviluppo del complesso museale archeologico di Firenze*, by various authors, in *Studi e Materiali*, 5, 1982, pp. 33-175

M. Marini, F. Razeto, *Museo Archeologico*, Firenze, Florence 1985

Museo degli Argenti

50125 Firenze
Palazzo Pitti
Piazza Pitti, 1
Tel. 055/212557

Large

Weekdays 9 a.m.-2 p.m., Sundays and public holidays 9 a.m.-1 p.m.; closed on Mondays

Entrance fee

Partially accessible

By arrangement

The education section of the Uffizi Gallery (Via della Ninna 5, Firenze, tel: 055/218341-284272) organizes educational activities in the museum for schools at every level.

Situated on the ground floor of Palazzo Pitti, the museum contains the treasures amassed by the Medicis and the Dukes of Hapsburg-Lorraine: from the splendid antique vases belonging to Lorenzo the Magnificient to the artistic treasures of the Precious Stone Room of the Uffizi, to the jewels of the Electress Palatine to the treasures of the Salzburg Princes (brought to Florence in 1814 by Ferdinando III); precious stones, ivory, amber, painted glass, lace, cloth, tapestries and cameos which make it one of the most varied and valuable princely collections in the world. It is housed in sumptuous rooms decorated with frescoes, once the summer apartments of the grand-dukes: the magnificent Sala degli Argenti decorated by various artists (Giovanni da San Giovanni, F. Furini, C. Bravo, O. Vannini) beginning in 1634 on the occasion of the marriage of Ferdinando II de' Medici and Vittoria della Rovere, a small Chapel and other rooms decorated with Florentine tapestries from the 16th-17th C. It is part of the Palazzo Pitti museum complex, run by the Soprintendenza per i beni artistici e storici di Firenze.

Objects in pietre dure (goblets, vases, cups etc., some antique with 15th and 16th C. mountings) beloging to the Medici collections of Piero and Lorenzo and then Cosimo, Francesco and Ferdinando. Reliquaries in silver and pietre dure from the 16th and the 17th C. Sculptures and other objects in ivory of the Italian, German and Flemish schools from the 15th-18th C. Turned ivory vases, polyhedrons and goblets produced in Germany in the 16th and 17th C. Northern European sculptures and decorative objects in amber.

Ferdinando III's treasure: objects in horn, coconut,, ostrich egg, briar wood, shells, rocks crystal, enamelled silver and gold of German production from the 14th-19th C.
Silver tableware and church silver from the 18th C. 17th and 18th C. enamelled glass. Furniture (prie-dieus, cabinets) in ebony and pietre dure. Precious stones, cameos and jewels.

A. J. Rusconi, *Il Museo degli argenti in Firenze*, Rome 1935

K. Aschenreen Piacenti, *Il Museo degli argenti*, Milan 1968

K. Aschengreen Piacenti, *Capolavori del Museo degli argenti*, Florence 1969

K. Aschengreen Piacenti, M. Chiarini, E. Spalletti, *Palazzo Pitti*, Florence 1988

Museo Bardini

50125 Firenze
Piazza de' Mozzi, 1
Tel. 055/2342427

The important and varied collection preserved in the museum was formed by Stefano Bardini (1836-1922) and reflects the taste typical of a collector and antiquarian with the uncommon gifts of a connoisseur and art dealer. The Palazzo, commissioned in 1883 by Bardini to house his Antique Gallery was built using original antique

Large

Weekdays 9 a.m.-2 p.m., Sundays and public holidays 8 a.m.-1 p.m.; closed on Wednesdays. Evening opening during the summer period, with dates and times decided each year.

Entrance fee

Partially accessible

By arrangement

Occasional exhibitions and conferences.

pieces (altars, staircases, doorways and columns) and acts as an authentic and fitting frame to the collection. On the death of Bardini in 1922 the building and what was left of the vast collection passed according to the collector's express wish to the Council. The museum was opened in 1925. Alonside the masterpieces of painting and sculpture it contains many important examples of the minor arts such as carpets, arms and armour, bronzes, medals and various fittings and furniture. After extensive damage suffered in the 1966 flood it underwent comprehensive restoration. On the second floor of the museum is the Galleria Corsi, presently closed to the public, containing over six hundred works from various periods from the 12th-19th C., donated to the Council in 1937 by Fortunata Carobbi Corsi.

Etruscan, Roman and Romanesque architectural fragments and sculptures (corbel with *Lady's head* by N. Pisano), from the Gothic

Antonio del Pollaiolo; St. Michael Archangel

period (*Charity* by T. di Camaino), from the Renaissance (*Madonna 'dei Cordai'* by Donatello and collaborators; *Madonna with Angels* by A. della Robbia; *Bust of St. John the Baptist* attributed to A. Sansovino); *Madonna and Child* in plaster attributed to Donatello. Painting on wood and canvas and detached frescoes from the 13th-17th C., including *Madonna and Child* from the school of A. Lorenzetti, *Madonna 'dell'orecchio'* by S. dei Crocifissi, *St. John the Baptist* by M. Giambono, *Madonna and Child* by Benvenuto di Giovanni, *St. Michael Archangel* by A. del Pollaiolo; also works by G. Bugiardini, F. Salviati, B. Passarotti, Guercino. 17th C. Florentine paintings by G. da San Giovanni, Cecco Bravo, Volterrano, C. Dolci. Drawings by G. D. Tiepolo. Renaissance pottery, 15th and 16th C. bronzes; oriental carpets; furniture, cassoni (decorated chests), tapestries from various periods; glass, goldsmith's work and enamel; arms and armour; musical instruments.

San Niccolò Oltrarno, *La Chiesa, una famiglia di antiquari*, by various authors, Florence 1982

F. Scalia, C. De Benedictis, *Il Museo Bardini a Firenze*. I dipinti e i disegni, Milan 1984

F. Scalia, L.G. Boccia, *Museo Bardini*. Le armi, Florence 1985

E. Neri Lusanna, L. Faedo, *Il Museo Bardini a Firenze. Le sculture*, Milan 1986

Natura morta italiana del Sei-Settecento dalla Galleria Corsi e dal Museo Bardini, exhibition catalogue, edited by M. Chiarini, Florence 1987

Museo del Bigallo

50123 Firenze
Piazza San Giovanni, 1
Tel. 055/215440 (Istituto Sant'Agnese)

Owned by the Opera Pia Orfanatrofio del Bigallo, the museum was opened in 1976, after reorganization and restoration arranged by the Soprintendenza of Florence with contributions from private individuals and companies. Situated in the Loggia del Bigallo, the old headquarters of the charitable society, it contains an important group of works of art from the 13th-16th C. of great historical and artistic interest (including works by the Maestro del Bigallo, B. Daddi, Niccolò di Pietro Gerini, Domenico di Michelino, J. del Sellaio, R. del Ghirlandaio, C. Portelli, A. Arnoldi). Presently closed to the public the museum can be visited for approved study purposes.

Il Museo del Bigallo, edited by H. Kiel, Milan 1977

Museo Botanico

Sezione del Museo di storia naturale dell'Università di Firenze
50121 Firenze
Via La Pira, 4
Tel. 055/284411-218525

Medium

Weekdays: Monday,

Contains herbariums and various collections of botanical material. The original core, the Erbario Centrale Italiano, was set up in 1842 for the grand-duke Leopoldo II of Lorraine by the famous botanist Filippo Parlatore at the Imperial Regio Museo di Fisica e Storia Naturale. The museum has been subsequently enriched with numerous collections including the splendid Webb herbarium acquired in 1854. Between 1833 and 1890 it was transferred to the new site in Via La Pira. In 1918 the Erbario Tropicale from Rome containing over three thousand botanical specimens mainly from Africa was added to it.
One of the most important in Italy both in its richness and scientific value, the museum contains today over four million items from throughout the world.

Wednesday and Friday 9 a.m.-noon. From November to June it is also open occasionally on Sunday morning

Free

No access

By arrangement

Guided visits

Laboratory for the preparation of samples, palinology laboratory, seed bank. Open for consultation

Series of conferences, occasional exhibitions and study meetings organized by the Natural History Museum of the University of Florence.

A Bundle from the 18th C. Herbarium of P.A. Micheli

F. Parlatore general herbarium (3,500,000 specimens). Webb herbarium (250,000 specimens from the 18th-19th C. from Africa, South America and Oceania). Beccari Herbarium (20,000 specimens from the 19th C. from Indonesia). Micheli herbarium (18th C.). Cesalpino herbarium (16th C.).

18th-19th C. wax models (by C. Susini, L. Calamai and L. Calenzuoli). Paintings on botanical subjects by B. Bimbi, G. Napolitano. 18th C. illustrated manuscripts. Plant fossils. Objects of ethnographical value produced from plant products from the 19th and 20th C. Sections of tree trunks. Plaster models of fungi.

G. Moggi, *Il Museo botanico ed il Giardino dei Semplici dell'Università di Firenze*, in *Boll. Soc. It. Iris*, 1975, pp. 26-39

A. Berzi, C. Cipriani, M. Poggesi, *Florentine scientific museums*, in *J. Soc. Bibl. nat. Hist.* (1980) 9(4), pp. 413-425

G. Moggi, *Il Museo botanico*, in *I musei scientifici a Firenze. Problemi di restauro e ricomposizione museale. Parte seconda*, edited by F. Gurrieri, L. Zangheri, Florence 1981, pp. 13-19

G. Moggi, *Storie di collezioni di piante: gli erbari fiorentini*, in *Atti Società Leonardo da Vinci*, 5, Florence 1984, pp. 49-66

G. Moggi, *L'Erbario*, Florence 1984

Una visita al museo botanico, edited by G. Moggi 1985

Il Museo di storia naturale dell'Università di Firenze, by various authors, Florence 1987

Museo delle Carrozze

50125 Firenze
Palazzo Pitti
Piazza Pitti

Presently closed for restoration, the museum contains several splendid 18th and 19th C. carriages, mainly belonging to the Court of Lorraine. It is part of the Palazzo Pitti museum complex, administered by the Florence Soprintendenza per i beni artistici e storici and is situated in the right wing of the palace.

K. Aschengreen Piacenti, M. Chiarini, E. Spalletti, *Palazzo Pitti*, Florence 1988

Museo del Conservatorio di Musica Cherubini

50122 Firenze
Palazzo Vecchio
Piazza della Signoria
Tel. 055/210502 (Conservatorio di musica Luigi Cherubini)

Contains a unique and priceless collection of musical instruments. The collection's origins go back to the acquisitions of musical instruments made by the Medici court, in particular by Ferdinando (1663-1713) the son of the grand-duke Cosimo III, 'a passionate music-lover'. Enlarged over the years with further acquisitions, the collection was transferred in 1863 from Palazzo Pitti to the Luigi Cherubini Music Conservatoire where the museum was opened in 1926.
Part of the collection is presently housed in the Palazzo Vecchio museum, and the museum is temporarily closed to the public.

Musical instruments from 1568 to the 20th C.: of particular note, *violins*, *violas* and *'cellos* by *Antonio Stradivarius*, *Amati' cello*, *upright piano* by D. Del Mela, *Floriani spinet*; numerous wind instruments including the *'bimbonifono'*, *Giorgi flute* and *Briccialdi flute*.

V. Gai, C. Calzolari, *Gli strumenti musicali della corte medicea e il Museo del Conservatorio «Luigi Cherubini» di Firenze*, Florence 1969

Antichi strumenti. Collezione dei Medici e dei Lorena, exhibition catalogue, Florence 1980

Museo della Fondazione Herbert Percy Horne

50122 Firenze
Via dei Benci, 6
Tel. 055/244661

Medium

Weekdays 9 a.m.-1 p.m.; closed on Sundays

Entrance fee

No access

Contains a rich collection of paintings, sculptures, drawings, furniture and pottery presented to the nation, along with his house, by the English art historian Herbert P. Horne (1864-1916). An interesting and celebrated scholar and collector, Horne bought Palazzo Corsini in Via dei Benci 6 in 1911 and dedicated himself over the following years to its complete redevelopment with the intention of creating, also in the decoration of the rooms and the arrangement of the works, the original appearance of a Renaissance mansion. On his death the decoration of the rooms was completed by the art historian Carlo Gamba, who was also the first president of the Foundation set up the following year (1917). In addition to the interesting and varied collections of works of art, the Foundation also has at its disposal a well-stocked library and an important collection of archival material.

Paintings of the Sienese and Florentine schools from the 14th C. (Giotto, *St. Stephen*; P. Lorenzetti, *Three Saints*; B. Daddi, *Crucifixion*; S. Martini, *Diptych with Madonna and Child and Pietà*); also 15th and 16th C. works by Masaccio, B. Gozzoli, Filippino Lippi (front of a cassone with *Queen Vasthi leaving the royale palace*), P. di Cosimo,

By arrangement

Guided tour by appointment

Archive and library open to consultation on request

Exhibitions and conferences

L. Signorelli, Giovanni di Paolo, D. Beccafumi, D. Dossi (*Allegory of music*). 17th C. Florentine canvases by F. Furini, F. Curradi, C. Dolci.

14th-17th C. sculpture:
St. John by D. da Settignano, two *Madonnas* in plaster attributed to A. Rossellino, *Madonna* by J. Sansovino, terracotta studies by Giambologna, sketch with *Angels in glory* by G.L. Bernini.

Collection of Italian ceramics (Florence, Orvieto, Faenza etc.) from the 14th-17th C.

Religious and decorative art (15th C. crosses and chalices, plaquettes and seals, chess-boards and mirrors) and domestic implements (15th-17th C. cutlery; firedogs etc.).

Furniture and wooden fittings from the Renaissance to the 17th C.

The collection of drawings (with works by Raphael, A. del Sarto, A. Carracci, Guercino, S. Rosa, G.B. Tiepolo) is currently stored in the Prints and Drawings Rooms at the Uffizi.

Catalogo illustrato della fondazione Horne, Florence 1921
C. Gamba, *Il Museo Horne a Firenze*, Florence 1961

F. Rossi, *Il Museo Horne a Firenze*, Milan 1966

L. Bellosi, *Il Museo Horne. Luci e ombre dei musei fiorentini*, in *Atti della Società Leonardo da Vinci*, III, 6, 1975, pp. 229-241

Chest

Museo di Geologia e Paleontologia

Sezione del Museo di storia naturale dell'Università di Firenze
50121 Firenze
Via La Pira, 4
Tel. 055/262711

Large

Weekdays 9 a.m.-1 p.m., Monday 2 p.m.-6 p.m.; closed on Fridays.
From November to June the museum is occasionally open also on Sundays

The origins of the university museum go back to the grand-ducal collections of the Imperial Regio Museo di Fisica e Storia Naturale founded by Pietro Leopoldo in 1775. In 1870 the geological and paleontological collection was transferred to the «Gabinetto di Geologia» and in 1925 was moved to its present site. It contains one of the richest collections in Italy of almost three hundred thousand specimens of fossils and rocks. The present exhibition areas contain a collection of mammal remains mainly from the Upper Valdarno area, a recently opened room on the evolution of the horse and the Invertebrate and Plant Room with specimens from the Quaternary to Precambrian periods.

Invertebrate, plant and rock section.

Vertebrate section: original skeleton of the *Orephithecus bambolii*, an ape found in lignite near Grosseto; collection of impressions from the Mesozoic period, including a unique impression of an Italian dinosaur; skeletons found in the Upper Valdarno including *Ursus minimus*, *Tapirus arvenensis*; skull of the *Cervus diacronios*; skeletons of *Anancus arvenensis*, *Hippopotamus antiquus*, *Di-*

Free

♿
Accessible

By arrangement

☞
Guided visits for teachers by appointment

Library of the University Department of Earth Sciences open to consultation 9 a.m.-1 p.m. / 3 p.m.-6 p.m. by prior arrangement

Series of conferences, occasional exhibitions and study meetings organized by the Natural History Museum of the University of Florence.

cerorhinus etruscus, *Leptobos etruscus*.

Interesting fully mounted specimen of *Elephas meridionalis*.

V. Schiff, *Il Museo di storia naturale e la Facoltà di Scienze Fisiche e Naturali di Firenze*, in *Archeion*, IX, Rome 1928, pp. 1-98

A. Berzi, M. Mazzini, *Il Museo di Geologia e Paleontologia dell'Università degli Studi di Firenze*, in *I Musei Scientifici a Firenze*, Florence 1976, pp. 65-68

A. Berzi, C. Cipriani, M. Poggesi, *Florentine Scientific Museums*, in *J. Soc. Bibl. nat. Hist.* (1980) 9(4), pp. 413-425

M. Mazzini, *Guida del Museo di Geologia e Paleontologia dell'Università di Firenze*, San Giovanni Valdarno 1982

Il Museo di storia naturale dell'Università di Firenze, by various authors, Florence 1987

Room on the evolution of Equidae

Museo e Istituto Fiorentino di Preistoria

50122 Firenze
Via Sant'Egidio, 21
Tel. 055/295159

Large

Founded in 1946 on the initiative of a group of scholars it is situated in the rooms of the former convent of the lay-sisters owned by the Council. It was opened to the public in 1975 following comprehensive restoration and restructuring. The material in the museum covers the period between the early Stone Age and the late prehistorical period. The collections comprising stone and bone objects, pottery, copper and bronze weapons and documents concerning the arts accompanied by animal and human remains from excavations and studies undertaken by Societies (Comitato per le ricerche di Paleontologia umana, Istituto Italiano di Preistoria e Protostoria) and by individual scholars in Europe, Africa, Asia and America. The material, with the exception of the educational room

Weekdays 9.30 a.m.-12.30 p.m., closed on Sundays
Evening opening during the summer period with dates and times decided annually

Free

No access

By arrangement

Educational activities organized annually in collaboration with the Council (Assessorato pubblica istruzione) consisting in series of meetings, lectures and guided visits; educational and scientific material available

Library open to the public from 9.30 a.m.-12.30 p.m.
Archive, photograph library, research and restoration laboratories open only to students and scholars

Conferences

is displayed chronologically and geographically, starting from the earliest prehistorical period in Italy.

The earliest Italian Prehistory, with human hunter-gathered groups dating from the Lower Paleolithic period, is represented by remarkable collections of stone objects from the terraces of Tuscany, and deposits in Abruzzo and Basilicata. From the Middle Paleolithic period items from famous Tuscan caves: Onda, Equi, Buca del Tasso; in addition to those coming from the Grottoes 'dei Balzi Rossi' (Liguria), the fruit of early 20th C. researches; the result of modern excavations are the collections from the Grotta Spagnoli (Puglia) and Grotta del Poggio (Campania). Of particular importance regarding ancient human relics is the famous Olmo skull (Arezzo) long held to be the most evolved human type existing at the time. From the Upper Paleolithic period there are four groups of material which show particular variety and completeness: Vado all'Arancio (Tuscany), Romito (Calabria), Romanelli (Puglia), Levanzo (Sicily); these complexes, in addition to having exposed stone age sites which have given their name to cultural types, are famous for the artistic evidence: rock and bone carvings with naturalistic and schematic illustrations, artistic expressions from the «Mediterranean Province»; from the excavations in Romito there is a 'bisoma' tomb, evidence of the existence even at such an early date of the cult of the dead. From this period there is a remarkable collection of carved stones from Salento (Puglia). And also the San Teodoro (Messina) excavations with the famous human skull and contemporary stone works. Of note, from a Neolithic agricultural settlement, a group of imprinted, painted and carved pottery accompanied by objects in stone and bone (Puglia) and the reproductions of the famous neolithic paintings from the cave in Porto Badisco (Puglia) and those of the neoneolithic paintings in Levanzo. From the Metal Age, of note are the grave-goods, with black pottery, copper daggers and arrow-heads (Lazio) as well as the collections from the pile-dwellings of the Lago di Ledro (Trentino), from the Grotta dello Scoglietto (Tuscany) with bronze daggers, pendants, necklaces, amber.From the Iron Age the important group of urns from the Benacci and Arnoaldi tombs (Emilia). Of particular interest are the collections from the earliest prehistorical discoveries, the French collections from the region of the Somme, of Le Moustier, La Madeleine and those from the pile-dwellings on French and Swiss lakes, still displayed in the original 19th C. presentation.
Valuable African collections: exceptional example of grave-goods from the preislamic tomb in Ghira with wooden vases and combs and the stelae and altars for funeral offering from the necropolises of El Agial and the original fragments of rock carved by Arrechin. From Somalia, of particular interest is the material from the Bur region.
From Asia, worthy of particular note is the impressive collection of material from the Lower Paleolithic period from the alluvion of the Soan River (Pakistan) and the pottery and stone objects from the acropolis of Morgah.
From America, Argentine ethnographical material and stone objects from the late Stone Age in North America.

Text edited by M. Guerri

Museo fiorentino di Preistoria, Florence 1975

Avvio alla conoscenza del Museo di geologia e paleontologia dell'Università di Firenze e del Museo e Istituto fiorentino di Preistoria, Florence 1986-1987

Museo Marino Marini

50123 Firenze
Piazza San Pancrazio, 1

Large

All week 10 a.m.-6 p.m.
Closed on Tuesday

Entrance fee

Accessible

Yes

The museum, opened in 1988, contains the donation to Florence Council of a considerable group of works (over 200 including paintings, drawings, sculptures in terracotta, plaster, bronze and wodd) by the sculptor Marino Marini (1901-1980). It has been designed using the most modern of museum display Techniques and is housed in the former church of San Pancrazio, owned by the State and comprehensively restructured by the Soprintendenza per i beni architettonici e ambientali for the Provinces of Florence and Pistoia.

F. Russoli, *Marino Marini. Pitture e disegni*, Milan 1963

H. Read, P. Waldberg, G. di San Lazzaro, *Marino Marini*, Milan 1970

A.M. Hammacher, *Marino Marini. Sculture, pitture, disegni*, London 1972

C. Pirovano, *Marino Marini scultore*, Milan 1972

Marino Marini. Sculture, pitture, disegni dal 1914 al 1977, exhibition catalogue, by various authors, Florence 1983

Marino Pittore, exhibition catalogue, edited by M. De Micheli and C. Pirovano, Milan 1987

Marino Marini, a cura di C. Pirovano, Firenze 1988

Museo di Mineralogia e Litologia

Sezione del Museo di storia naturale dell'Università di Firenze
50121 Firenze
Via La Pira, 4
Tel. 055/216936

Medium

Weekdays 9 a.m.-1 p.m. / 3 p.m.-6 p.m. From November to June the museum is also occasionally open on Sundays

Free

Accessible

By arrangement

Originally housed with the other grand-ducal scientific collections at the «Specola» (the Imperial Regio Museo di Fisica e Storia Naturale founded in 1775) the museum, one of the most important in Italy, has been at its present home since 1915. It contains an extraordinary collection of worked stones of Medici origin and comprehensive collections of minerals from throughout the world comprising c. 30,000 specimens. There is the world-famous topaz of 151 kilograms (755,000 carats) from the Fazenda do Fenil in the Brazilian state of Minas Gerais. Among the regional collections, the five thousand mineralogical specimens from Elba are of great interest.

Specimens of minerals and rocks divided into the following collections: general collection; regional collection; collection of worked stones and gems; Elban collection; lithological collection; collection of antique scientific instruments; meteorites.

Tourmalin, San Piero — Island of Elba

By prior arrangement, visits for schools and groups on Tuesdays, Wednesdays and Thursdays. Specialized meetings for teachers.

Historical library open to consultation during opening hours

Series of conferences, temporary exhibitions and study meetings organized by the Natural History Museum of the University of Florence.

G. Grattarola, *Guida e pianta del Museo e Laboratorio di mineralogia*, Florence 1881

F. Millosevich, *I 5000 Elbani del Museo di Firenze*, Florence 1914

G. Carobbi, *Un secolo di attività mineralogica a Firenze (1870-1970)*, in *Atti Ac. Tosc. Sc. Lett.. «La Colombaria»*, XXXVII, Florence 1972

C. Cipriani, *Il Museo di mineralogia e litologia*, in *Atti Società Leonardo da Vinci*, Florence 1975, 6, pp. 51-63

A. Berzi, C. Cipriani, M. Poggesi, *Florentine Scientific Museums*, in *J. Soc. Bibl. nat. Hist.* (1980) 9(4), pp. 413-425

I musei scientifici a Firenze. Problemi di restauro e ricomposizione Museale. Part Two, by various authors, Florence 1981

Il Museo di storia naturale dell'Università di Firenze, by various authors, Florence 1987

Museo Nazionale del Bargello

50122 Firenze
Via del Proconsolo, 4
Tel. 055/210801

Large

Weekdays 9 a.m.-2 p.m., Sundays and public holidays 9 a.m.-1 p.m.; closed on Mondays

Entrance fee

Partially accessible

By arrangement

The education section of the Uffizi Gallery (Via della Ninna 5, Firenze, tel.: 055/218341-284272) organizes educational activities in the museum for schools at every level.

Organization of temporary exhibitions on individual sections of the museum with the publication of accompanying catalogues.

This museum is known throughout the world as the museum of Donatello, the Della Robbia family and Michelangelo. The Bargello contains outstanding collections of sculpture and the minor arts (ivory, arms and armour, majolica, jewellery, goldsmiths' work, seals and medals), an immense heritage which arrived here in the second half of the last century. It is housed in the celebrated medieval Palazzo del Capitano del Popolo or del Podestà (whose origins date back to 1255) the seat of the Capitano di Giustizia or Bargello (head of the police) from 1574. Pietro Leopoldo, transferring the prisons to the Murate in 1857, decreed its complete restoration which was carried out by the architect Francesco Mazzei. The museum's official foundation dates from a few years later, on the initiative of the Provisional Government of Tuscany (1865), and groups of works were gradually transferred to the Palazzo: Robbian ceramics (from the suppressed convents), various sculptures from Palazzo Vecchio (including Michelangelo's *Victory* and *Virtue overcoming Vice* by Giambologna) and in 1874 the most important group of works arrived from the Uffizi (including *David* by Donatello, the *David-Apollo* and *Brutus* by Michelangelo and the collections of coins from Zecca (Mint) of Florence). Over the following years it was enlarged with valuable collections of the minor arts: the Carrand collection (1889), the Ressman collection of arms and armour (1899) and the collection of antique fabrics presented by the Barone Franchetti in 1906. The museum has for some years been undergoing a programme of continuous partial modernization as part of a general plan to reorganize its numerous collections.

Important sculptures by Donatello (*St. George*, *St. John*, *David* in bronze), Michelangelo (*Brutus*, *Apollo*, *Bacchus drunk*, Tondo of *Madonna and Child with the infant St. John*), B. Cellini (*Ganymede* and *Cosimo I*), Giambologna (*Virtue overcoming Vice*, *Mercury* in bronze, and *Eagle*, *Peacock*, *Turkey*, *Goshawk*).

Sculptures in stone and marble from the 14th C. (M. Arnoldi, T. di Camaino, A. di Cambio, school of N. Pisano).

15th C. Florentine works in wood, marble, bronze and terracotta: panels with *Sacrifice of Isaac*, by L. Ghiberti and F. Brunelleschi; *David* and *Bust of a lady holding flowers* by Verrocchio; *Portrait bust of a man* by Pollaiolo; *Bust of a young woman* and *Bust of a boy* by

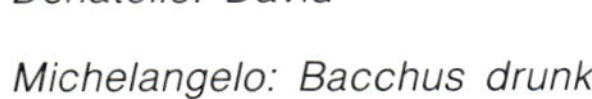

Donatello: David

Michelangelo: Bacchus drunk

Desiderio da Settignano; *The young St. Bernard* by Vecchietta; *Madonna and Child* by Michelozzo; *St. Peter freed from prison* and *Crucifixion of St. Peter*, *Madonna 'della mela'*, *Madonna 'del roseto'* by L. della Robbia; also sculptures by Mino da Fiesole, B. da Maiano, B. Rossellino, Agostino di Duccio. 16th C. works by A. della Robbia (*Bust of young boy*), G. della Robbia (*Crib*), Pierino da Vinci, Tribolo, V. Danti, B. Bandinelli, P. Francavilla, B. Ammannati, J. Sansovino and from the 17th C. by G.L. Bernini (*Portrait bust of Costanza Bonarelli*), F. Mochi.

Collection of small Renaissance bronzes (by Pisanello, B. Cellini, L. Leoni). collection of arms and armour (fragments of *armour «alla romana»* belonging to Cosimo I de' Medici), of glass (*Goblet* from Murano, 15th C.), of ivories, majolica from Florence, Siena, Urbino, Gubbio, Deruta from the 15th-16th C., of goldsmiths' work and medieval enamels from the 12th-16th C., of Italian, French, Limoges and Rhenish art.

Flemish and Italian paintings from the 14th-16th C. (*Diptych* by the Maestro di San Giorgio).

I.B. Supino, U. Rossi, *Catalogo del R. Museo Nazionale di Firenze (Palazzo del Podestà)*, Rome 1898

F. Rossi, *Il Museo Nazionale di Firenze. Palazzo del Bargello*, Rome 1951

Il Palazzo del Bargello e il Museo Nazionale, guide, Florence 1960

L. Berti, *Museo Nazionale «Bargello»*, new guide, Florence 1972

Andrea e Giovanni della Robbia, edited by G. Gentilini, Florence 1983

P. Barocchi, G. Gaeta Bertelà, *Itinerario e guida*, Florence 1984

Medaglie italiane del Rinascimento nel Museo Nazionale del Bargello, vol. 3, edited by J.G. Pollard, Florence 1984

Oreficeria sacra italiana, edited by A. Capitanio and M. Collareta, Florence 1987

Series «*Lo Specchio del Bargello*» (catalogues by Italian and foreign specialists concerning the minor arts).

Museo dell'Opera di Santa Croce

50122 Firenze
Piazza Santa Croce, 16
Tel. 055/244619

Large

Winter, from 1st October to 28th February: all week 10 a.m.-12.30 p.m. / 2.30 p.m.-5 p.m.

Summer, from 1st March to 30th September: all week 10 a.m.-12.30 p.m. / 2.30 p.m.-6.30 p.m.

Entrance fee

Accessible

By arrangement

Archives of the Opera di Santa Croce open to consultation by students and scholars by prior arrangement

Occasional exhibitions and conferences

Contains important works, mainly frescoes and sculptures, predominantly from the Basilica and Convent of Santa Croce. Opened in 1900 with a first group of exhibits displayed in the large refectory, it was subsequently enlarged and enriched (1952-59). Badly damaged by the 1966 flood, it was reopened to the public in 1976 after a radical reorganization of the exhibits. The exhibition space today comprises the old refectory (first half of the 14th C.), the small refectory, the Cappella Canigiani or 'dei Cerchi' with another three adjoining rooms. The two 15th C. cloisters, the Cappella Pazzi and the Gallery of 19th C. funerary monuments underneath the wing of the first 14th C. cloister adjacent to the Basilica are also open to visitors. In rooms adjoining the Cappella Pazzi there is also a permanent exhibition of woodcuts by P. Parigi.

Cimabue: Crucifix

In the museum's six rooms are displayed detached frescoes and sculptures from the 14th-17th C. from throughout the Santa Croce complex (church, cloisters, refectory) and from other religious buildings in the city: in addition to the celebrated *Crucifix* by Cimabue, damaged by the flood in 1966 and subsequently restored by the Opificio delle Pietre Dure, there are works by T. Gaddi (*Tree of the Cross*, *Last Supper*, *St. Francis' stigmata*, *St. Ludovico serves the poor people at table*, *Episode from the life of St. Benedict*, *Jesus at supper in the house of the Pharisee*), M. di Banco, G. del Biondo, A. Orcagna (fragments of the cycle of the *Triumph of Death*, *Final Judgement* and *Hell*), N. di Pietro Gerini, G. Starnina, D. Veneziano (*St. Francis* and *St. John the Baptist*), J. Ligozzi, M. Rosselli. Sculptures in stone, marble, terracotta and bronze from the 14th-16th C.: *Annunciata* and *Tomb of Gastone della Torre* by Tino da Camaino, *St. Ludovic of Toulouse* by Donatello, *altar-frontal* attribuited to Andrea della Robbia and other figures and reliefs from the bottega of the della Robbias.

G. Cocci, *Guida al Museo di Santa Croce*, Florence 1964

L. Becherucci, *I Musei di Santa Croce e di Santo Spirito*, Milan 1983

Santa Croce, by various authors, Florence 1983

E. Micheletti, *Santa Croce*, Florence 1983

Santa Croce nell'800, exhibition catalogue, by various authors, Florence 1986

M. Franchi, *Santa Croce*, Florence 1987

Museo dell'Opera di Santa Maria del Fiore

50122 Firenze
Piazza Duomo, 8
Tel. 055/213229

Large

Winter, from 1st November to 28th February: weekdays 9 a.m.-6 p.m., Sundays and public holidays 10 a.m.-1 p.m.

Summer, from 1st March to 31st October: weekdays 9 a.m.-8 p.m.; Sundays and public holidays 10 a.m.-1 p.m.

Entrance fee

Partially accessible

By arrangement

Founded in 1891 in the building of the Opera administration, converted by the architect Luigi del Moro, the museum contains a large and valuable collection of material from the Duomo, the Baptistery and Giotto's Campanile: sculpture, architectural fragments, paintings, rich goldsmiths' work and liturgical ornaments. Among the works of sculpture, in addition to the material which has survived the modifications to the buildings - the sculptures by Donatello, Nanni di Banco, Bernardo Ciuffagni, Nanni di Bartolo and Arnolfo di Cambio are from the old facade demolished in 1587 - there are also many pieces transferred here for conservation reasons: from the celebrated *Cantorie* by Donatello and Luca della Robbia, to the sixteen large statues by Andrea Pisano and Donatello, to the relief panels from the Campanile. Of great artistic as well as historical interest are the models, instruments and materials concerning the construction of the Cupola. Seriously damaged in the 1966 flood - of over fifty precious illuminated manuscripts only four are currently on display - it has been partly restructured and enlarged with the addition of important new masterpieces.

13th-17th C. sculpture: statues by Arnolfo di Cambio and his studio for the original facade; *Cantorie* by Donatello and Luca della Robbia; 16 statues by A. Pisano and Donatello from the Campanile; 49 *panels* with bas-reliefs by A. Pisano which previously decorated the first and second tiers of the Campanile; 5 panels by L. della Robbia, marble fragments and other material from restorations to the Duomo, the Baptistery and the Campanile. *St. Mary Magdalen* by Donatello, formerly in the Baptistery; Michelangelo's *Pietà*, formerly in the Duomo; 2 panels by L. Ghiberti, formerly in the

Archives of the Opera del Duomo (Via della Canonica 1-2, Firenze) open to students and scholars by prior arrangement

'Porta del Paradiso' (*Story of Joseph*, *Story of David*). Goldsmiths' work and religious ornaments and hangings from the 13th-16th C. (*Altar-frontal* in silver by S. Giovanni, from the Baptistery, 1366-1480; '*Paramento di S. Giovanni*', a liturgical tapestry designed by A. del Pollaiolo).
13th and 14th C. paintings (Neri di Bicci, B. Daddi). 13th-15th C. mosaics. Illuminated manuscripts from the 16th C.
Models of various plans for the facade, the cupola and the lantern.

L. Becherucci, G. Brunetti, *Il Museo dell'Opera del Duomo a Firenze*, Milan 1970

E. Settesoldi, *Museo dell'Opera del Duomo di Firenze*, Florence 1982

E. Settesoldi, *Donatello e l'Opera del Duomo di Firenze*, Florence 1986

Luca della Robbia: Cantoria, singers with book

Museo dell'Opificio delle Pietre Dure

50121 Firenze
Via degli Alfani, 78
Tel. 055/263414-210102

Medium

Weekdays 9 a.m.-1 p.m.; closed on Sundays

Entrance fee

Partially accessible

This unusual and very interesting collection is the exhibition section of the Opificio delle Pietre Dure, a national Institute which is also a workshop and restoration school housed in the large Fortezza da Basso complex (tel. 055/470991). The original core of material comes from the grand-ducal workshops, set up in 1588 by Ferdinando I in a wing of the Uffizi and transferred by Pietro Leopoldo in 1796 to its present site in Via degli Alfani. The present museum layout was designed between 1952 and 1976. In addition to works in polychrome marble and pietre dure (hard or semi-precious stones) which make up the vast majority of the material in this unusual and valuable museum, there are also displays of scagliolas, paintings on stone, paintings in oil (from models for works in pietre dure) and various instruments for the working of the materials.

Works in inlaid pietre dure and polychrome marbles from the 16th-19th C.: pictures, panels, sculptures, furniture and cabinets, table-tops (*Medici coat-of-arms* in porphyry; 18th C. *Model* of the Cappella dei Principi; *Portrait of Cosimo I* in pietre dure from 1597; *La*

By arrangement

Guided visits by prior arrangement. The educational section of the Uffizi Gallery (Via della Ninna 5, Firenze, tel.: 055/218341-284272) organizes educational activities in the museum for schools at every level.

Book and photograph library, archive open from 8 a.m.-2 p.m. by prior arrangement. Laboratories only open to qualified experts.

Occasional exhibitions and conferences.

Scultura, a picture in pietre dure from a design by G. Zocchi; *Table-top with instruments and floral garlands*, in pietre dure inlaid in porphyry, from 1849).

Paintings on stone (17th C.), paintings in oil (models for works in pietre dure).

Collection of samples of stones and gems; printed material and technical instruments for working pietre dure.

A. Pampaloni Martelli, *Il Museo dell'Opificio delle pietre dure*, Florence 1975

A.M. Giusti, A. Pampaloni Martelli, P. Mazzoni, *Il Museo dell'Opificio delle pietre dure*, Milan 1978

Giorgi Panel, Temple

Museo di Palazzo Davanzati

50123 Firenze
Via Porta Rossa, 13
Tel. 055/216518

Large

Weekdays 9 a.m.-2 p.m.; Sundays and public holidays 9 a.m.-1 p.m.; closed on Mondays
Schools wishing to visit the museum are asked to book in advance by telephone.

Entrance fee

Accessible

By arrangement

Conceived with the aim of reconstructing a typical example of a medieval nobleman's house in Florence, the museum contains a selection of furnishings and examples of the decorative arts from various periods arranged in their appropriate environment. Paintings, sculptures and other works of art embellish the rooms. The magnificent building, an integral part of the museum display, is an example almost unique in Florence of that style of 14th C. urban house which lies between the medieval tower and the Renaissance Palazzo. It was built by the Davizzi family as a private house, passed in 1516 to the Bartolini family and in 1578 to the Davanzatis who were in possession of it until the last century. Divided up, altered and in a state of serious decay it was bought in 1904 by the antiquarian Elia Volpi who restored it completely and furnished it with pieces from his collection. Resold in 1927, it passed through various owners before being purchased by the State in 1951. After the subsequent additions to the museum, of particular interest is a section dedicated to Italian and foreign lacework and embroidery, opened in 1977 with the Bargagli and Nugent collections from the Museo degli Argenti and rapidly enriched with numerous donations and acquisitions. The museum provides extensive educational resources and apparatus aimed at a variety of users.

The works of varied styles and periods constitute as a whole the furnishings of a typical Florentine nobleman's house from the 14th-17th C.
14th-16th C. paintings, with secular and religious subjects (altars with images of private devotion), including works by S. Aretino, Maestro del Cassone Adimari (*The flirt's game*), F. Granacci

☞
The education section of the Uffizi Gallery (Via della Ninna 5, Firenze, tel.: 055/218341-284272) organizes educational activities in the museum for schools at every level.
Services for the elderly. Room for blind visitors. Audiovisual projection: *The Davanzatis, merchants and patrons of the arts. Public and private life in the Middle Ages.*

Organization of exhibitions

The courtyard

(*Joseph being led to prison*), P.F. Foschi. 15th and 16th C. sculptures (*Bust of a young boy* by A. Rossellino, *Madonna Annunciata* by A. Rizzo).

14th-17th C. furniture: chairs and chests, credences, tables (16th C. Florentine *Table* in the style of Ammannati), cabinets (*gun cupboard* from a Sienese worshop from the early 16th C.), beds, cradles; painted cassoni and coffers (14th C. Sienese iron-reinforced *coffer*, 15th C. *wedding-chest* with *Stories of Paris*; 4 panels from a wedding-chest with *Triumphs of Petrarch* by the Maestro del Cassone Adimari). Domestic and kitchen implements (mixer, spit, fruit squeezer, lamp) and instruments for work by women (looms, irons, spinning-wheels). Collection of ceramics and majolica from the 14th-18th C. (pottery bowls and jugs; plates, centre-pieces etc. by various makers from the 15th-18th C.; collection of 18th C. Northern European hand-warmers in the shape of shoes).

15th and 16th C. Flemish and Florentine tapestries. Collection of lacework with some excellent examples illustrating the various European styles from the early 17th-20th C. (examples of '*punto Venezia*', *in relief*, '*a pointe de France*', '*valenciennes*' etc.).

Embroideries from the 17th-20th C. in Sicily; collection of *samplers*).

The rooms are decorated with wall paintings in geometrical designs, as imitation wall-paper and free-hand (14th C.); in the bedroom on the second floor a freize depicts episodes from the chivalric legend «The lady of the castle of Vergi», taken from a medieval French poem.

Il Museo di Palazzo Davanzati a Firenze, edited by L. Berti, Milan-Venice 1971

Palazzo Davanzati, Museo della Casa fiorentina antica, edited by M. Fossi Todorow, Florence 1979

M. Carmignani, M. Fossi Todorow, *Merletti a Palazzo Davanzati. Manifatture Europee dal XVI al XX secolo*, exhibition catalogue, Florence 1981

M. Carmignani, M. Fossi Todorow, '*Imparaticci-Samplers*'. *Esercizi di ricamo delle bambine europee ed americane dal Seicento all'Ottocento*, exhibition catalogue, Florence 1986

Palazzo Davanzati, edited by M. Fossi Todorow, Florence 1986

M. Carmignani, M. Fossi Todorow, *Eleganza e civetterie: merletti e ricami*; exhibition catalogue, Florence 1987

A. Chiostrini Mannini, *I Davanzati mercanti, banchieri, mecenati*, Florence 1988

Museo di Palazzo Strozzi

50123 Firenze
Piazza Strozzi
Tel. 055/215990 (Gabinetto Vieusseux)

Small

Weekdays 9 a.m.-12.30 p.m., by arrangement 3.30 p.m.-6.30 p.m.

Opened in 1971 this small museum was created by the INA (National Institute of Assurers) who have owned the building since 1937. It comprises various documentary material on the building; photographs of the restoration work, reproductions of drawings and plans of the city. Of considerable interest is the wooden model of the first Palazzo Strozzi design by Giuliano da Sangallo, probably dating from between 1489 and 1490.

G. Pampaloni, *Palazzo Strozzi*, Rome 1982

Free

No access

By arrangement

Museo di Palazzo Vecchio

50122 Firenze
Piazza della Signoria
Tel. 055/2768465

Large

Weekdays 9 a.m.-7 p.m., Sundays and public holidays 8 a.m.-1 p.m.; closed on Saturdays

Evening opening during the summer, dates and times set annually

Entrance fee

Accessible

By arrangement

Exhibitions, conferences, meetings and various other events

This fortress-palace was built between 1299 and 1314 to a design by Arnolfo di Cambio to house the city's government. Over the centuries it has undergone numerous alterations and additions. The most significant were: in 1466 by Michelozzo, the trusted architect of the Medicis, from 1555 to 1574, under the influence of Savonarola, by Cronaca and in 1540 by Vasari following the restoration of the Medici family who took up residence here. The transfer of the «family» to their new residence in Palazzo Pitti led to the gradual plundering of the building which was cleared of its works of art and used principally as a government building. With the extinction of the Medici dynasty and the advent of the Dukes of Lorraine the Palazzo suffered various alterations.
Subsequently the annexation to the Kingdom of Savoy and the transfer of the capital to Florence (1864) saw extensive and radical conversions to adapt it to its new bureaucratic and administrative functions. In 1872 it was finally presented to the Council which set up its own offices here and which still occupies much of the building.
The museum area open to the public comprises the Quartieri Monumentali, with the Salone dei Cinquecento and the adjoining Studiolo of Francesco I, the Sala dei Dugento and the Quartiere of Duke Cosimo, the Sala dei Gigli, the Sala delle Udienze, the Appartamento di Eleonora and the Quartieri degli Elementi. The collection of sculpture and paintings presented to the Council in 1928 by Charles Loeser and the museum of musical instruments (see entry on the museum) temporarily closed to the public are situated on the mezzanine floor; the third floor houses the exhibition «L'Opera ritrovata. Omaggio a Rodolfo Siviero» opened in 1984 and containing works stolen by the Nazis and recovered after the war.

Sala dei Dugento with carved wood ceiling by B. and G. da Maiano (1472) and series of ten Medici tapestries with *Stories of Joseph* from cartoons by Bronzino, Pontormo and F. Salviati (1545-53), presently being restored. *Sala dei Gigli* with carved wood ceiling by B. and G. da Maiano (1472-76), marble doorway by the same artists (1476-81) and frescoes with *St. Zanobius and other figures* by D. del Ghirlandaio (1482-85). *Salone dei Cinquecento* restored and decorated with panelled ceiling and frescoes by G. Vasari and helpers (G. Stradano, J. Zucchi, G.B. Naldini) between 1563 and 1572 with *Allegories and stories of Florence and the Medicis*; sculptures by Michelangelo (*Victory*), B. Bandinelli (*Cosimo I, Giovanni delle Bande Nere, Alessandro de' Medici, Clement VII*), Vincenzo de' Rossi (*Hercules and Cacus, Hercules and Hippolyta, Hercules and Antaeus*) and Giambologna (*Florence triumphs over Pisa*).
Studiolo di Francesco I (1570-75) with paintings and frescoes on panels and wood by J. Zucchi, F. Poppi, G. Butteri, G. Stradano, M. Cavalori, I. Coppi, G. Macchietti, G.B. Naldini, G. Vasari, S. di Tito, A. Allori, M. da San Friano; small bronzes on the walls by

Giambologna, Vincenzo de' Rossi, D. Poggini, B. Ammannati, V. Danti.

Sala delle Udienze with marble doorway by B. and G. da Maiano (1476-81) and frescoes with *Stories of Furio Camillo* by F. Salviati (1543-45).

Quartiere degli Elementi with frescoes by G. Vasari, G. Gherardi, M. da Faenza (1555-58); Flemish tapestries. *Quartiere di Leone X* with floor in red and white terracotta by S. Buglioni; frescoes by G. Vasari, G. Stradano and M. da Faenza (1555-61). *Quartiere di Eleonora*: in the chapel frescoes and paintings on wood (*Deposition* by Bronzino) (1540-45); in the rooms frescoes by G. Vasari and G. Stradano (1561-62).

Loeser Collection containing paintings and scuptures of the Tuscan school from the 14th-16th C. by P. Lorenzetti, T. di Camaino, P. di Cosimo, Bronzino, Pontormo, A. Berruguete, Giambologna.

Permanent exhibition «L'Opera ritrovata. Omaggio a Rodolfo Siviero», comprising 141 paintings and sculptures from ancient times to the 19th C.

A. Lenzi, *Palazzo Vecchio*, Rome-Milan 1929

A. Lenzi, *La donazione Loeser in Palazzo Vecchio*, Florence 1934

U. Baldini, *Palazzo Vecchio e i Quartieri monumentali*, Florence 1950

L. Berti, *Il principe dello Studiolo*, Florence 1967

G. Lensi Orlandi, *Il Palazzo Vecchio di Firenze*, Milan-Florence 1977

F. Scalia, *Palazzo Vecchio. Arte e storia*, Florence 1979

E. Allegri, A. Cecchi, *Palazzo Vecchio e i Medici*, Florence 1980

L'opera ritrovata. Omaggio a Rodolfo Siviero, exhibition catalogue, Florence 1984

Sala dei Gigli

Museo delle Porcellane

50125 Firenze
Casino del Cavaliere del Giardino di Boboli
Piazza Pitti, 1
Tel. 055/212557

Medium

Weekdays 9 a.m.-2 p.m., Sundays and public holidays 9 a.m.-1 p.m.; closed on Mondays

Entrance fee

♿
No access

📷
By arrangement

The education section of the Uffizi Gallery (Via della Ninna 5, Firenze, tel.: 055/218341-284272) organizes educational activities in the museum for schools at every level.

Organization of exhibitions

Part of the Palazzo Pitti museum complex administered by the Florence Soprintendenza per i beni artistici e storici, the museum is situated in the Boboli rose garden in the 'Casino del Cavaliere'. It is a 17th C. building, converted to museum use and opened in 1973. It contains an important collection of Italian, European and Asian porcelain from the collections of the Tuscan grand-dukes and the dukes of Parma and Piacenza.

18th and 19th C. porcelain from the Doccia factory and the Royal factory in Naples, from French, Viennese and German factories.

Illustrated vases, *panel with portrait of Napoleon* presented by the Emperor to the grand-duke Ferdinando III. 18th C. bisque statuettes depicting *Neapolitan Women*; bisque groups.

G. Liverani, *Catalogo delle porcellane dei Medici*, Florence 1936-38

S. Eriksen, *Le porcellane francesi a Palazzo Pitti*, Florence 1973

Porcellane dell'Ottocento a Palazzo Pitti, exhibition catalogue, edited by K. Aschengreen Piacenti, Florence 1983

A. D'Agliano, *Le porcellane italiane a Palazzo Pitti*, Florence 1983

K. Aschengreen Piacenti, M. Chiarini, E. Spalletti, *Palazzo Pitti*, Florence 1988

Vienna Factory: Breakfast service

Museo di San Marco

50121 Firenze
Piazza San Marco, 3
Tel. 055/210741

Large

Weekdays 9 a.m.-2 p.m., Sundays and public holidays 9 a.m.-1 p.m.; closed on Mondays

Entrance fee

The museum is housed in the historic San Marco complex (14th-15th C.), originally the monastery of the Silvestrine monks and subsequently presented to the Dominican friars of Fiesole. The national museum was founded in 1869 following the suppression of the monastery in 1866. Dedicated to the works of the 'Blessed' Fra' Angelico who lived and worked at San Marco (1387/1400-1455), it contains in addition to the celebrated frescoes a considerable collection of paintings transferred here from the territory of Florence between 1919 and 1923. Among the many masterpieces on display worthy of particular note are the two *Last Suppers* in the small refectory (D. Ghirlandaio) and the large refectory (G.A. Sogliani), the works by Fra' Bartolommeo della Porta (1475/77-1517) and Mariotto Albertinelli as well as the collection of illuminated choirbooks and psalters in the library. Of mainly historical interest are Savonarola's rooms containings relics and other material. Extensive restoration work undertaken by the Florentine Soprintendenza between 1967 and 1980 and still in progress have enabled further areas of the monastery to be converted for museum use:

♿
No access

📷
By arrangement

The education section of the Uffizi Gallery (Via della Ninna, Florence, tel.: 055/218341-284272) organizes educational activities in the museum for schools at every level.

nearing completion are the old guest-rooms adjoining the second cloister and the underground rooms containing architectural fragments and fragments of sculpture and other stone material recovered during the 19th C. demolitions of the old centre of Florence and other more recent projects.

Paintings by Fra' Angelico (*Tabernacle of the Linaioli, Madonna and Child with Saints, Deposition, Coronation of the Virgin, Universal Judgement, Stories from the life of Christ*), by Fra' Bartolommeo (*Madonna and St. Anne with Saints, Final Judgement, Portrait of Savonarola, Christ carrying his Cross, Ecce Homo, St. John the Baptist, St. Catherine*), G.A. Sogliani, Fra' Paolino (*Sacred Family, Pietà*). Also sculptures by Baldovinetti, Michele di Ridolfo del Ghirlandaio, C. Portelli, F. Tarchiani, J. Ligozzi, L. Lippi, C. Gamberucci.

Sculptures in stone, wood, marble and terracotta from the 14th-16th C. (works by B. da Montelupo, the della Robbias), architectural fragments and stone material.

In the Chapter House, *Crucifixion*, a fresco by Fra' Angelico; in the large cloister, *St. Dominic at the foot of the Cross*, by Fra' Angelico. In the large refectory and the small refectory *Last Supper* by D. Ghirlandaio and *Last Supper* by G.A. Sogliani.

In the library designed by Michelozzo, illuminated codices from the 14th, 15th and 16th C. (by Fra' Eustachio, Filippo di Matteo Torelli, Z. Strozzi).

On the first floor of the monastery, in the cells and other areas, frescoes by Fra' Angelico (*Noli me tangere, Annuciation, Transfiguration, Christ mocked*).

📖

F. Rondoni, *Guida del R. Museo fiorentino di San Marco con aggiunta di brevi notizie sulla chiesa annessa*, Florence 1872

G. Sinibaldi, *Il Museo di San Marco in Firenze*, Rome 1936

L. Berti, *Il Museo di San Marco*, 1959-60

L. Berti, *L'Angelico a San Marco, in Forma e Colore*, 13, 1965

G. Bonsanti, *Il Beato Angelico nel Convento di San Marco*, Novara 1982

Fra' Angelico: Annunciation

Museo di Santa Maria del Carmine

50124 Firenze
Piazza del Carmine
Tel. 055/212331

In rooms leading off the cloister in the Carmine complex paintings on wood and canvas and detached frescoes from the Convent and Church have been exhibited since 1973. Among the most important works: *Confirmation of the rule*, by Filippino Lippi, fragmentary picture of *Saints* in aedicules and *Stories of St. Jerome*, by G. Starnina (1404), *Flagellation, Last Supper* and *Saints*, parts of frescoes (1402-1404) attribuited to Lippo Fiorentino, *Crucifixion* by an artist close to Fra' Angelico, *Last Supper* by F. Vanni.
The museum is temporarily closed for restoration.

Museo di Santa Maria Novella

50123 Firenze
Piazza Santa Maria Novella
tel. 055/282187

Large

Weekdays 9 a.m.-2 p.m., Sundays and public holidays 8 a.m.-1 p.m.; closed on Fridays

Evening opening during the summer, dates and times set annually

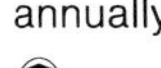
Entrance fee

Accessible

By arrangement

The museum, run by the Council, is situated in part of the historic complex of the Dominican Basilica of Santa Maria Novella (14th C.) which passed to the Italian state following the 1866 suppressions and was acquired by the Council in 1868. The present museum area was opened in 1983 after restoration of the rooms and frescoes organized by the Council as part of a huge programme of restoration of the whole conventual complex. The area open to the public includes the 14th C. Chiostro Verde with the series of frescoes illustrating stories from Genesis by Paolo Uccello, the Chapter House or Cappellone degli Spagnoli and the Chiostrino dei Morti with the twelve frescoed chapels. There is also a selection of ecclesiastical hangings and ornaments from the Basilica's splendid collection.

Paolo Uccello: The Flood

In the Chiostro Verde: *Stories from Genesis*, cycle of frescoes by P. Uccello (c. 1425 : *Episodes from the creation of Adam and Eve*; 1446-48: *Flood*, *Sacrifice* and *Noah's drunkeness*) and pupils. In the Cappellone degli Spagnoli frescoes painted in 1365 by Andrea di Bonaiuto of Florence (*Allegory of the Church and the Dominican order*, *Crucifixion*, *Descent to Limbo*); in the Chapel of the Chapter House works by A. Allori (*St. James*, on the altar) and by B. Poccetti (frescoes in the vault, *Apotheosis of Spain*). Chiostrino dei Morti: chapels with frescoes from the second half of the 14th C. in the style of Orcagna.

In three 14th C. rooms (entrance room, Cappella degli Ubriachi, Refectory) are displayed church ornaments from the sacresty of Santa Maria Novella: Goldsmiths' work from the 15th-19th C. (15th-16th C. *Reliquary of St. Catherine*; 15th C. *Reliquary of St. Jerome*; 15th C. *Reliquary of the Cross*; 17th C. silver *chalice*) hangings, vestments and frontals, from the 15th-19th C.

Santa Maria Novella, by various authors, Florence 1981

R. Lunardi, *Arte e Storia in Santa Maria Novella*, Florence 1983

Museo dello Spedale degli Innocenti

50122 Firenze
Piazza Santissima Annunziata, 12
Tel. 055/243670

Large

Weekdays 9 a.m.-2 p.m., Sundays and public holidays 8 a.m.-1 p.m.

Entrance fee

No access

Francesco Granacci: Madonna 'degli Innocenti'

The museum contains a rich collection of works donated in the past to the Institution enriched with numerous bequests and donations. The historic complex of the Spedale which houses it was built during the 15th C. as a foundling hospital. The original structure designed by Filippo Brunelleschi has through the centuries undergone many alterations, the most radical being during the Lorraine period. From 1964 to 1970 it was comprehensively restored by the Soprintendenza per i beni ambientali e architettonici for the Provinces of Florence and Pistoia. It is thanks to this restoration programme that the rooms housing the museum have been made available: the room above the colonnade and the corridors looking into the entrance courtyard. When the museum was reopened in 1971 it had also been enriched with a remarkable collection of detached frescoes formerly in the Cenacolo di Ognissanti, from the Ospedale di Santa Maria Nuova.

14th-17th C. detached frescoes from the Spedale and other ecclesiastical buildings in the city and surrounding territory (*Madonna 'della neve'* by an anonymous artist from Pistoia; *Prophets* by A. Allori; *St. Catherine's dispute* by B. Poccetti). Sculptures in wood, stone, marble and terracotta from the 14th-19th C. (L. della Robbia, *Madonna and Child*; A. della Robbia, *Annunciation*; Studio of G. della Robbia, *Madonna enthroned with St. Francis and St. Dominic* from 1520). Paintings on wood and canvas of the Tuscan school from the 14th-19th C. including *Coronation of the Vergin* by Neri di Bicci, *Triptych* by G. Toscani, *Madonna and Child* by S. Botticelli, *Adoration of the Magi* by D. Ghirlandaio, *Madonna and Child with Saints* by Piero di Cosimo; also works by Tuscan artists from the Late Mannerist period such as J. del Conte, G.B. Naldini, Poppi and 17th C. canvases by M. Rosselli, J. Vignali, G. Bilivert, O. Vannini; collection of material on the Spedale's founders, protectors and benefactors, mainly 19th C.

16th-18th C. furnishings

Illuminated manuscripts of the 14th C. (from the Monastery of St. Salvatore in Settimo) and 15th C. (from the studio of Gherardo di Giovanni).

L. Bellosi, A. Piccini, G. Vailati Schömburg Waldemburg, *Il Museo dello Spedale degli Innocenti*, Milan 1977

M. Bietti, A. Piccini, *Spedale e Museo degli Innocenti*, Florence 1977

Museo Stibbert

50134 Firenze
Via Federico Stibbert, 26
Tel. 055/475520

Large

Weekdays 9 a.m.-1.30 p.m., Sundays and public holidays 9 a.m.-1 p.m.

It contains a huge collection started in 1859 by the Englishman Frederick Stibbert (1838-1906), the celebrated collector, patron of the arts and influential businessman. On his death the rich collections were left to Britain; they were then presented to the city of Florence which set up the Fondazione Opera Museo Stibbert in 1908. This «private collection» is distinguished by its exceptional eclecticism: splendid collections of antique European and Oriental arms and armour and costumes which are the two main themes, accompained by a well-stocked picture gallery and library; the museum also contains sculptures, porcelain, tapestries comprising in all over fifty thousand items, divided into over forty sections. In addition there is an important archive containing about eighty thousand documents. The building housing this vast heritage consists of a series of rooms some of which were built by Stibbert over a number of years; the most characteristic rooms date back to 1878-1891 ('Sala della Cavalcata', 'Sala della Malachite', 'Salone dell'Armeria', 'Sala Moresca', 'Fumoir Cantagalli').

The largest of the museum's sections is dedicated to arms and armour and costumes from the Late Middle Ages to modern day. Of particular note: a valuable collection of 18th C. clothes, a fine group of costumes with accessories, the uniform for the coronation of Napoleon as King of Italy; the armour worn by Giovanni delle Bande Nere, armour belonging to Pompeo della Cesa and the Maestro del Castello, German armour with pieces made by the major armourers, pieces from the Medici, Este and Hapsbourg armouries.
Also tapestries (series from cartoons by G. Romano, 16th C. tapestries from the Casa Bourbon del Monte); ecclesiastical vessels and vestments; furnishings and ornaments with fine examples of Florentine and Tuscan craftsmanship from the 19th C. Series of stone eschutcheons on the facade overlooking the park.

Ch. Buttin, *Le Musée Stibbert à Florence*, in *Les Arts*, Sept. 1910, pp. 1-32

F. Stibbert, *Abiti e fogge civili e militari dal I al XVIII secolo*, Bergamo 1914, revised, Florence 1975

A. Lensi, *Il Museo Stibbert. Catalogo della sala delle armi europee*, Florence 1917-18

H.R. Robinson, *Il Museo Stibbert: armi e armature orientali*, Milan 1973

G. Cantelli, *Il Museo Stibbert*, Milan 1974

L.G. Boccia, *Il Museo Stibbert: l'armeria europea*, Milan 1975

L.G. Boccia, G. Cantelli, F. Maraini, *Il Museo Stibbert: i depositi e l'archivio*, Milan 1976

Sala della Cavalcata

Entrance fee

Partially accessible

By arrangement with the Administrating Committee

Courses for teachers and school visits on specific themes

Important and extensive library open by prior arrangement only to specialist scholars. Historical photograph library and Archive

Exhibitions, conferences, study meetings. Research on the problems of lexicon and the recording of the material. Visiting curatorships for Italian and foreign scholars.

L.G. Boccia, *Il Museo Stibbert*, Florence 1981 (8mm film)

Guerre e assoldati in Toscana 1260-1364, by various authors, Florence 1982

IAMAN. Third international symposium, computer cataloguing of historic arms and armour, by various authors, Florence 1982

L.G. Boccia, M. Scalini, *The Stibbert Museum - Il Museo Stibbert*, Florence 1982 (audiovisual)

Armi e cimeli della rivoluzione e dell'epopea napoleonica 1789-1815, by various authors, Florence 1983

L.G. Boccia, *Guida al Museo Stibbert*, Florence 1983

O. von Hessen, *Il materiale altomedievale nelle collezioni Stibbert di Firenze*, Florence 1983

Oggetti d'arte italiani - Italian works of art - Objets d'art italiens, by various authors, Florence 1985

De Italia (L'arte extra-europea nei musei italiani: il Museo Stibbert di Firenze), by various authors, Turin 1987 (video record)

C. Adelson, *Costumi: doni e acquisiti - gifts and acquisitions, 1978-1988, Florence 1988.*
L'armatura europea del secondo Cinquecento, by various authors, Florence 1988 (being printed)

L. Desideri, S. Di Marco, *Catalogo della libreria Stibbert*, being printed

L.G. Boccia, *Un «caso museale», lo Stibbert*, in *L'Ippogrifo*, I, 1, 1988

Museo di Storia della Fotografia Fratelli Alinari

50123 Firenze
Via della Vigna Nuova, 16
Tel. 055/213370

Small

All week 10 a.m.-7.30 p.m.; Saturday 10 a.m.-11 p.m.

Entrance fee

Partially accessible

By arrangement

Audiovisual show on the history of photography

Opened in 1985 the museum contains material on the history of photography and in particular on the work of the Società Alinari (founded in 1852), the oldest society active in the field of photography. Housed in several specially restored and converted rooms of Palazzo Rucellai it contains a permanent exhibition of photographic apparatus and prints. It is also equipped with rooms and laboratories where both preservation work and continual scientific-historical researches are carried out. This activity is the basis for a continuous series of photographic exhibitions on specific themes and historical retrospective shows. The museum contains a photograph library with over three hundred thousand prints, a "sala di posa" currently under restoration equipped with period and contemporary instruments (in addition to providing an idea of the original working environment of the Alinari brothers it is also used periodically by specialists) and an exhibition space for temporary shows. An adjacent bookshop connected to the museum (Via della Vigna Nuova 46-48r, tel. 055/218975) offers a wide selection of material including photographs, catalogues and posters.

Period photographic equipment: cameras, lenses, plates and photographic accessories.

Photographic and labelled panels on the history of photography

Fotologia, quarterly magazine, published by Edizioni Alinari

Archive and photographic library open from Monday to Friday 9 a.m. to 1 p.m., by prior arrangement

Temporary exhibitions with accompanying catalogue

Museo Storico Topografico «Firenze com'era»

50122 Firenze
Via dell'Oriolo, 24
Tel. 055/298483 (Comune)

Opened in 1908 at the Casa Buonarroti on the initiative of Corrado Ricci, since 1955 the museum has been housed in the conventual complex of the lay-sisters owned by the Council which was restored during the 1970's. By means of paintings, drawings and prints the museum illustrates the most significant transformations in Florence from the 15th C. to the present day; it also has an archive containing important topographical and cartographical material. A permanent collection of works by Ottone Rosai presented to Florence Council by the artist is also housed here.

Large

Weekdays 9 a.m.-2 p.m., Sundays and public holidays 8 a.m.-1 p.m.; closed on Thursdays

Entrance fee

Accessible

By arrangement

The museum's archive, situated at 21 via Sant'Egidio at the Ufficio Musei, contains graphic and iconographic material on Florence; it is open to scholars by prior arrangement

Occasionally houses exhibitions organized as part of the cultural activities of the Ufficio Musei of Florence Council

Antique maps of Florence: *Perspective view of Florence*, 19th C. tempera reproduction of the famous *Carta della Catena* of 1470 preserved in the Museum of Berlin; *Topographical plan of Florence* by S. Buonsignori (1594 ed.); *Prints* by V. Spada (1650), by F. Ruggieri (1731), G. Vascellini; C. Zocchi (1738), F. Fantozzi (1843-1866).

Paintings in oil and tempera depicting the city and surroundings, with scenes of games, historical episodes, (lunettes in oil with *Medici Villas* by G. Utens (1599); series of etchings by T. Signorini).

Series of prints (from the 18th-19th C.) including the etchings with views of churches, palazzos and villas by G. Zocchi (1744 and 1754).

Drawings and plans of the town-planning projects for Florence when it was the capital of Italy (G. Poggi).

Mostra permanente delle opere di Ottone Rosai donate al Comune di Firenze, Florence 1963

F. Scalia, *Visioni Fiorentine dalle raccolte del Museo storico-topografico Firenze com'era*, Turin 1971

E. Allegri, *Il Museo «Firenze com'era». Luci ed ombre dei musei fiorentini*, in *Atti della società Leonardo da Vinci*, III, 1976, pp. 29-43

D. Mignani, *Le Ville Medicee di Giusto Utens*, Florence 1980

Lunette with Piazza della Signoria

Museo di Zoologia «La Specola»

Sezione del Museo di storia naturale dell'Università di Firenze
50125 Firenze
Via Romana, 17
Tel. 055/222451

Large

Zoology: Tuesday and Thursday 9 a.m.- noon; Sundays 9.30 a.m.-12.30 p.m.

Wax models: Saturday 2 p.m.-5 p.m.; from 1st June to 30th September: Saturday 3 p.m.-6 p.m.

Free

No access

By prior arrangement, guided visits for groups and meetings on specific themes for teachers

Departmental library of Animal Biology open by arrangement

Series of conferences, temporary exhibitions and study meetings organized by the Natural History Museum of the University of Florence

Founded in 1775 by the grand-duke Pietro Leopoldo with the title of Imperial Regio Museo di Fisica e Storia Naturale, it has always been better known as «La Specola», after the astronomical telescope situated on top of the Palazzo. It was founded to preserve and display the rich natural history and science collections formed by the Medicis and the Dukes of Lorraine. The museum's first director, the chemist and physiologist Felice Fontana (1730-1805) ordered the collections and provided the museum with a ceroplastics workshops (active until 1895) whose output, human and comparative anatomical models, still constitute one of its major attractions. During the second half of the 19th C. the collections were broken up and divided between various university institutes (in 1869 the Physics and Astrology department was transferred to Arcetri, in 1880 the Geology, Paleontology and Mineralogical museums moved to Piazza San Marco, closely followed by the Botanical Museum). The Zoological Museum alone remained at «La Specola». The museum's collections, of great scientific value, are only partly open to the public. Among the more important groups are the collection of molluscs (donated to the museum towards the end of the 19th C. by the Marchesa Paolucci), the Verity butterfly collection, the beetle collection from Eritrea, the main collection of Italian Vertebrates and many specimens from East Africa collected by the C.N.R. centre for Tropical Fauna and Ecology. Of the building itself, of note is the Tribuna di Galileo, a rare example of Neo-Classical architecture commissioned by Leopoldo II in 1841 and opened on the occasion of the Third Congress of Italian Scientists.

Zoology Collection
Invertebrate section: Porifera and Coelenterata, Molluscs, Insects, Crustaceans, Annelida, Echinoderma
Vertebrate section: Mammals, Birds, Reptiles, Amphibians, Fishes, 3 dioramas.
Collection of wax anatomical models
C. 1400 examples from the 16th-19th C. by C. Susini, F. and C. Calenzuoli, L. Calamai and F. Tortoli.
An outstanding head from the end of the 17th C. and four models known as the 'Cere della Peste' ('Plague Models') by the Sicilian wax-modeller Gaetano Zumbo

One of the rooms of the Collection of anatomical wax models

M.L. Azzaroli Puccetti, *Il Museo della Specola: un conflitto tra antico e moderno*, in *Atti della Società Leonardo da Vinci*, Florence 1976, pp. 7-27

M.L. Azzaroli, *La Specola. The zoological museum of Florence University*, in *Atti del primo Congresso Internazionale sulla Ceroplastica nella scienza e nell'arte*, Vol. I, Florence 1977, pp. 1-22

B. Lanza, M.L. Azzaroli Puccetti, M. Poggesi, A. Martelli, *Le cere anatomiche della Specola*, Florence 1979

A. Berzi, C. Cipriani, P. Poggesi, *Florentine scientific museums*, in *J. Soc. Bibl. nat. Hist.* (1980) 9(4), pp. 413-425

Il Museo di storia naturale dell'Università di Firenze, by various authors, Florence 1987

Orto Botanico «Giardino dei Semplici»

Sezione del Museo di storia naturale dell'Università di Firenze
50121 Firenze
Via P.A. Micheli, 3
Tel. 055/284696

Large

Weekdays: Monday, Wednesday and Friday 9 a.m.-noon.
From November to June it is also open occasionally on Sunday mornings

Free

Accessible

By arrangement

Guided visits for schools and groups by prior arrangement on Mondays, Wednesday and Fridays

The Giardino dei Semplici was founded by Cosimo de' Medici in 1545 for the study of medicinal plants by the students of Florence University. It is one of the oldest botanical gardens in the world after the one in Pisa (1543) and Padova (1545). Designed by the famous architect Niccolò Tribolo it was initially organized and run by the celebrated botanist Luca Ghini. Radically altered during the 18th C. it became in 1783 the experimental agricultural nursery of the Accademia dei Georgofili and enjoyed a new period of splendour under the direction of Ottaviano Targioni Tozzetti from 1801 to 1829. After a period of mixed fortunes it was once again handed over to the Istituto di Studi Superiori (founded in 1859). Today connected with the Department of Plant Biology at Florence University it covers an area of about two hectares (c. 5 acres) three quarters of which is made up by the original 16th C. botanical garden. It contains botanical specimens of all types including rare collections of cicadea and bromeliaceae, three magnificent arancarie and an important collection of ferns. Among the secular plants worthy of mention is the cork oak from the early 19th and the famous yew planted by Pier Antonio Micheli in 1710.

Main avenue with azaleas in bloom

Laboratory for the preparation of plant specimens, palinological laboratory and seed bank. Open by prior arrangement.

Series of conferences, temporary exhibitions and study meetings organized by the Natural History Museum of the University of Florence

Cold glass houses: cicadea, citrus plants, palms, agave. Hot houses: tropical plants. Six smaller hot houses: collection of exotic plants, collection of bromeliaceae, ferns, orchids, begonias, araceous plants.
Outdoors are: secular trees including Quercus suber L., Taxus baccata L., Zelkova crenata Spach. Medicinal plant section. Coniferous section. Collection of spontaneous plants from Tuscany. Collection of monocoltyledons including narcissi, irises, dwarf palms and yuccas.

A. Chiarugi, *Le date di fondazione dei primi orti botanici del mondo: Pisa (Estate 1543); Padova (7 luglio 1545), Firenze (1 dicembre 1545)*, in *Nuovo Giornale Botanico Italiano*, n.s., 60, 1953, pp. 785-839

G. Moggi, *Il Museo botanico ed il Giardino dei Semplici*, in *Atti della Società Leonardo da Vinci*, Florence 1974, pp. 373-393

A. Berzi, C. Cipriani, M. Poggesi, *Florentine scientific museums*, in *J. Soc. Bibl. nat. Hist.* (1980) 9(4), pp. 413-425

G. Ciuffi Cellai, *Il Giardino dei Semplici*, in *I Musei scientifici a Firenze. Problemi di restauro e ricomposizione museale*. Part Two, edited by F. Gurrieri and L. Zangheri, Florence 1981

F. Fabbri, *L'Orto Botanico di Firenze*, in *Agricoltura*, 12, 4, 1983, pp. 73-86

G. Ciuffi Cellai, *Guida alla visita del Giardino dei Semplici*, Florence 1987

P. Luzi, *Guida alle piante medicinali coltivate nell'Orto botanico*, Florence 1987

Il Museo di storia naturale dell'Università di Firenze, by various authors, Florence 1987

Palazzo Medici Riccardi

50129 Firenze
Via Cavour, 1
Tel. 055/2760 (Provincia)

Medium

Weekdays 9 a.m.-12 p.m. / 3 p.m.-5 p.m.; Sundays and public holidays 9 a.m.-12 p.m.; closed on Wednesdays

Free

No access

By arrangement

Built from a design by Michelozzo between 1444 and 1452 the Palazzo was the permanent residence of the main branch of the Medici family. Sold in 1659 to the Marchese Gabriello Riccardi it was substantially altered by G.B. Foggini; after returning to the grand-dukes of Tuscany in 1818 it was acquired by the Provincial Government in 1871. Around 1929 the ground floor was used for a museum on the Medici dynasty which was dismantled to make way for temporary exhibitions. Within the Palazzo, presently the seat of the offices of the Provincial Government and the Prefettura, the Chapel with frescoes by Benozzo Gozzoli and the Galleria di Luca Giordano are open to the public.

On the first floor, in the Chapel designed by Michelozzo are frescoes by B. Gozzoli (1459-60) with the *Journey of the Magi to Bethlehem*; on the altar *Nativity*, a contemporary copy of the original by Filippo Lippi now in the Museum of Berlin.
In the Galleria, decorated with stucco-work, mirrors and carved panels is the vault decorated with frescoes by L. Giordano (1682-3) depicting the *Apotheosis of the Medicis*.

B. Santi, *Palazzo Medici Riccardi*, Florence 1983

Raccolta d'Arte Arciconfraternita della Misericordia

Piazza del Duomo, 20
50122 Firenze
Tel. 055/212509

Small

By arrangement to scholars

Free

No access

By arrangement

Library and archive open for consultation by arrangement with the Soprintendenza archivistica della Toscana

At the seat of the Arciconfraternita is a substantial and valuable collection of works of art and furnishings, brought together through donations and acquisitions during the society's seven centuries of activity (founded in 1240). There is also an extensive historical archive and library.

Paintings on wood and canvas of the Tuscan school from the 14th-20th C. from the collection owned by the Confraternity (works by G.A. Sogliani, G.B. Naldini, S. di Tito, F. Tarchiani, G. Bianchi) and from more recent acquisitions (works by F. Bachiacca, G.M. Butteri, Valentin de Boulogne, D. Van Baburen, C. Dolci). Group of statues in wood, marble, terracotta and bronze from the 15th-19th C. by B. da Maiano (*Madonna and Child*, *St. Sebastian*), in the style of L. Ghiberti (*Madonna and Child*), by A. della Robbia (*Madonna and Child with Saints*) and G. della Robbia. Painting in oil (*A brother of the Misericordia carries an invalid*) and series of sketches and drawings by P. Annigoni. Church ornaments from the 16th-20th C. (furniture and carvings, goldsmiths' work, ceramics, fabrics).

La Misericordia di Firenze. Archivio e Raccolta d'Arte, vol. 1, by various authors, Florence 1981

La Misericordia di Firenze. Archivio e arredi, vol. 2, by various authors, Florence 1982

Raccolta d'Arte Contemporanea Alberto Della Ragione

50122 Firenze
Piazza della Signoria, 5
Tel. 055/283078

Large

Weekdays 9 a.m.-2 p.m., Sundays and public holidays 8 a.m.-1 p.m.; closed on Tuesdays
Evening opening during the summer, dates and times set annually

Entrance fee

No access

By arrangement

Temporary exhibitions

The collection, formed by the Genoese collector and patron of the arts Alberto Della Ragione (1892-1972), contains examples of the major movements in Italian art between the wars: from Futurism through the Metaphysical period to the most recent currents of the Sixties. It was donated in 1970 to the Council which housed it in its present home in Piazza Signoria in rooms provided by the Cassa di Risparmio di Firenze. A small group of twelve canvases by Filippo De Pisis (1896-1956) presented by the poet Palazzeschi to the Faculty of Letters and Philosophy of Florence University has recently been set up here.

Contemporary paintings and sculptures from 1910 to 1950 by G. De Chirico, F. De Pisis, O. Rosai, V. Guidi, M. Sironi, F. Casorati, C. Carrà, M. Campigli, F. Depero, G. Morandi, Scipione, M. Mafai, R. Guttuso, R. Birolli, E. Morlotti, B. Cassinari, M. Maccari, G. Migneco, E. Vedova.
Sculptures by G. Manzù, M. Marini, A. Martini.
Ceramics by L. Fontana, A. Tosi, O. Licini.

R. Monti, F. Ragghianti, *La Raccolta Alberto Della Ragione*, introduction by C.L. Ragghianti, Florence 1970

L. Caprile, *Guttuso a Genova nel nome Della Ragione*, exhibition catalogue, Genoa-Milan 1985

Raccolta d'arte contemporanea Alberto Della Ragione, edited by F. Scalia, Florence 1987

Sala Capitolare della Chiesa di Santa Maria Maddalena de' Pazzi

50121 Firenze
Borgo Pinti, 58
Tel. 055/2478420

Small

All week 9 a.m.-12 p.m. / 5 p.m.-7 p.m.

Free

No access

By arrangement

In the Chapter House of the old Benedictine monastery, today the Community of the Augustinian Fathers of the Assumption the fresco painted by Perugino between 1493 and 1496 takes up the end wall and is divided into three arches: in the centre *Christ on the Cross with Mary Magdalen*, on the left *St. Bernard and Mary*, on the right *St. John and St. Benedict*. It is reached through the Church of Santa Maria Maddalena de' Pazzi.

Perugino: Crucifixion

Villa Medicea La Petraia e Giardino

50141 Firenze
Via della Petraia, 40
Tel. 055/451208

Large

Villa: all week 9 a.m.-1.30 p.m.
Garden: from 1st November to 28th February 9 a.m.-4.30 p.m.; from 1st March to 30th April 9 a.m.-5.30 p.m.; from 1st May to 31st October 9 a.m.-6.30 p.m.

Among the most outstanding of the Medici residences near Florence the villa (rebuilt perhaps under the direction of Buontalenti between 1576 and 1589) was lived in by Ferdinando de' Medici, then by his son don Lorenzo. It then passed into the ownership of the Dukes of Lorraine (1745) and then of Savoy (1865). During Florence's period as capital city it was the summer residence of Vittorio Emanuele II and the Contessa di Mirafiori until 1870. Since passing to State ownership it has been open to the public regularly. It is surrounded by a magnificent park with a garden all'Italiana restored by Leopoldo II between 1830 and c. 1850.

Volterrano: Cosimo's entrance into Siena

Free

Partially accessible

By arrangement

Guided tours. Collaboration with the Council's education department

In the courtyard frescoes by Volterrano (1636-48) celebrating the *Deeds of the House of Medici and the Knights of St. Stephen*. Inside on the ground floor and the piano nobile furniture and fittings from the 19th C. in Empire style; 16th and 17th C. Florentine tapestries and 19th C. wall-coverings; Vittorio Emanuele II's apartment with mid-19th C. furnishings. In store under the management of the Florence Soprintendenza, a series of 17th C. Florentine canvases from the collection of the Cardinal Carlo de' Medici, including works by M. Rosselli, F. Curradi, Passignano.
In the Italian garden can be found an elegant marble fountain by Tribolo and P. da Vinci (1545-1550) depicting *Fiorenza wringing her hair* in bronze by Giambologna (1572).

Fiorenza in Villa, edited by C. Acidini Luchinat, Florence 1987.

Pinacoteca del Monastero della Certosa

50124 Galluzzo — Firenze
Buca di Certosa, 2
Tel. 055/2049226

The picture-gallery is part of the historic complex of the Certosa del Galluzzo. It was set up in 1960 after restoration work on the whole structure. Owned by the State it contains in its two large rooms important detached frescoes by Pontormo, originally in the main cloister, in addition to a group of paintings from the 14th-17th C. (Fra' Angelico, R. del Ghirlandaio, J. da Empoli, G. Bilivert, R. Manetti, O. Fidani).

C. Chiarelli, G. Leoncini, *La Certosa del Galluzzo*, Milan 1982

Medium

All week 9 a.m.- noon / 4 p.m.-7 p.m.; closed on Mondays

Free

No access

By arrangement

Guided tour

Pontormo: Resurrection

Villa I Tatti

The Harward University Center for Italian Renassance Studies
50135 Settignano — Firenze
Via di Vincigliata 26
Tel. 055/603251

Contains the collection of the art historian B. Berenson comprising works from various periods and in particular paintings on wood of the Italian school from the 14th-16th C. On his death in 1959 it passed according to his wishes, along with the Villa «I Tatti», the photograph library and the library, to Harward University which has set up a Centre for the study of the Italian Renaissance. It is open to scholars by prior appointment.

F. Russoli, *La Raccolta Berenson*, Milan 1962

Museo Civico

50054 Fucecchio (FI)
Via Poggio Salamartano, 1
Tel. 0571/20349 (Local Library)

Small

By arrangement with public library

Free

No access

By arrangement

Opened in the former Chapel of the Misericordia, the museum contains religious works and church ornaments from the nearby Collegiate Church and from other parishes in the area. Since 1983 there has also been a display of archaeological finds, the fruit of organized digs and chance discoveries in the Council territory.

Archaeological section. Fossil remains of local animals from the Villafranchian and Post-Pleistocene periods; stone objects from the Lower Paleolithic to the Eneolithic periods; pottery fragments and stone tools from the Bronze Age. Clay objects from the Iron Age and the Etruscan and Roman periods; Roman altar in marble and various metal objects. Unglazed pottery and majolica, metal objects from disappeared medieval settlements. Selection of Post-Classical ceramics produced in the Valdarno area.
13th-16th C. Tuscan paintings including works by the 'Maestro di Fucecchio' (*Madonna and Child with Saints*), Z. Macchiavelli (*Madonna and Child*), Maestro dei Paesaggi Kress (*Nativity scene with Saints*, *Trinity with Saints*), Santi di Tito (lunette with *The Lord blessing*); also 17th C. canvases of the Sienese, Florentine and local schools (G.D. Ferretti, *St. Luigi Gonzaga in glory*).
Ecclesiastical ornaments and goldsmiths' work from the 12th-19th C. (*Shepherd's crook* in ivory from the end of the 12th to the early 13th C.); vestments from the 17th-19th C.

Museo di Fucecchio, edited by P. Dal Poggetto, Fucecchio 1969, *Archeologia del territorio di Fucecchio*, edited by A. Vanni Desideri, Fucecchio 1985

Museo del Tesoro di Santa Maria

50023 Impruneta (FI)
Basilica di Santa Maria dell'Impruneta
Piazza Buondelmonti, 28
Tel. 055/2011700 (Comune)

Small

Winter, from 1st October to 31st May: Friday 10 a.m.-1 p.m., Saturday 3.30 p.m.-7 p.m., Sunday 10 a.m.-1 p.m. / 3.30 p.m.-7 p.m.

Summer, from 1st June to 30th September: Thursday and Friday 10 a.m.-1 p.m., Saturday and Sunday 10 a.m.-1 p.m. / 4.30 p.m.-8 p.m.

Founded recently thanks to the collaboration of various organizations (the Council, the Bishop's See, the Soprintendenza of Florence) the museum preserves a priceless collection of goldsmiths' work, vases, candlesticks, reliquaries, the fruit of centuries of worship at the Church of Santa Maria dell'Impruneta. They are the ex votos donated in a contest of religious fervour and social rivalry from the 14th C. until the early years of the last century. Among the collection's greatest contributors were the grand-ducal court of the Medicis and the noble families, the Florentine corporations and professional organizations. For this reason the treasure of Santa Maria has an important part in the panorama of Tuscan museums.

Votive vase

Entrance fee

No access

By arrangement

Bas-relief in marble depicting the *Rediscovery of the Sacred Images of the Virgin* from the mid-15th C. attribuited to followers of Filarete (Pasquino da Montepulciano ?).
Gothic and Renaissance goldsmiths' work (*Astylar Cross* attributed to L. Ghiberti, two *Paxes* attributed to Antonio di Salvi from 1515); 17th C. ornaments and silver of grand-ducal origin and manufacture (*Reliquary of St. Sisto* by S. Pignoni from 1614; *Reliquary of the Holy Cross* attributed to C. Merlini the Elder from 1620; early 18th C. *Altar set* with four candlesticks and cross in rock crystal from the grand-ducal workshops; silver *Pyx* by C. Merlini from 1637; fifteen votive vases in silver presented to the Sanctuary in 1633). Various ecclesiastical objects from the 18th and 19th C.

A. Paolucci, B. Pacciani, R. Proto Pisani, *Il tesoro di Santa Maria all'Impruneta*, Florence 1987

Museo Parrocchiale

50055 Lastra a Signa (FI)
Propositura di San Martino a Gangalandi
Tel. 055/8720008

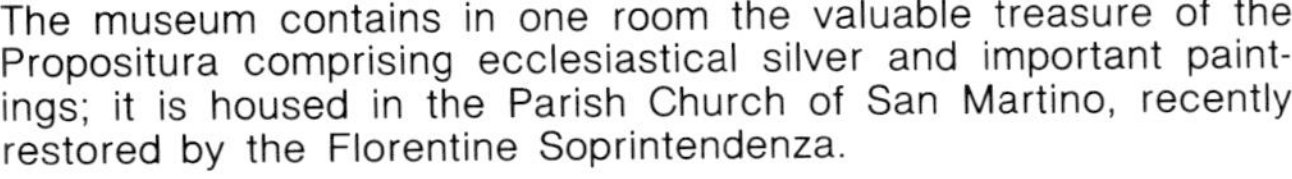
The museum contains in one room the valuable treasure of the Propositura comprising ecclesiastical silver and important paintings; it is housed in the Parish Church of San Martino, recently restored by the Florentine Soprintendenza.

14th-17th C. paintings on wood including *Madonna 'dell'umiltà'* by L. Monaco and the tabernacle with *Madonna and Child* by J. del Sellaio. 17th C. canvases of the Florentine school (J. Confortini). Ecclesiastical silver mainly from the 17th-18th C. (three *reliquaries* in silver foil from 1743).

Small

By arrangement

Free

By arrangement

Museo Comunale

Circolo mineralogico e paleontologico Val d'Elsa
50050 Montaione (FI)
Via Cresci, 15
Tel. 0571/69031-69032
(Comune)

The museum was founded in 1982 by the Council in collaboration with the Mineralogy and Paleontology Society of Val d'Elsa. It displays animal, mineral and fossil remains found in the territory of Montaione and a substantial collection of prehistoric stone tools.

Local zoological collection.

Mineral collection.

Pliocene fossilized remains from the territory of Montaione.

Collection of stone tools from the Paleolithic period, Neolithc arrowheads and impressed pottery from Libya.

Small

By arrangement with the Council

Free

Partially accessible

By arrangement

Guided tours for schools by prior arrangement

Museo della Ceramica e del Territorio

50056 Montelupo Fiorentino (FI)
Via Baccio Sinibaldi, 45
Tel. 0571/51352

Opened in 1983 by the Council and housed in the former Palazzo Pretorio (14th C.), the museum contains systematically arranged examples of local ceramics from the 13th C. onwards. There is also a prehistoric section with material from sites in the Middle Valdarno, the area of Montalbano and the Lower Val di Pesa. The «territory» section is under completion, and displays protohistoric, Etruscan and Roman material from the same area. The Azzati donation has recently been acquired, comprising protohistorical, classical and Hellenistic ceramics. The museum undertakes extensive research and study and has useful documentary and educational material at its disposal.

Large

All week 2.30 p.m.-7.30 p.m.; closed on Mondays

Entrance fee

No access

By arrangement

Educational service, book in advance. Information and audiovisual material available

Book, photograph and tape library on pottery from Montelupo. Information sheets on the history of pottery. Restoration workshop (32 Via XX Settembre). Open to visits and consultation by prior arrangement.

Occasional conferences. Training courses organized by the Scuola di formazione professionale di ceramisti, 24 Via Caverni, Montelupo

Stone objects from the Lower Paleolithic to the Eneolithic periods; fossilized remains of Pliocene and Villafranchian animals from the Middle Valdarno area; Bronze age metal objects. Metal, glass and other remains from excavations of Post-Classical sites in the urban area of Montelupo. Numerous examples of majolica and ceramics produced by Montelupo factories between the 13th and 18th C., accompained by examples of the material used for the manufacture. Ceramics from various periods from the Azzati collection.

F. Berti, G. Pasquinelli, *Antiche maioliche di Montelupo*, Pontedera 1984

O. von Hessen, *Il bacile bronzeo romanico da Empoli*, Florence 1984

Preistoria del medio Valdarno fiorentino, edited by F. Martini, Empoli 1984

F. Berti, *La maiolica di Montelupo*, Florence 1987

Decorated jug (16th C.), Pozzo dei Lavatoi

Museo della Civiltà Contadina e Artigiana

50035 Palazzuolo sul Senio (FI)
Piazza del Podestà, 8
Tel. 055/8046125-8046154

The museum contains a substantial and continually growing collection of objects and a variety of other material on peasant and artisan culture in the territory. It is house in the 14th C. Palazzo del Capitano.

Medium

From 1st September to 31st December and from 1st March to 30th June: Sundays and public holidays 3 p.m.-6 p.m.; closed on weekdays

From 1st July to 31st August: all week 4 p.m.-7 p.m.

Closed in January and February

Free

♿
Partially accessible

📷
Yes

☞
Guided tours by prior arrangament

Agricultural tools and machines, peasant clothes and products, domestic utensils, furniture, sacred images and devotional objects (including a *Crucifix* in wood probably from the 14th-15th C.). Photographs and explanatory panels describe the items displayed, their use and their origins.

A. Poli, E. Donatini, *Museo della civiltà contadina e artigiana. Usi e costumi del primo Novecento*, Palazzuolo sul Senio 1984

Show-room

Villa Medicea di Poggio a Caiano

50046 Poggio a Caiano (FI)
Piazza dei Medici, 12
Tel. 055/877012

The Villa, designed by Giuliano da Sangallo on commission from Lorenzo the Magnificent between 1480 and 1485 passed to the State in 1919. It contains furnishings and important frescoes. Already partly restored there are plans for further reconstruction work to convert it for museum use.

Large

All week 9 a.m.-1.30 p.m.; closed on Mondays

Afternoon visits during the opening hours of the park

Free

♿
Accessible

📷
By arrangement

Furniture and fittings from the 17th-19th C.; 16th C. frescoes depicing *Roman stories* by A. del Sarto, Franciabigio, A. Allori; fresco by Pontormo (lunette with *Vertumno and Pomona). Remains of*

Façade, central section

Educational activities by prior arrangement (contact the Soprintendenza per i beni architettonici e ambientali per le province di Firenze e Pistoia, 1 Piazza Pitti, Florence, tel. 055/218741)

Exhibitions and meetings

frescoes by Filippino Lippi (Death of Laocoon). Ceiling in decorated and polychrome mortars and frieze in glazed terracotta attributed to A. Sansovino in the Loggia.

S. Bardazzi, E. Castellani, *La Villa Medicea di Poggio a Caiano*, Florence 1981
L. Medri, P. Mazzoni, M. De Vico Fallani, *La Villa Medicea di Poggio a Caiano*, Florence 1986

Centro per l'Arte Contemporanea Luigi Pecci

50047 Prato
Viale della Repubblica
Tel. 0574/452018

Large

All week 10 a.m.-7 p.m.; closed on Tuesday

Entrance fee

Accessible

No

In the Museum's internal workshops the Education Department organizes an interesting programme of didactic activities aimed mainly at school pupils. Special courses for teachers. Audiovisual material.

I.D.C.: Library specializing in contemporary art opening soon.
Extensive programme of cultural activities organized by the Events Department: performance, avant-garde theatre, musical recitals and modern dance in the open-air amphitheatre; conferences, series of films and art videos in the museum's internal spaces.

Founded on the initiative of the industrialist Enrico Pecci in memory of his son Luigi, the recently opened Centre is administered by a group of several public and private organizations (the local Council, the Cassa di Risparmi e Depositi, the Unione Industriale Pratese and over seventy founding members). It covers an area of over five thousand square metres (over fifty three thousand square feet) of which one thousand five hundred square metres (sixteen thousand square feet) are indoors. The building was designed by the architect Italo Gamberini. The museum — the first purpose-built modern art museum in Italy — constitutes a multi-disciplinary cultural organization with interesting exhibitions, acquisition and educational programmes centred on the art of the last decade. The museum will organize quarterly temporary exhibitions and will act as a true permanent collection through the acquisition of some of the works periodically exhibited. The internal education department carries out extensive didactic activities, the Events Department organizes cultural shows and the Graphics Department takes care of the preservation and display of drawings, prints and photographs. There is also the IDC (Information and Documentation Centre - Visual Arts) founded in 1983 and subsequently passed to the direction of the Pecci Museum, which will be set up as a study and research centre.

Until 10.11.1988 *Europe Now. Contemporary Art in Western Europe*, an exhibition of painting, sculptures, video and installations from the last decade, with works by John Armeleder, Marco Bagnoli, Richard Basquiá, Joseph Beuys, Domenico Bianchi, Francesco Clemente, Tony Cragg, Enzo Cucchi, Jiri Georg Dikoupil, Albert Hien, Anish Kapoo, Per Kirkeby, Willi Kopf, Jannis Kounellis, Marie-Jo Lafontaine, Bertrand Lavier, Mario Merz, Vittorio Messina, Julian Opie, Mimmo Paladino, Giulio Paolini, Michelangelo Pistoletto, Fabrizio Plessi, Annee and Patrick Poirier, Gerhard Richter, Georges Rousse, Hubert Scheibl, Hob Scholte, Thomas Schutte, Susana Solano, Mauro Staccioli, Thomas Virnich, Gilberto Zorio.
From 10.11.1988 the exhibition *Space '88*, installations by ten international artists.
Outside: Enzo Cucchi, *Fountain*, 1988, marble and mosaic; Mauro Staccioli, *Prato Sculpture*, 1988, concrete; Anne and Patrick Poirier, *Exegi Monumentum Aere Perennius*, 1988, stainless steel.

Europa Oggi. Arte contemporanea nell'Europa Occidentale, edited by Amnon Barzel, Centro Di/Electa, Florence Milan 1988.
Spazi '88, installazioni, edited by Amnon Barzel, Centro Di/Electa, Florence Milan 1988.

Collezioni Scientifiche del Liceo Classico Cicognini di Prato

50047 Prato (FI)
Via Baldanzi, 16
Tel. 0574/40780

The museum contains rich natural history and scientific collections whose creation is closely linked with the history of the Liceo founded in 1699 as a boarding school by the Jesuit Fathers. In 1854 it passed to the grand-ducal Government as a Pubblico Liceo and in 1925, permanently detached from the Collegio, it was taken over by the State. The collection has been restored and rearranged since 1970 by the school's principals and teachers.

Small

By arrangement on weekdays from 9 a.m.-1 p.m.

Free

No access

Yes

Antique library and historical archive open only to scholars

Natural History collection: exotic objects; stuffed birds, mammals and reptiles; invertebrates and vertebrates in formalin and alcohol; shells and coelenterates; minerals (natural elements, sulphides, haloids, oxides, carbonates, silicates, sulphates); rocks (ligneous, sedimentary and metamorphic); various plant species in formalin; fungi in formalin and models; stereoscopes with respective anatomical stereographs; skeletons of various animal species. Antique physics apparatus divided into the following sections: Mechanics; Electromagnetics (electrostatics; electrical currents and magnetic fields; variable electromagnetic field); Thermology; Optical acoustics; Properties of solids, liquids and gasses.

In preparation *Catalogo degli antichi strumenti di fisica restaurati*

Galleria di Palazzo degli Alberti

50047 Prato (FI)
Via degli Alberti, 2
Tel. 0574/4921 (Cassa di Risparmi e Depositi di Prato)

Opened in 1983 the museum is housed in rooms of the historic Palazzo degli Alberti, headquarters of the Cassa di Risparmi e Depositi di Prato. It contains an extensive collection of paintings, mainly 17th C. Tuscan works, arranged chronologically and thematically. Sculptures by the Prato artist Lorenzo Bartolini (1777-1850) are also displayed.

Medium

Weekdays 4 p.m.-6 p.m., Saturday 9 a.m.- noon (for groups) by prior arrangement with the Secretary's office of the Bank

Free

Accessible

By arrangement

Guided tours by arrangement

15th and 16th C. paintings on wood: F. Lippi (*Madonna and Child*), G. Bellini (*The Crucifix*), S. di Tito (*The Virgin Mary received into Heaven and various Saints*). 17th C. canvases: Caravaggio (*Christ crowned with thorns*), with particular attention to the Tuscan school, M. Rosselli, J. Vignali, L. Lippi, F. Furini, G. Dandini, C. Dolci, V. Dandini, S. Coccapani, M. Balassi, G. Martinelli, B. Mei, P. Paolini. Also G. Sustermans (*Portrait of Vittoria della Rovere*), L. Mehus, P. Reschi, N. Van Houbraken. 18th C. paintings by P. Dandini, C. Sagrestani, F. Conti, D. Ferretti.
Sculptures by L. Bartolini, *Bust of M. Luisa of Austria*, of *Elisa Baciocchi*, *Bust of Anatolio Demidoff*, *Model for a monument to Leopoldo II of Lorraine*, *Faith in God*.

G. Marchini, *La Galleria di Palazzo degli Alberti*, Milan 1982

G. Marchini, *La Galleria di Palazzo degli Alberti*, *100 opere d'arte*, Prato 1985

Tutti i Musei di Prato, by various authors, Milan 1985.

Museo Civico

50047 Prato (FI)
Piazza del Comune
Tel. 0574/452302

The museum's origins date back to a collection started by the Grand Duke Pietro Leopoldo in 1788; set up officially by the local scholar Gaetano Guasti in 1858 it grew considerably as a consequence of the 1866 religious suppressions. Since 1912 it has been housed in the historic Palazzo Pretorio.
Reorganized and enlarged many times over the years it today boasts a magnificent collection of important works (14th-19th C. paintings, drawings, sculptures, casts, ceramics and archaelogical remains) only partly exhibited due to the reconstuction work currently under way. There is also an educational section.

Large

Weekdays 9 a.m.-1 p.m. / 3 p.m.-7 p.m.; closed on Sundays

Entrance fee

By arrangement

The museum's education department (opening times Monday to Thursday 8 a.m.-2 p.m., Friday 9 a.m.-1 p.m.) organizes historical and artistic tours in the town and guided visits of the museum. Audiovisual and documentary material available

Conferences and lectures on the museum and the town's artistic heritage

14th-19th C. paintings on wood and canvas of the Florentine school, as well as a considerable collection of Flemish, Roman and Neapolitan works. Of particular note paintings by B. Daddi (*Madonna and Child with Saints*), predella wiith *Legend of the Sacred Cincture*, Giovanni da Milano (*Madonna and Child with Saints*), L. Monaco, Andrea Giusto, Filippo Lippi (*Adoration of the Child*, '*Pala del Ceppo*' from 1453), fra' Diamante, Filippino Lippi (tabernacle with the *Madonna with Saints*; *Madonna and Child, St. Stephen and St. John the Baptist* from 1503), L. Signorelli, Poppi (*Archangel Raphael and Tobiolo* from 1572), G.B. Naldini, G.B. Caracciolo (*Noli me tangere*), L. Mascagni, O. Fidani, G. Bilivert (*Annunciation* from 1630), M. Balassi, follower of Vanvitelli, G.D. Ferretti, A. Marini, A. Franchi. Sculptures by the della Robbias, Michele da Firenze and plaster models by L. Bartolini.

G. Guasti, *Alcuni quadri della Galleria comunale di Prato descritti e illustrati*, Prato 1858

G. Guasti, *I quadri della Galleria d'arte del Comune di Prato descritti e illustrati*, Prato 1888

G. Carocci, *Catalogo della Galleria comunale*, Prato 1900

R. Papini, *Catalogo della Galleria comunale di Prato*, Bergamo 1912

G. Marchini, *La Galleria comunale di Prato*, catalogue of the works, Florence 1958

G. Datini, *Musei di Prato: Galleria di Palazzo Pretorio, Opera del Duomo, Quadreria comunale*, Bologna 1972

Il materiale archeologico nel Palazzo Pretorio, edited by R. Francovich and G. Vannini, Florence 1978

Tutti i Musei di Prato, by various authors, Milan 1985

Museo dell'Opera del Duomo

50047 Prato (FI)
Piazza Duomo, 49
Tel. 0574/29339

Founded in 1967 by the Cathedral Chapter, the Florentine Soprintendenzas and the Azienda Autonoma di Turismo di Prato, the museum contains important paintings, sculptures, goldsmiths' work and ecclesiastical ornaments from the Duomo and various other churches in the Diocese. It was comprehensively restored and enlarged in 1974. Also open to the visitor are the «Vaults» (14th C. tombs under the chapels in the apses opened in 1980), and a small Antiquarium beneath the Cathedral.

Medium

Weekdays 9.30 a.m.-12.30 p.m. / 3 p.m.-6.30 p.m., Sundays and public holidays

In the museum: frescoes, paintings on wood and canvas from the 13th-18th C. including works by Niccolò di Tommaso, G. Toscani, P. Uccello (*Il Beato Iacopone da Todi*, detached fresco), Maestro della Natività di Castello, Filippino Lippi (*St. Lucy*), Michele di Ridolfo,

9.30 a.m.-12.30 p.m.; closed on Tuesdays

Entrance fee

No access

By arrangement

Guided tours by prior arrangement with the local Tourist Organization's Information Office, 48 Via Cairoli, tel. 0574/24112

Maso da San Friano, C. Dolci (*Guardian Angel* from 1675); L. Mehus (*Communion of St. Teresa* from 1683). Church ornaments (*Cappella della Cintola* by Maso di Bartolomeo from 1446; *Reliquary of St. Anne*, by Antonio di Salvi from 1490). Cloths and hangings from the 15th-18th C. (16th C. *Parato di S. Stefano* in damask). 15th-16th C. illuminated choirbooks from the Cathedral. 15th C. sculptures (reliefs depicting *Dancing Putti* from the external pulpit by Donatello, Michelozzo, Maso di Bartolomeo and Pagno di Lapo from 1428).
In the Antiquarium and the Vaults: remains of the Romanesque cloister, architectural and sculptural fragments from the 14th-18th C., stone and ceramic pieces from excavations in the Cathedral, cycles and fragments of frescoes from the 14th and 15th C.

Tutti i Musei di Prato, by various authors, Milan 1985

Museo di Pittura Murale

50047 Prato (FI)
Piazza San Domenico, 8
Tel. 0574/24112 (Azienda autonoma di turismo)
Tel. 0574/20665-460392 (Amici dei musei)

Founded in 1974 on the initiative of the Azienda Autonoma di Turismo di Prato the museum displays detached frescoes, sinopias and wall drawings from the city and the territory of Prato (the churches of San Donato and San Giorgio, the Cathedral, Tabernacle of Figline di Prato, Palazzo Vaj). Housed in the Convent of St. Dominic with modern display criteria it also offers interesting educational material. There is also a large collection of ex votos (17th C.), paintings and ornaments and fittings from the Convent.

Medium

Sundays and public holidays 9.30 a.m.-12.30 p.m.; weekdays by arrangement with the Friends of the Museum Association

Free

No access

By arrangement

Guided tours by prior arrangement

Detached frescoes and sinopias from the 14th-17th C. by Pietro di Miniato, N. Gerini (*Tabernacolo del Ceppo* from 1391), Maestro delle Madonne, A. Gaddi (*Tabernacolo di Figline*), Antonio di Miniato, Andrea di Giusto and P. Uccello (*Life of the Madonna*, *Stories of St. Stephen*, *Virtue*, *Saints*, from the Cathedral), Volterrano (*Christ served by the Angels* from 1650). Mid-15th C. wall drawings. 14th-18th C. paintings on wood and canvas (T. Gaddi, *St. Dominic*). 17th-19th C. cloths and hangings; church ornaments (17th-19th C. silver) and furniture from the convent. Collection of 17th C. votive tablets dedicated to the Beato Benedetto Bacci.

Pittura murale nel S. Domenico di Prato. Il Museo, l'architettura e le opere d'arte del complesso conventuale, edited by F. Gurrieri, Prato 1974

Tutti i Musei di Prato, by various authors, Milan 1985

Museo del Tessuto

50047 Prato
Istituto Tecnico industriale «Tullio Buzzi»
Viale della Repubblica, 9
Tel. 0574/570352

Opened in 1975, the museum is housed in the Istituto Buzzi, specialists in the various branches of textile production. The most important part of the collection consists of a precious collection of fabrics in part from the Salvadori collection, presented by the industrialist Loriano Bertini. The museum has the use of the school's modern equipment and undertakes extensive educational and research activities.

Small

By appointment

Free

Accessible

By arrangement

Educational service for schools. Visit to the school's textile and chemistry departments

Library and archive open only to scholars by prior arrangement

Examples of fabrics from the 15th-18th C. including many silks. Sample books. Late 19th C. 1:20 scale models of textile machines; textile machines and original tools.

R. Bonito Fanelli, *Il Museo del tessuto a Prato. La donazione Bertini*, Florence 1975

R. Bonito Fanelli, *Five centuries of Italian textiles: 1300-1800*, exhibition catalogue, Prato 1981

Tutti i Musei di Prato, by various authors, Prato 1984

Museo della Pieve di San Pietro

50040 Figline di Prato — Prato (FI)
Via Vecchia Cantagallo, 4
Tel. 0574/460555

Small

By arrangement

Free

No access

By arrangement

Guided tours on request

Founded in 1975 by the Azienda Autonoma di Turismo di Prato the museum, owned by the parish of San Pietro Apostolo, displays works of art and church ornaments from the adjacent Romanesque parish church and a small group of archaeological remains found in the area.

14th-17th C. paintings on wood and canvas, by Tommaso di Piero (*Madonna and Child with Saints* from 1529), by L. Mascagni (*The entrusting of the keys to St. Peter*).
Ecclesiastical ornaments and church silver (Early 15th C. *Chalice* in silver and gilded copper; *Processional Cross* in gilded copper and silver).

F. Gurrieri, A.M. Maetzke, *La Pieve romanica di Figline di Prato*, Prato 1970

Tutti i Musei di Prato, by various authors, Milan 1985

Centro di Scienze Naturali

50047 Galceti — Prato (FI)
Via di Galceti, 74
Tel. 0574/460503

Housed in a former convent and surrounded by a large park of over 6 hectares (15 acres) the Natural History Centre undertakes ecological, scientific, research and educational activities as well as environmental protection and improvement schemes. It is also involved in an effective programme aimed at the protection and reintroduction of wild animals into the natural environment.

Medium

Winter, from 1st October to 31st March: weekdays 9.30 a.m.-12.30 p.m. / 3 p.m.-6 p.m., Sundays and public holidays 3 p.m.-6 p.m.

Summer, from 1st April to 30th September: weekdays 9.30 a.m.-12.30 p.m. / 3.30 p.m.-7.30 p.m., Sundays and public holidays 3.30 p.m.-7.30 p.m.

Closed on Mondays and Tuesdays

Entrance fee

♿
Partially accessible

By arrangement

Guided tours by prior arrangement. Refresher courses for teachers. Seminars

Electronic data bank on the animals and natural environment of the Region, Ecology and Natural History library open by arrangement

Environmental education activities. Information centre on ecological and environmental problems. Tours and outings organized to nature reserves and parks. Forest fire-fighting service. Exhibitions, meetings, training courses, conferences

Birds, mammals, fishes, reptiles, insects, shells, herbarium, minerals, palethnological finds from Galceti and stone objects from the Bronze Age from Monferrato. Animal dioramas with living animals.

Atti del Primo convegno di studi sul Monferrato, by various authors, Prato 1973

Parco naturale del Monferrato. Piano studio di fattibilità, by various authors, Prato 1981

P.V. Arrigoni, C. Ricceri, A. Mazzanti, *La vegetazione serpentinicola del Monferrato di Prato in Toscana*, Prato 1983

Parco Bisenzio, Rivisitazione e riuso di un fiume urbano, by various authors, Prato 1986

Female roe-deer with her young

Arboreto Sperimentale di Vallombrosa

50060 Reggello (FI)
Tel. 055/862008 0575/353021
(Istituto sperimentale per la selvicotura di Vallombrosa)

Founded in 1880 by Vittorio Perona the Vallombrosa arboretum, today administered by the Institute of experimental forestry of Arezzo, is without doubt one of the most important in Europe. It contains a collection of about four thousand specimens including over one thousand five hundred species of forest plants and shrubs. Attached to the arboretum is an experimental nursery, a seed bank and a collection of wood samples which can be consulted by arrangement and a small tree museum currently under restoration.

Large

Open by prior arrangement with the Istituto sperimentale per la selvicotura (80 Viale Santa Margherita, Arezzo)

Free

No access

Yes

Guided tours

Experimental nursery section. 1884 Siemoni arboretum section. 1886 Tozzi arboretum section. 1914 Perona arboretum section. 1923-1958 Pavari arboretum section. 1976 Allegri arboretum section.

E. Allegri, *Index plantarum vallis umbrosae*, catalogue of the Vallombrosa arboretums, in *Annali dell'Istituto sperimentale per la selvicoltura di Arezzo*, vol. I, 1970

L'Arboreto di Masso del Diavolo a Vallombrosa, by various authors, in *Annali dell'Istituto sperimentale per la selvicoltura di Arezzo*, vol. XI, 1980

Museo della Vite e del Vino della Val di Sieve

50068 Rufina (FI)
Villa di Poggio Reale
Tel. 055/839377 (Consorzio Vitirufina)

Founded by the Consorzio Vitirufina the museum displays over a thousand objects concerned with vine cultivation and wine-making, the principal activity in the Valdisieve. It also has at its disposal extensive archives and documents on the technical and commercial aspects of the sector and on the territory. It is housed in the Villa Spalletti di Poggio Reale recently acquired by the local council.

Medium

By prior arrangement

Free

No access

By arrangement

Guided tours by prior arrangement with the Council's education office

Archival material and library open for consultation by prior arrangement

Tools for disinfestation, pruning, hoeing, the grape harvest, wine making, bottling and wine analysis. Section dedicated to the cooper with tools for making casks, containers for wine and 'vinsanto', including examples of 18th C. blown glass.

Raccolta di Arte Sacra

50037 San Piero a Sieve (FI)
Convento del Bosco ai Frati
Tel. 055/848111

Opened in 1971 the collection is housed in one room of the 15th C. Franciscan monastery of Bosco ai Frati. It contains the ornaments and works of art from the Church and the Monastery.

Small

By arrangement

Free

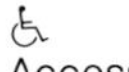
Accessible

By arrangement

16th-19th C. ecclesiastical vessels and vestments and hangings. 16th-18th C. paintings on wood. 15th and 16th C. Florentine sculptures (wooden *Crucifix* by Donatello)

Museo di Doccia

50019 Sesto Fiorentino (FI)
Viale Pratese, 31
Tel. 055/4210451

Large

Tuesday, Thursday and Saturday 9.30 a.m.-1 p.m. / 3.30 p.m.-6.30 p.m.

Entrance fee

Accessible

By arrangement

Educational activities concerning the historical and artistic study of the Doccia factory. Printed and audiovisual material available

Book and photograph library and archive open for consultation by prior arrangement

Occasional exhibitions and series of conferences

Opened in 1965 the museum contains the precious porcelains produced by the famous factory founded in 1737 by the Florentine patrician Carlo Ginori and managed by his heirs until 1896. The firm was then taken over by the Richard Ginori company which still owns the factory and the museum. Set out according to the most modern museum standards it undertakes extensive educational and research activities.

Over 3000 items divided into five periods (from 1737 to the present century). Each chronological section is further arranged by theme, colour and pattern to aid an understanding of the delicacy and art of making porcelain.
The tableware is mainly multi-coloured apart from some characteristic designs such as the stencilled design in blue and landscape scenes in monochrome purple. The fine services have «fruit and flower», «rose», «villages», «quadruped», «town views», marine subjects and archaeological designs (with scenes taken from archaeological remains) as their motifs.
The chinoiserie, «eggshell» porcelain and stoneware belong to the selective high technology production imported to Doccia during the 1840's and 1850's. The 19th C. ceramics are characterized by a high artistic level, with some beautiful examples in Liberty style. Great refinement and innovation can be seen in the Gio Ponti style from the 20's and 30's.
Among the exceptional large scale pieces from the 18th C. Ginori factory are the life size statues (reproduction of famous Greek sculptural groups) and a very unusual fireplace over 3 metres (9 1/2 feet) tall. The Galleria dei Modelli which displays a collection of samples in wax (original models by Florentine Baroque artists) also exhibits several statuettes in terracotta and original clay moulds for the casting of the porcelain model. The goldsmith's die from a limited production from the early period of Doccia is accompanied by the series of medals, of Renaissance leads and by the series of casts (in sulphur and red lead) taken from cameos in pietre dure. There are a number of 18th C. Glass vessels with bases and lids in turquoise-painted majolica which show the whole range of coloured earths used for hard-fired painting on porcelain.

Text edited by E. Maggini Catarsi

G. Liverani, *Il Museo delle porcellane di Doccia*, Milan 1967

G. Ponti, *Ceramiche 1923-1930. Le opere del Museo Ginori di Doccia*, exhibition catalogue, Florence 1983

Museo della Cultura Contadina

50019 Colonnata — Sesto Fiorentino (FI)
Scuola Media Statale «C. Lorenzini»
Via delle Porcellane, 46
Tel. 055/4490992

Founded in 1972 as part of the school's educational activities, the museum contains a collection of objects from the territory of Sesto and other areas in Tuscany. It is currently closed to the public.

The museum is divided into the following sections: hay and straw; work in the fields both pastoral and agricultural the stable; shed and threshing floor; treatment of oil, wine and bread; tools for making and repairing work implements and domestic objects; various iconographical documents; weaving; the kitchen; sanitation; games; school; religion.

Museo Beato Angelico

50039 Vicchio (FI)
Piazza Giotto
Tel. 055/844460 (Biblioteca)

Small

Thursday, Saturday and Sunday 10 a.m.- noon.

Free

Accessible

By arrangement

Guided tours by prior arrangement

Founded in 1967 by the Council the museum is housed in rooms on the ground floor of the Town Hall. It comprises a medieval and modern section with paintings, sculptures and ecclesiastical objects and an archaeological section with remains found on surface sites and excavations in the territory.

Stone objects (building material and utensils; impasto, purified clay and bucchero pottery); weapons and metal utensils dating from the middle of the 7th C. B.C. and the Hellenistic period found in the area of Poggio di Colla.
Sculptures in stone, wood and terracotta (*Holy water stoup* with sculptured relief; *escutcheons* of the Podestà of Vicchio; 15th C. Florentine *Madonna and Child*; *St. John the Baptist*, bust by A. della Robbia).
14th-16th C. Detached frescoes of the Florentine school. Ecclesiastical goldsmiths' work and other objects (16th and 17th C.).

R. Chiarellii, F. Nicosia, A. Santoni, *Museo «Beato Angelico»*, Florence 1975

Museo Casa di Giotto

50039 Vespignano — Vicchio (FI)
Tel. 055/844782

Small

All week 3 p.m.-7 p.m.; closed on Mondays

Free

Traditionally held to be the artist's birthplace the museum, owned by the Council, houses a permanent educational exhibition created by the International University of Art of Florence. The display comprises seventy reproductions with respective critical comment regarding Giotto's work.

L. Collobi Ragghianti, *Giotto*, Vicchio 1987

Accessible

By arrangement

Documentary material available

Giotto's house

Museo Leonardiano

50059 Vinci (FI)
Via della Torre, 2
Tel. 0571/56055

Housed in the 11th-12th C. Castello dei Conti Guidi the museum contains a collection of several models of machines built from original designs by Leonardo. The original collection, opened in 1953 on the occasion of the 500th anniversary of his birth, was recently enlarged with the material from the travelling exhibition «Laboratorio di Leonardo» arranged by IBM Italy.
The new exhibition opened in 1986 benefits from educational material and a variety of material on the life and work of Leonardo as scientist.

Medium

All week 9.30 a.m.- noon / 2.30 p.m.-6 p.m.

Entrance fee

No access

By arrangement

Video library open to visitors. Documents on Leonardo available on request

Library (Via La Pira, Vinci, tel: 0571/56590)

Letture vinciane organized by the Leonardo Library

Original section with working models of machines (1930-52) built to scale from designs by Leonardo.
Section containing material from the travelliing exhibition «Laboratorio di Leonardo» divided into three parts: Leonardo and vehicles in the air, in water and on land.

M. Cianchi, *Le macchine di Leonardo*, Florence 1981

Il Museo leonardiano di Vinci, edited by A. Marinoni, Milan 1986

Casa Natale di Leonardo

50059 Anchiano — Vinci (FI)
Tel. 0571/56055 (Museo leonardiano)

Presented to the Council by the Count Rasini di Castel Campo the house is traditionally believed to be the place where Leonardo spend his childhhood. Completely restored, it contains educational and documentary material and is part of the «Leonardo Itinerary» created at Vinci by the local Council in collaboration with IBM Italy.

Small

All week 9.30 a.m.- noon / 2.30 p.m.-6 p.m.

Free

Accessible

Yes

Leonardo's house

Museo Archeologico
58040 Vetulonia — Castiglione della Pescaia (GR)
Via Garibaldi
Tel. 0564/933870 (Comune)

Contains important remains found in the area of Vetulonia, dating from the 8th C. B.C. to the Hellenistic period. Among the most important items the grave goods from the «Tomba dei Leoncini» and the terracottas from the Costa Murata complex.
The museum is temporarily closed to the public for important rebuilding work.

Museo Archeologico e d'Arte della Maremma
58100 Grosseto
Piazza Baccarini, 3
Tel. 0564/27290

Large

Weekdays 9 a.m.-1 p.m. / 4 p.m.-7.30 p.m.; Sundays and public holidays 9 a.m.-1 p.m.; closed on Wednesdays

Entrance fee

No access

By arrangement

In preparation

Archive and library open to consultation on weekdays from 8 a.m. to 2 p.m., by prior arrangement

Founded in 1865 with a donation from the canon Chelli and enlarged with further acquisitions and donations by the State (including the Lotti and Ciacci collections), the museum was totally restructured in 1975. It contains a wide range of exhibits and extensive documentary material on various archaeological centres in the Province of Grosseto (Roselle, Populonia, Vetulonia, Talamone, Vulci, Sovana, Pitigliano, Saturnia, Magliano) including a particularly interesting section dedicated to the Roselle excavations.
The museum also houses the Diocesan Museum of Sacred Art (transferred here in 1975) comprising a valuable group of paintings of the Sienese school dating from the 14th-17th C., and examples of the minor arts. There is also a section dedicated to medieval archaeology and collections of majolica and coins. The museum has extensive technical and scientific support apparatus at its disposal and a programme is currently underway to modernize the educational facilities available.

Material mainly from Vulci and the surrounding country, from Populonia and from archaeological sites in the Province of Grosseto. Stone tools, pottery and copper and bronze objects (remarkable Eneolithic grave goods, the relics from the «ripostiglio di Campese» (Isola di Giglio) and from the necropolises of Nomadelfia at Roselle). Of particular note in the topographical section the series of impasto pottery, utensils and ornamental objects in bronze from Vetulonia, the vases in late geometrical style from Pescia Romana and other locations around Vulci, also the source of numerous Corinthian, Etrusco-Corinthian and Attic material; also the rich and varied production of impasto and bucchero, as well as examples of Vulci funenary sculptures (*male torso* and *ram's head*). Also of great interest a *Bust of Hadrian* from Castiglione della Pescaia. Permanent exhibition on the material found in the Roselle excavations, including ceramics (oustanding Attic imports), architectural terracottas (facing tiles with floral and illustrated decora-

Exhibitions and annual series of conferences

Geometric krater with lid

tion, antefixes in the form of heads of maenads and satyrs), metal and glass remains. An important group of statues representing members of the Giulio-Claudia family from the site of the city's forum. There is a recently acquired substantial group of archaeological material from the Fiora and Albegna valleys, previously in the Ciacci collection, dating from the prehistorical period to the Late Middle Ages. Also worthy of mention a collection of late medieval ceramics and metal objects and some sets of grave goods from Longobardian tombs containing mainly personal ornaments and weapons. The medieval collection contains too pottery of local production (Fortezza di Grosseto, remains from Burano, Badiola al Fango, Monte Argentario), dating from the 13th-18th C.
13th-17th C. paintings on wood of the Sienese and Florentine schools, including works from the studio of Guido da Siena (*Christ the Judge*), Ugolino di Neri, Segna di Bonaventura, Sassetta (*Madonna 'delle ciliegie'*), Gerolamo di Benvenuto, from the school of Sodoma.
17th and 18th C. canvases of the Bolognese, Genoese, Florentine and Roman schools. Sculptures in wood from various periods. 14th and 15th C. illuminated manuscripts. Church ornaments (15th-18th C.).
Paintings and sculptures by local artists of the 19th and 20th C.

A. Mazzolai, *Grosseto. Il Museo archeologico della Maremma*, Grosseto 1977

Roselle, gli scavi e la mostra, by various authors, Pisa 1977

L. Donati, M. Michelucci, *La collezione Ciacci nel Museo archeologico di Grosseto*, Rome 1981

Museo Civico di Storia Naturale

58100 Grosseto
Via Mazzini, 61
Tel. 0564/414701

Small

Winter, from 1st November to 30th March: weekdays 9 a.m.-12.30 p.m. / 3.30 p.m.-7.30 p.m., Sundays and public holidays 9 a.m.-12.30 p.m.

Summer, from 1st April to 31st October: weekdays 9 a.m.-12.30 p.m. / 4 p.m.-7.30 p.m., Sundays and public holidays 9 a.m.-12.30 p.m.
Closed on Mondays

Free

Accessible

Opened in 1971 on the initiative of the Natural History Society of Maremma the museum is housed in rooms of the local elementary school. It contains material on the natural history of the Province of Grosseto with various collections including also mineralogical material and interesting fossil remains.

Collections of lithology, mineralogy, paleontology, osteology, entomology, malacology, ornithology, erpetology and prehistoric remains.

Atti, four-mounthly publication produced by the museum

C. Del Prete, H. Ticky, G. Tosi, *Le orchidee spontanee della provincia di Grosseto*, Pitigliano 1982

G. Guerrini, *Guida catalogo del Museo civico di storia naturale*, Grosseto 1984

C. Del Prete, G. Tosi, *Flora e vegetazione dei litoranei sabbiosi della Maremma*, Milan 1985

G. Guerrini, *Grosseto, città e natura*, Montepulciano 1985

Yes

Guided visits by prior arrangement

Library open to consultation by prior arrangement

Museo delle Tradizioni Popolari della Maremma
58010 Alberese — Grosseto
Tel. 0564/407111 (Parco Naturale della Maremma)

The foundation of the museum, presently under preparation, was promoted by the Consortium of the Maremma Natural Park in collaboration with the Archivio of popular traditions of the Council of Grosseto. Situated in the former oil-mill in Alberese it will house material and documents on the popular traditions of Maremma and will also offer hints and starting points for a deeper knowledge of the Park. The restored oil-mill will form an integral part of the display. The opening of the museum is planned for late 1988

Museo di Preistoria e Protostoria della Valle Del Fiora
58014 Manciano (GR)
Via Corsini, 5
Tel. 0564/629222 (Comune)

Opened in 1985 and administered by the local Council of Manciano the museum contains material from archaeological researches in the valley of the River Fiora. It has been designed with a very flexible educational format so as to be able to adapt itself to eventual changes in the Museum. One of the aims is to create a real and true educational centre for the territory.

Small

Winter, from 1st October to 31st May: all week 9.30 a.m.-12.30 p.. / 2.30 p.m.-5.30 p.m.

Summer, from 1st June to 30th September: all week 10 a.m.-1 p.m. / 4 p.m.-7 p.m.
Closed on Mondays

Entrance fee

No access

Yes, by arrangement

Stone tools and animal remains from the Paleolithic period. Neolithic tools in obsidian and impressed pottery. Pottery including examples of flask-shaped vases, eneolithic metal and bone objects from various burial sites, particularly the Grotta dei Sassi Neri. Samples of antimonite, malachite and other minerals. Axes and daggers from the Montemerano store; stone utensils, pottery from Bronze Age sites at Scarceta and Sorgenti della Nova. Grave goods from a cremation tomb of the Late Bronze Age from Cavallini del Bufalo (Manciano). Iron Age bronze ornaments.

Museo di preistoria e protostoria della Valle del Fiume Fiora, edited by N. Negroni Catacchio, Roccastrada 1988

Mostra della Civiltà Contadina
58024 Massa Marittima (GR)
Ex Castello di Monteregio
Piazza Beccucci
Tel. 0566/902289 (Servizio turistico musei)

The permanent exhibition, owned by the local Council, comprises material illustrating country life and agricultural work from the territory of Massa Marittima. Since its foundation in 1979 it has been housed in one large room on the ground floor of the Fortezza di Monteregio. Work is currently underway on rearrangement, restoration and transfer to another site.

Small

Winter, from 1st October to 30th June: by arrangement. Summer, from 1st July to 30th September: 10 a.m.-12.30 p.m. / 3.30 p.m.-7 p.m.; closed on Mondays

Free

Accessible

Yes

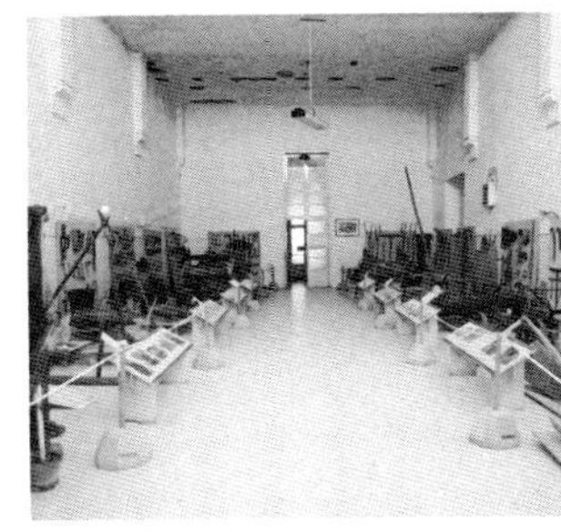
Show-room

Museo Civico Archeologico, Risorgimentale e Pinacoteca

58024 Massa Marittima (GR)
Piazza Garibaldi
Tel. 0566/902289 (Servizio turistico musei)

The impressive Palazzo del Podestà in Massa Marittima, built in 1230, houses on several floors the municipal collections which have been accumulated here over the centuries.
The archaeological museum, recently partly renovated, was founded in 1867 following the donation of a collection of relics found mainly in southern Etruria; it was then expanded with the remains from various excavations carried out in the area by Doro Levi between 1928 and 1931 and more recently with material from the excavation of the Etruscan dwelling beside the Lago dell'Accesa.
The picture gallery was opened in 1980. Situated on the second floor it contains important 14th and 15th C. works of the Sienese school, including the famous *Maestà* by Ambrogio Lorenzetti.
Finally there is the section dedicated to the Risorgimento, completely reorganized in 1987 and comprising arms, medals and relics.

Medium

Winter, from 1st October to 31st March: 9 a.m.-1 p.m. / 3 p.m.-5 p.m.

Summer, from 1st April to 30th September: 10 a.m.-12.30 p.m. / 3.30 p.m.-7 p.m.

Closed on Mondays

Entrance fee

No access

By arrangement

Ambrogio Lorenzetti: Maestà

Occasional conferences to present the results of the excavations in progress in the territory, held in collaboration with the Universities of Florence and Siena

Archaeological section
Stone tools from the Lower and Upper Paleolithic periods. Eneolithic statue-stelae in sandstone. Grave goods from the burial grounds of Lago dell'Accesa, dating mainly from between the Villanova and the Archaic periods, including stone and metal objects (among the latter some remarkable fragments of two *belts* and of two *kantharoi* in bronze foil). Funerary material from the late 4th to early 3rd. B.C. and the Roman period. Bucchero pottery, bricks and metals from the Etruscan settlement recently excavated in the same area. Hellenistic pottery with carved inscriptions. Vases from the former Galli collection including painted examples of Laconian, Etruscano-Corinthian production and from Rhodes and bucchero pottery.

Risorgimento section
Collection of souvenirs and relics of the Risorgimento: arms, flags, uniforms and jackets worn by Garibaldi and other important figures from the period, photographs and medals.

Picture-gallery
14th-19th C. paintings on wood and canvas (a total of 30 works) including important paintings of the Sienese school by A. Lorenzetti (*Maestà*), by Sassetta (*St. Gabriel*) and by Sano di Pietro.

G. Monaco, *Museo Civico: collezioni archeologiche*, Empoli 1964

L'Etruria mineraria, exhibition catalogue, by various authors, Milan 1985

Museo della Miniera

58024 Massa Marittima (GR)
Via Corridoni
Tel. 0566/902289 (Servizio turistico musei)

Open for guided tours at the following times:

Winter, from 1st October to 31st March: all week 11 a.m.-1 p.m. / 3 p.m.- 5 p.m.

Summer, from 1st April to 30th September: all week 10 a.m.-12.30 p.m. / 4 p.m.-7.30 p.m.
Closed on Mondays

Entrance fee

No access

By arrangement

Guided tour

Set up in 1980 by the local Council in collaboration with the local mineralogy society the museum is situated in underground tunnels (about 3000 ft. below the surface) built as anti-aircraft shelters during the Second World War. It contains material on the various mining methods and strengthening of the tunnels, valuable evidence of an activity which has played a fundamental role in the local economy and history.

Machines, tools and equipment from mines in the territory; exhibition of typical local minerals and rocks; examples of chronological growth of metal ore deposits.

Tunnel

Museo di Storia e Arte della Miniera
58024 Massa Marittima (GR)
Palazzetto delle Armi
Tel. 0566/902289 (Servizio turistico musei)

Founded by the mineralogy society of Massa it is housed in the historic Palazzetto delle Armi (15th C.). Opened in 1985 it contains a rich collection of maps and instruments associated with mining in the area from the Etruscan period onwards.
It is presently closed to the public.

Antiquarium Civico
58015 Orbetello (GR)
Tel. 0564/862427 (Comune)

It contains interesting remains dating from between the 8th. C. B.C. and the Imperial period found in the surrounding area, from the Isola del Giglio and from wrecks discovered near the coasts of Giannutri and Argentario.
It is presently closed while awaiting transfer to another site.

Antiquarium di Cosa
58015 Ansedonia — Orbetello (GR)

Set up by the American Academy of Rome in collaboration with the Soprintendenza of archaeology it is presently closed to the public. The small museum contains archaeological material from excavations undertaken over the last decades on the site of the Roman city and port of Cosa.

Museo Storico Naturalistico Rocca di Talamone
58015 Talamone — Orbetello (GR)
Rocca di Talamone
Tel. 0564/407111 (Parco Naturale della Maremma)

Small

Currently closed to the public

Entrance fee

No access

Yes

Opened in 1982 it is housed in the restored Rocca di Talamone, a defensive castle built in the 14th C. On the southern tip of the Parco Naturale the museum offers the visitor an introduction to the area with maps, plans, historical information and extensive photographical material. Administered by the Consorzio del Parco Naturale the museum is an introduction to and an integral part of the many itineraries on offer to visitors.

General information on the site of the Park and the Rocca and of the main historical and artistic treasures of the area as a whole.
Historical section with information on the Rocca and the restoration work, on the Forte delle Saline and on the systems of defence and coastal observation.
S. Rabano section: historical analysis and information on the restoration work.
Natural history section: forestry and management aspects in the Park.
Archaeological section: material on archaeological aspects of the Park and the surrounding area.

The Rocca

Raccolta d'Arte

58053 Roccalbegna (GR)
Oratorio del Santissimo Crocifisso
Tel. 0564/989122

The small parish museum is housed in the Oratory of the Santissimo Crocifisso; opened in 1981 it contains church ornaments and 14th-17th C. paintings on wood and canvas of the Sienese school including a Crucifix by Luca di Tommé. It can be visited by prior arrangement.

Museo Etnografico Santa Caterina

58053 Santa Caterina — Roccalbegna (GR)
Via Roma, 15
Tel. 0564/989032 (Comune)

Small

By arrangement

Free

♿
Accessible

Yes

The privately owned museum administered with the collaboration of the local Council was opened recently (November 1987). Housed in the former forge of the local blacksmith it contains material on the life and traditions of the hills around Grosseto. Further enlargement of the collection and an increase in the exhibition space is planned.

Work tools and various objects with photographic material and explanatory panels.

The annual cycle: Rite of May, Rite of Holy Week, Fire festivals in the hills of Grosseto (the 'Torciata' in Pitigliano, the 'Fiaccolata di Santa Fiora', the 'Rito dello Stallo' and 'Focarazza di Santa Caterina').

The cycle of human life: the trade of the charcoal-burner, the kilnman, the potter, the blacksmith, the cycle of harvest and hay-making; country childrens' games and toys.

David Lazzaretti and the Comunità di Monte Labbro: material on local religion and in particular on David Lazzaretti and the Jurisdavidic Community

---

Mostra Archeologica Media Valle dell'Albegna

58054 Scansano (GR)
Via XX Settembre
Tel. 0564/633023 (Comune)

Housed in rooms in the Town Hall, the museum comprises a selection of excavated material (pottery, metal objects) from the Etruscan dwelling at Ghiaccioforte. It can be visited by prior arrangement with the Council.

A. Talocchini, *Il Ghiaccioforte*, Scansano 1986

Centro di Documentazione dell'Area Archeologica di Sovana

58010 Sovana — Sorano (GR)
Piazza Pretorio
Tel. 0564/633023 (Comune)

The centre which is currently under preparation in the Palazzetto Pretorio in the main square in Sovana will offer an introduction to the territory. Established by the Council in collaboration with the Tuscan Soprintendenza for archaeology it will contain informative material (plans, a scale model and panels showing the various itineraries) and will display fragments of sculpture from the Hildebrand tomb.
The opening is planned for late 1988.

Museo Archivio Giosuè Carducci

57022 Castagneto Carducci (LI)
Piazzetta dell'Arco, 1
Tel. 0565/763624-25 (Comune)

Opened in 1967 the museum contains a variety of material on the poet and the historical-literary period in which he lived. In establishing the museum the local Council seeks to create a permanent centre for the study of local history whose activities also include a series of periodicals, the *Quaderni del Museo*. The material from private collections, from the library of the Carducci home in

Small

Winter, from 15th September to 15th June: weekdays 7 a.m.-1 p.m.

Summer, from 16th June to 14th September: weekdays 7 a.m.-1 p.m. / 6 p.m.-11 p.m., Sundays and public holidays 6 p.m.-11 p.m.

Free

Accessible

By arrangement

Bologna and from the Forteguerriana of Pistoia is housed on the ground floor of the Town Hall.
Further expansion is planned.

Documentary material on Carducci and the historical and literary period in which he lived: various writings, portraits and photographs. Paintings and drawings representing Carducci, caricatures and Carduccian sites. Patriotic, political and propaganda pictures.

Materiale per un Museo Archivio, in *Quaderni del Museo-Archivio «Giosuè Carducci»*, by various authors, July-August 1982

Museo del Menù

57022 Bolgheri — Castagneto Carducci (LI)
Via dei Colli 3

Small

Restricted to experts on written request

Free

Accessible

By arrangement

Small library of gastronomical, food and wine books

The museum was opened in 1975 on the initiative of Enrico Guagnini. In one large and evocative room which was once a milking shed are displayed over ten thousand menus: from those of the royal houses for meals at the courts of Turin, Caserta, Naples and Rome to Mussolini's menu for the inauguration of the Pontine plain; from the Festessen menu offered by the Prussian emperor to the governor of German Africa to more recent ones created by the great chefs of France such as Paul Bacause, François Hinault. There are also about thirty drawings by the Pagot brothers, portraits of great gastronomes and an extensive library of works on gastronomy, food and wine.

C. 10,000 menus and wine lists from the 19th C. to the present day.
Portraits of great gastronomes by the painter Gianni Renna.
Drawings by the Pagot brothers representing the various phases of people at table.
Bronze bust of Luigi Carnacina by Pleikoff.

Museo Etrusco-Romano

57023 San Pietro in Palazzi — Cecina (LI)
Fattoria La Cinquantina
Tel. 0586/660411
0586/680145 (Library)

Founded in 1962 the museum contains various archaeological material from excavations or chance discoveries in the area, from donations and from acquisitions. Since 1980 it has been housed in the villa-farmhouse la Cinquantina (18th C.) bought by the Council and specially rebuilt. An ethnographical section is planned.

Prehistoric stone tools dating mainly from the Neolithic period. Collection of bones and bronze ornaments from a Villanovian tomb.

Medium

Winter, from 16th September to 14th June: Tuesday and Thursday 9 a.m.-12.30 p.m., Saturday 3 p.m.-6 p.m.

Summer, from 15th June to 15th September: Tuesday and Thursday 5.30 p.m.-7 p.m., Saturday 4.30 p.m.-7.30 p.m., Sunday 9.30 a.m.-12.30 p.m.

Free

Accessible

By arrangement

Guided visits by arrangement

Archaic stone urns. Amphoras and anchor stocks from wrecks dating from the late Republican period. Pottery, lanterns, glass and bronze remains from Roman burial sites. Two marble heads, pieces of architectural decoration, pottery and metal domestic utensils from the *Roman villa of San Vincenzino*. In the antiquities section: vases (painted Corinthian, Attic black-figured, Italo-geometrical, Etrusco-Corinthian, examples of buttero and Apulian pottery in the Gnathian style); terracotta statuettes from Magna Graecia; Hellenistic Etruscan urns; oil-lamps; crockery and other domestic objects in bronze (mirror with Dioscuri); illustrated bronzes (mainly Hellenistic); coins dating from the Republican to the Tetrarchan periods (a fine example of gold coin from Gaul).

La Cinquantina Villa

Acquario Comunale Diacinto Cestoni

57127 Livorno
Piazzale Mascagni
Tel. 0586/8095504

Medium

From 1st October to 30th October: all week 10 a.m.-noon / 3 p.m.-6 p.m.

From 1st November to 31st January: all week 10 a.m.-noon / 2.30 p.m.-5.30 p.m.

From 1st February to 28th February: all week 10 a.m.-noon / 3 p.m.-6 p.m.

From 1st March to 30th September: all week 10 a.m.-noon / 4 p.m.-7 p.m.

Closed on Mondays

Entrance fee

Accessible

The aquarium is housed in an early 20th C. building in a corner of the famous Terrazza Mascagni a short distance from the sea. The only institution of its kind in the Region it constitutes an important point of reference for all those interested in marine biology, containing in its tanks the most important and typical Mediterranean marine animals. The building also houses the Inter-university Centre of Marine Biology.

18 tanks of various sizes (from 1.3 cu.m to 6.7 cu.m.) containing the most representative examples of mediterranean plants and animals.

P. Meschini, *Acquario comunale Diacinto Cestoni*, Livorno 1988

By arrangement

Courses for teachers and students with practical activities on marine biology and environmental protection; documentary material available

The Centre's library open to consultation to scholars by prior arrangement

Exhibitions, courses and conferences

Tank with Sea Bream

Museo Mascagni

57125 Livorno
Via Calzabigi, 54
Tel. 0586/852695

Founded in 1985 by the local Council the museum is housed in three rooms on the first floor of the 19th C. Palazzina «Il Castelletto» at the entrance to the Villa Maria public park. The material displayed, comprising photographs, drawings, musical scores, instruments and various relics, was mainly donated by the composer's heirs. There are also extensive archives containing the «letters to my father» and numerous correspondence with other figures and with the composer's friend Tanzini from Livorno.

Small

Winter: weekdays 10 a.m.-1 p.m., Thursday and Saturday 10 a.m.-1 p.m. / 4 p.m.-7 p.m.

Summer: weekdays 10 a.m.-1 p.m. / Thursday and Saturday 4.30 p.m.-7.30 p.m.

Closed on Mondays

Letters and musical scores, libretti and play-bills, photographs and drawings, musical instruments and objects belonging to the composer, portraits in oil, diplomas and decorations.

Of particular importance: the «Cavalleria Rusticana» piano, two portraits in oil by T. Malesci and A. Tommasi, a portrait photograph of Gustav Mahler with a dedication, manuscript scores.

Entrance fee

No access

By arrangement

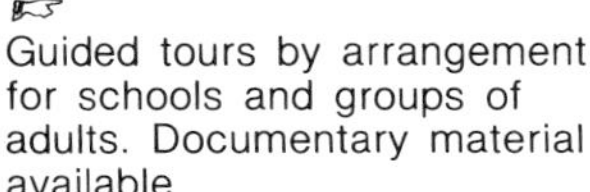

Guided tours by arrangement, for schools and groups of adults. Documentary material available

Mascagni archive, tape and video library, book library on the composer's life and work open to consultation by prior arrangement during the museum's opening hours.

Pietro Mascagni

Exhibitions, meetings and conferences organized annually

Museo e Pinacoteca Civica Giovanni Fattori

57127 Livorno
Piazza Matteotti, 19
Tel. 0586/808001

Medium

Winter, from 1st October to 30th April: weekdays 10 a.m.-1 p.m., Thursdays and Saturdays 10 a.m.-1 p.m. / 4 p.m.-7 p.m.; Sundays and public holidays 10 a.m.-1 p.m. Summer, from 1st May to 30th September: weekdays 10 a.m.-1 p.m., Thursdays and Saturday 10 a.m.-1 p.m. / 4.30 p.m.-7.30 p.m.; Sundays and public holidays 10 a.m.-1 p.m.

Closed on Mondays

The museum's origins date back to 1896 following the donation by Enrico Chiellini to the Council of prehistoric material, Etruscan and Roman material and a coin collection. It was subsequently enriched with a substantial collection of 19th C. Tuscan paintings: acquisitions of works by Giovanni Fattori and Enrico Pollastrini, donations by the families of Plinio Nomellini and Giuseppe Micheli and works on loan from the Uffizi Gallery. It was opened in 1950 in its present home in Villa Fabbricotti, a 19th C. building which also houses the Labronica library. The most interesting section is the Fattori collection, comprising 24 paintings, 236 drawings and 140 etchings. The archaeological collection (Greek, Roman and Etruscan material) and the coin collection (Ancient Greek and Roman, medieval and modern coins) are not open to the public.

Collection of Late Byzantine Greek and Russian icons from the Greek Orthodox Church in Livorno.
Antique painting section (on loan from the Soprintendenza per i beni artistici e storici di Firenze) with 14th-17th C. paintings on wood and canvas of various schools (B. Angelico, Neri di Bicci, Maestro della Natività di Castello, C. Cignani, Borgognone).
The most important section is the Fattori Collection comprising 24 paintings (*Straw-stack*, *Antignano*, *The Signora Martelli*, *Portrait of the artist's wife* and others), 236 drawings and 140 etchings. There are also works by the Macchiaioli painters S. Lega, V. Cabianca, T.

Giovanni Fattori: The signora Martelli at Castiglioncello

Entrance fee

No access

By arrangement

Films and slides on the museum available

Library and archive open to consultation by prior arrangement

Organization of occasional exhibitions with accompanying catalogue

Signorini, C. Banti, S. De Tivoli, G. Boldini and by the post-Macchiaioli painters Ulvi Liegi, M. Puccini, R. Gambogi, Adolfo, Ludoviico and Angiolo Tommasi, O. Chiglia, G. Bartolena, A. Modigliani, V. Corcos, E. Cecconi, L. Lloyd, B. Benvenuti, N. Cannicci, F. Fanelli, G. Gabrielli, V. Grubicy Dragon.

Giovanni Fattori al Museo civico di Livorno, edited by V. Durbé, Florence 1973

Enrico Pollastrini. Mostra dei disegni restaurati, edited by V. Durbé, Florence 1976

Plinio Nomellini. Disegni inediti, edited by V. Durbé, Florence 1979

Icone greche e russe del Museo civico di Livorno, edited by D. Dell'Agata Popova, Pisa 1979

La donazione Chiellini 1883-1983. Rinvenimenti monetari da Santo Stefano ai Lupi, edited by T. Volk, Cambridge 1983

Museo Progressivo d'Arte Contemporanea

57125 Livorno
Via Redi, 22
Tel. 0586/39463

Medium

Winter, from 1st October to 30th April: weekdays 10 a.m.-1 p.m., Thursdays and Saturdays 10 a.m.-1 p.m. / 4 p.m.-7 p.m.

Summer, from 1st May to 30th September: weekdays 10 a.m.-1 p.m., Thursdays and Saturdays 10 a.m.-1 p.m. / 4.30 p.m.-7.30 p.m.

Closed on Mondays

Entrance fee

No access

By arrangement

The museum was opened in 1974 on the initiative of the local Council at Villa Maria which was completely restored and converted to house it. It displays a permanent collection of works by contemporary artists.

Paintings, drawings, engravings and sculptures by contemporary artists (including V. Adami, V. Berti, A. Burri, P.P. Calzolari, F. Cannilla, C. Cappello, E. Castellani, P. Consagra, P. Dorazio, L. Fabro, F. Melotti, G. Nativi, M. Nigro, G. Paolini, C. Parmiggiani, A. Pomodoro, C. Pozzati, M. Reggiani, E. Scanavino, L. Fontana, G. Korompay, O. Licini, P. Manzoni, M. Schifano, A. Soldati, E. Vedova, L. Veronesi).

Museo Provinciale di Storia Naturale

57127 Livorno
Via Roma, 234
Tel. 0586/802294

Small

Weekdays 9 a.m.- noon / 4 p.m.-6 p.m., Saturdays 9 a.m.-12 p.m.; closed on Sundays

Free

Accessible

By arrangement

Guided tours on request

Library open to the public 9 a.m.- noon. Microscope and computer laboratory.
Planetarium open to schools by prior arrangement.
Observatory with astronomical telescope for use by astronomers

Congresses, training courses, conferences, guided natural history excursions

Founded in 1929 by the Province of Livorno the museum is housed in Villa Henderson. It contains collections of considerable scientific value comprising minerals, rocks, fossils, plants, animals, stone objects and pottery mainly from the area of Livorno, from the sea nearby and from the islands of the Tuscan archipelago. During recent years it has been expanded with natural history and prehistorical remains collected on scientific expeditions to Africa and Asia Minor. The museum undertakes extensive scientific and educational activities.

Educational exhibition, mainly for use by schools, covering the following disciplines: geology, mineralogy, petrology, sedimentology, paleontology, botany, zoology, anthropology and ethnology.
In the villa's park the «Mediterranean Garden» is laid out, containing about 300 species of Mediterranean plants and a section of officinal and aromatic plants.

Quaderni del Museo di storia naturale di Livorno with supplements, annual publication produced by the museum.

Raccolta di Ex voto

57128 Montenero — Livorno
Santuario di Montenero
Tel. 0586/579033

Medium

Winter, from 1st October to 30th April: all week 6.30 a.m.-12.30 p.m. / 2.30 p.m.-6 p.m.

This is a rich and valuable collection housed in rooms adjoining the Montenero Sanctuary. Of great historical, artistic and social interest it comprises mainly paintings on wood (c. 600) from the 19th-20th C., depicting nautical subjects.

Ex voto marinari del Santuario di Montenero, exhibition catalogue, by various authors, Pisa 1981

Ex voto marinari del Santuario di Montenero, exhibition catalogue, by various authors, Pisa 1984

Summer, from 1st May to 30th September: all week 6.30 a.m.-12.30 p.m. / 2.30 p.m.-7 p.m.

Free

Accessible

Yes

Ex voto

Museo Archeologico Comunale

57030 Marciana (LI)
Via del Pretorio
Tel. 0565/901076 (Comune)

Established by the Council in 1967 in the ancient Palazzo Pretorio the museum contains material on the archaeological discoveries which have taken place mainly in the central and eastern area of the island: of particular interest the material from the tomb-cave of San Giuseppe di Rio Marina and from the hill settlement of Monte Castello at Procchio. There are also numerous relics recovered from the waters off the coast of Elba.

Small

Winter: by arrangement

Summer, from 1st April to 30th September: all week 10 a.m.-1 p.m. / 4 p.m.-8 p.m.

Entrance fee

No access

Yes

Guided tour by prior request

Prehistoric relics (stone tools from the Paleolithic and Neolithic periods; objects in metal; flask-shaped vessels, Neolithic ornaments in bone from the Grotta di San Giuseppe at Rio Marina). Early Iron Age bronze axe. Crockery and other objects in clay from the Etruscan fort of Monte Castello di Procchio. Grave-goods from Hellenistic tombs from various sources. Transport vessels, black-painted pots, grindstones, anchor stocks and other material from the wrecks off Capo San Andrea and Procchio.

M. Zecchini, *Archeologia e storia antica dell'Isola d'Elba*, Lucca 1983

Museo Archeologico Gasparri

57020 Populonia — Piombino (LI)
Via di Sotto
Tel. 0565/29436-29338

Formed during the Thirties and opened to the public in 1959 by the Gasparri family the museum is housed in a building in the historic centre of this small hamlet. It displays relics mainly from tombs in the Populonia archaeological area.

Small

By arrangement

Free

Accessible

By arrangement

The material consists mainly in grave-goods dating from the Villanovian period onwards and includes: impasto and bucchero pottery, Corinthian painted pottery, Etrusco-Corinthian, Graeco-oriental ceramics, Attic black- and red-figured pottery, Etruscan red-figured and over-painted pottery etc.; crockery and metal implements, glass and amber ornamental objects; acroteria, cippi, a sarcophagus and stone urns, Latin inscriptions. A terracotta shell and several anchor stocks are the fruit of underwater explorations.

A. De Agostino, *La zona archeologica ed il museo*, Rome 1963

A. Romualdi, *Guida archeologica di Populonia*, Rome 1984

Palazzina dei Mulini

57037 Portoferraio (LI)
Piazzale Napoleone
Tel. 0565/915846

The 18th C. Palazzina dei Mulini was residence of Napoleon and his court during his exile on Elba. Today owned by the State it displays Napoleonic furnishings and relics in large rooms with original frescoes. It also houses the Emperor's personal library from Fontainebleau presented by him to the Municipality of Portoferraio. The library can be visited by prior appointment with the Soprintendenza per i beni artistici e storici di Pisa

Large

Winter, from 1st November to 31st March: all week 9 a.m.-4 p.m.

Summer, from 1st April to 30th October: all week 9 a.m.-6.30 p.m.

Entrance fee

No access

By arrangement

Occasional exhibitions

Gallery with period furniture. Reception room with furniture and two paintings by R. Morghen. Servant's room with French, German and Italian caricatures on Napoleonic subjects. Wardrobe room with the Elban Napoleonic flag. Napoleon's private library. Sala degli Ufficiali. Appartamento di Paolina Borghese. Busts by F. Rude.

P. Castelli, M. Ferretti, *Le residenze napoleoniche a Portoferraio*, Pisa 1986

Pinacoteca Foresiana

57037 Portoferraio (LI)
Salita Napoleone
Tel. 0565/92018 (Library)

The gallery contains a collection of paintings, prints, miniatures and furnishings from the 16th-19th C., donated to the local Council in 1814 by the scholar and man of letters Mario Foresi. Opened to the public in 1924 along with the Foresi Library on the top floor of the Town Hall, it was transferred during the war to the Galleria Demidoff adjacent to Napoleon's residence at San Martino. Open to the public until a few years ago it is currently closed. Work is underway to prepare its new seat, the Caserma de Laugier, a large 16th C. building situated in Portoferraio's historic centre.

E. Marini, *Catalogo della Pinacoteca Foresiana*, Empoli 1932

L. Damiani, *Catalogo della Pinacoteca Foresiana*, Portoferraio 1940

Villa Napoleonica di San Martino
57037 San Martino —
Portoferraio (LI)
Tel. 0565/92688

Medium

All week 9 a.m.-1.45 p.m.; closed on Mondays

Entrance fee

Accessible

By arrangement

Occasional exhibitions

Napoleon's summer residence during his stay on Elba it was purchased with the furnishings and various relics in 1851 by Prince Demidoff. It then passed to the State which set up a Napoleon museum. The Galleria Demidoff (situated in a building opposite the villa) was recently reopened to the public (1987) with an exhibition of prints from the Napoleonic period.

Appartamento del Maresciallo Bertrand. Sala delle Colombe. The Emperor's studio and bedroom with 19th C. Furnishings. Egyptian Room with frescoes by V.A. Revelli (1814).

P. Castelli, M. Ferretti, *Collezione Turini De Micheli: immagini napoleoniche per le Sale*, Pisa 1987

Napoleonic Villa at San Martino

Museo Naturalistico
57037 Portoferraio (LI)
Isola di Montecristo
Tel. 0566/40019 (Ufficio Amministrazione di Follonica foreste demaniali)

Set up the CNR on behalf of the State Forestry Corps in 1980-82 this small museum contains material on the principal aspects of the flora, fauna and geological formations of the island and is an ideal starting point for visits to the nature reserve. It is open only during the summer season (May-September) by prior appointment with the Ufficio Amministrazione Foreste Demaniali, Via Bicocchi 2, 58022 Follonica (for school and groups) or the Ministry of Agriculture and Forestry, Via Carducci 5, 00187 Rome (for individual visits).

Museo dei Minerali Elbani
57038 Rio Marina (LI)
Palazzo Comunale

Owned by the private society Gennai Tonietti the small museum founded in 1962 contains a comprehensive collection of the principal types of mineral found on the island. The exhibits (each of which is identified by its chemical formula) are arranged in twenty four glass cabinets and, together with sketches and photographs, give information on the sites where they can be found; geological maps and enlarged photographs of the most important mining areas on the island are displayed on the walls.

Small

Summer, from 1st April to 30th September: weekdays 9 a.m.-noon / 3 p.m.-6 p.m.; Sundays and public holidays 9 a.m.-noon

Closed during the winter

Entrance fee

No access

By arrangement

Museo Civico Archeologico

57016 Rosignano Marittimo (LI)
Via del Castello
Tel. 0586/799232

Founded during the 1950's and recently rebuilt, the museum is presently housed in the Palazzo of the archiepiscopal farm in the 16th C. Castello di Rosignano Marittimo. It contains material from excavations, surface sites and underwater explorations undertaken in the municipal territory and surrounding areas, arranged chronologically and topographically. Plans are underway to transfer the museum to Palazzo Bombardieri.

Medium

Winter, from 16th September to 14th June: weekdays 9 a.m.-1 p.m.; Sundays and public holidays 3.30 p.m.-6.30 p.m.

Summer, from 15th June to 15th September: all week 5 p.m.-midnight

Closed on Mondays

Entrance fee

No access

By arrangement

By prior arrangement guided tours of the museum and the excavations at Vada. Refresher courses for teachers

Prehistoric stone tools; Bronze Age impasto cup. Tomb material from the late Republican period (of particular note a *Volterran Urn* in alabaster from Castiglioncello illustrating the *Rape of Helen*, 2nd C. B.C.). Black-painted and achromatic pottery, amphoras, 2nd-1st C. B.C. bronze plate, grindstones found on the sea bed near Vada and Castiglioncello. Stone altar with relief decorations. Material from Roman sites in the Lower Val di Cecina (head from the Trajan period, statue of Nike in marble, pieces of architectural decoration, ceramic, oil-lamps, metal utensils, glass, cut gems, coins). Reconstruction of tombs roofed with tiles - «alla cappuccina» - from Rosignano Solvay, 3rd-4th C. A.D. Medieval and Renaissance ceramics from the Castello and the Palazzo of the archiepiscopal farm at Rosignano.
Material from various sources and periods (fine groups from the area of Vulci and from Belora): Villanovian urn; Villanovian bronzes; examples of impasto, bucchero, Etrusco-Corinthian and Attic black-figured vases; Fragment of Archaic statue of a horse rider; Etruscan bronzes with human figures, from the 6th-5th C. B.C. and the Hellenistic period; bronze mirror and belt; anatomical ex votos.

Museo Storico Archeologico del Territorio

55022 Bagni di Lucca (LU)
Villa Webb
Tel. 0583/86200 (Comune)

The museum is in the process of being set up by the Council in collaboration with the Soprintendenza for archaeology. It will display material from the area of Val di Lima from the Middle Paleolithic period to the early Middle Ages: paleontological remains (including *ursus spelaeus*), stone and bone tools Upper Paleolitic and Roman relics found in the Grotta della Piella.

Casa Pascoli

55020 Castelvecchio Pascoli — Barga (LU)
Via Caprone, 4
Tel. 0583/766147

Small

Winter, from 1st October to 31st March: 9 a.m.-noon / 2 p.m.-5 p.m.

Summer, from 1st April to 30th October: 9 a.m.-noon / 2 p.m.-6.30 p.m.

Entrance fee

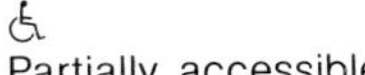
Partially accessible

By arrangement

Guided tours

Presented to the Council in 1935 on the death of the poet's sister Maria, Casa Pascoli, declared a national monument, was opened to the public in 1960. The rooms have survived intact with period furnishings and ornaments and various relics of the poet. The interesting material provides evidence of the period spent by Pascoli in the town. There is also the extensive library and archive with books, pamphlets, manuscripts and letters. Adjoining the house is the chapel containing the remains of the poet and his sister Maria in a marble tomb designed by Leonardo Bistolfi.

Quaderni Pascoliani, annual publication produced by the Council of Barga.

Exterior

Museo di Arte Sacra

55041 Camaiore (LU)
Via IV Novembre, 73
Tel. 0584/980268

Small

Winter, from 1st October to 31st May: Saturday 10 a.m.-noon

Summer, from 1st June to 30th September: Tuesday and Saturday 4 p.m.-6 p.m.

The museum is housed in rooms adjoining the Confraternità del SS. Sacramento di Camaiore (17th C.). It contains ecclesiastical vessels and vestments, goldsmiths' work and precious ornaments from churches in the area.

Ecclesiastical silver and ornaments from the 14th-18th C. (astylar *Cross* of the Florentine school; Late 15th C. *Chalice* in silver and enamel; fine 18th C. silverwork of the Luccan school including three statuettes dating from 1700: *Immaculate Conception* and *Holy Trinity* by G. Vambré, *Pietà* by G.F. Chelucci). 14th-18th C. sculptures in wood (*The Virgin Mary* by M. Civitali). Ecclesiastical hangings, cloths and embroidery (*Abbot's Mitre* embroidered in the 15th C.; Flemish tapestry with *The Last Supper* from 1516). Paintings from churches in the town and surrounding area.

Free

No access

By arrangement

U. Procacci, *Catalogo del Museo d'arte sacra di Camaiore*, Camaiore 1936

Civica Raccolta di Ceramiche Rinascimentali

58031 Camporgiano (LU)
Piazza San Giacomo
Tel. 0583/618888 (Comune)

Small

Winter: by prior arrangement

Summer, from 1st June to 30th September: all week 3 p.m.-6 p.m.; open by prior arrangement from Tuesday to Saturday 9 a.m.-1 p.m.

Free

No access

Yes

Educational service by prior arrangement for schools and tourist groups

Situated in the 15th C. Rocca belonging to the ducal family of Este the collection was opened in 1973. It contains ceramic remains mainly discovered in the Rocca.

Early Medieval terracottas and ceramics; 15th-16th C. slipped and inscribed ceramics; Archaic and Renaissance majolica; early 16th C. painted ceramics.

G.L. Reggi, *Ceramiche medioevali e rinascimentali a Camporgiano in Garfagnana*, in *Bollettino Musei Ferraresi*, 1974, pp. 147-170

Mostra Permanente Archeologica «Il Mesolitico della Garfagnana»

55032 Castelnuovo Garfagnana (LU)
Via Vallisneri, 5
Tel. 0583/65010 0583/62746 (Comune)

Small

Opened in 1986 the exhibition illustrates various aspects of the Mesolithic period which have come to light following research carried out in the Garfagnana area by the Institute of Human Anthropology and Paleontology at the University of Pisa and by local archaeological groups. It is arranged according to educational criteria in a room adjoining the local library.

Mesolithic relics from the Garfagnana valley, with information about the oldest archaeological traces to be found in the valley and the earliest settlements in the area.
Material on the origins and physical evolution of Man, as well as the techniques for chipping stone and the relationship between Prehistoric Man and his natural environment.

Tuesdays 8.30 a.m.-1 p.m. / 3 p.m.-6 p.m.; Friday 8.30 a.m.-1 p.m.

Free

No access

By arrangement

Guided tours by prior arrangement

O. Guidi, G. Rossi, M. Pioli, *Il Mesolitico della Garfagnana*, Castelnuovo Garfagnana 1985

Museo della Campagna e della Vita di Ieri

55030 San Pellegrino in Alpe — Castiglione Garfagnana (LU)
Via del Voltone, 14
Tel. 0583/665033

Medium

Winter, from 1st October to 31st May: 9 a.m.-noon / 2 p.m.-5 p.m.; closed on Mondays

Summer from 1st June to 30th September 9.30 a.m.-1 p.m. / 2.30 p.m.-7 p.m.

Entrance fee

No access

By arrangement

Guided tours by prior arrangement

Meetings and exhibitions

Founded in 1970 on the initiative of Don Luigi Pellegrini the museum contains a rich collection of over 3000 objects concerning agricultural, pastoral and artisan life in the area; the material comes mainly from the Garfagnana valley and from large areas of the Appennines near Modena and Reggio Emilia. It is housed in large and evocative rooms in the 12th C. Ospizio di San Pellegrino, an ancient refuge for travellers during the crossing of the Appennine pass. The museum was recently presented to the Provincial government which is planning its expansion and reorganization.

Pieces from the early 19th C. to the present day arranged in three main groups, the peasant's home, agricultural work and the work of the artisan: reconstructions of rooms (kitchen, bedroom and cellar) and material illustrating the main domestic activities (spinning, weaving, embroidery); large collection of agricultural implements covering the whole range of work in the fields throughout the year; tools and other material illustrating the various trades (blacksmith, knife-grinder, shoe-maker, carpenter, candle-maker).

Il Museo di S. Pellegrino in Alpe e l'affresco di Luciano Guarnieri, edited by P.L. Biagioni, Lucca 1987

Show-room

Museo della Figurina di Gesso e dell'Emigrazione

55025 Coreglia Antelminelli (LU)
Via del Mangano, 17
Tel. 0583/78082

Medium

Winter, from 1st October to 31st May: weekdays 10 a.m.-1 p.m.; closed on Saturdays and Sundays

Summer, from 1st June to 30th September: weekdays 10 a.m.-1 p.m.; Sundays and public holidays 10 a.m.-1 p.m. / 4 p.m.-7 p.m.; closed on Saturdays

Entrance fee

No access

By arrangement

Guided tours on request

Opened in 1982 this original civic museum is dedicated to the manufacture of plaster and the activities of the statuette sellers who have had a great influence on the economic and social fabric of the area, bringing about considerable emigration. The six hundred examples exhibited illustrate the progressive changes and improvement in the production: from the busts of poets and philosophers and the representation of Greek Gods and Goddesses to the depiction of figures from European and American artistic and political life, up until the first sacred subjects and the figures for cribs. They come largely from the Carlo Vanni School of Drawing and Modelling, from the Remo Molinari collection and from various donations by the residents of Coreglia.

Drawings and plaster models made by the students of the Scuola di Disegno e Plastica founded by the Barone C. Vanni in 1878. 18th-19th C. plaster models. Photographs and other material on the emigration of the model-maker. Permanent exhibition of cribs. Methods of plaster-working.

Show-room

Casa Natale Museo Puccini

55100 Lucca
Via di Poggio
Corte S. Lorenzo, 9
Tel. 0583/584028

Small

Winter, from 1st October to 31st March: all week 10 a.m.-4 p.m.

Summer, from 1st April to 30th September all week 10 a.m.-6 p.m.

Closed on Mondays

This is Puccini's birthplace, owned by the foundation of the same name. It displays documents and souvenirs of the composer, including the 'Turandot' piano, medals and letters. It is one stage in a larger Puccini itinerary taking in Torre del Lago, the composer's last home, and his family home at Celle (Pescaglia).

Free

No access

By arrangement

Esposizione Permanente Costumi XVIII-XIX-XX Secolo

55100 Lucca
Palazzo Controni Pfanner
Via degli Asili
Tel. 0583/44136

Medium

Winter, from 1st October to 31st March: all week 10 a.m.-1 p.m.

Summer, from 1st April to 30th eptember: all week 10 a.m.-5 p.m.

Closed on Mondays

Entrance fee

No access

By arrangement

Guided tours by prior arrangement with the Tourist Office of Lucca Council (0583/53888)

Opened in 1980 the exhibition set up by the local Council displays clothes and fabrics from the 18th-20th C. donated mainly by families in Lucca. It is housed on the piano nobile of Palazzo Controni-Pfanner, a splendid 17th C. private house.

Men and women's clothes and costumes, with accessories from the 18th-20th C. (fine 18th and 19th C. men's clothes belonging to members of the Garzoni family; also women's clothes in the Charleston and Art Déco styles and from the 40's and 70's). Fabrics, hangings and furnishings from the 18th and 19th C.

Costumi del XVIII e XIX Secolo, by various authors, Lucca 1980

Show-room

Museo Botanico «Cesare Bicchi»

55100 Lucca
Via San Micheletto, 5
Tel. 0583/41311-46665

The museum contains interesting herbaria (over twenty thousand specimens of local flora) started in 1830 by Benedetto Puccinelli and subsequently enlarged by Cesare Bicchi. It is housed in the Botanical Garden of Lucca. There is also an historical library which can be consulted by prior arrangement with the management.

Small

Winter, from 1st October to 31st March: weekdays 8.30 a.m.-12.30 p.m.

Summer, from 1st April to 30th September: all week 9 a.m.-noon / 4 p.m.-7 p.m.

Closed on Mondays

Entrance fee

Accessible

By arrangement

Collection of fruits in painted plaster. Models of 19th C. agricultural implements. Fossilized plants from Monte Pisano.
Herbarium Lucensis. Herbarium Bicchianum.
Oil paintings of Lucca grapes. Watercolours of Lucca mushrooms. Wood collection.

P.E. Tomei, *L'Orto botanico di Lucca*, in *Informatore Botanico Italiano*, VI, 1974, pp. 134-136

Museo Civico di Storia Naturale del Liceo Classico Machiavelli

55100 Lucca
Palazzo Lucchesini
Via degli Asili, 35
Tel. 0583/42761

Medium

To be arranged

Entrance fee

No access

By arrangement

Guided tours, lectures and educational activities for schools by prior arrangement

Book and photograph library open to consultation by scholars by prior arrangement

Thematic exhibitions on aspects of the natural history of the territory of Lucca

The museum is housed in the Liceo Classico Machiavelli, in the historic 17th C. Palazzo Lucchesini. Its origins date back to the rich scientific and natural history collections of the old Univeristy of Lucca (1785) transferred to the school by the Grand Duke Leopoldo II in 1860. It was opened recently (1987) by the local Council after a long process of research, cataloguing and restoration. It undertakes extensive educational and research programmes mainly directed toward the natural sciences. The museum is temporarily closed to the public.

Rich collection of samples of various classes of minerals. Important collection of fossilized fishes from Bolca; numerous specimens of Pliocenic fossils; vertebrates of the Quaternary period of local origin.
Over 30 000 examples of shells and 1 000 species of marine mollusc; collection of land gasteropoda belonging to the Conte Ernesto Turati.
Collection of beetles and butterflies from the Province of Lucca. Italian, European and exotic bird species.
Various material regarding the history of the museum.

Museo Nazionale e Pinacoteca di Palazzo Mansi
55100 Lucca
Via Galli Tassi, 43
Tel. 0583/55570

Large

All week 9 a.m.-7 p.m., Mondays 2 p.m.-7 p.m.

Entrance fee

No access

By arrangement

The museum's internal education department provides a service for schools on annual work programmes concerning the museum, the town and the surrounding area

Educational weaving workshop as part of the exhibition, apply to the museum's education centre

Exhibitions and series of conferences organized annually

The museum is housed in Palazzo Mansi, an 18th C. patrician residence acquired by the State in 1965. Opened in 1977 it consists of the Palazzo's monumental rooms with 17th-18th C. furnishings, unique in Tuscany for their quality and completeness. In the rooms which once held the now broken up Mansi art collection is housed the Picture-gallery comprising paintings presented to the city of Lucca by the Grand Duke Leopoldo II: about eighty works from the 16th-18th C. including paintings by Tintoretto, Veronese, Pontormo and Beccafumi as well as a selection of Flemish works. On the ground floor, an integral part of the museum's display, is the Niemack artisan weaving workshop, still functioning and closely linked to the activities of museum's internal educational centre. In the other rooms on the piano nobile (presently being prepared) 17th-18th C. paintings from private collections and Luccan period furnishings recently acquired by the nation will be displayed. Two new sections dedicated to 19th C. Luccan painting and to 16th-19th C. textile production are currently being set up to the top floor of the building.

Pontormo : Portrait of Alessandro dei Medici

'Appartamenti monumentali' with period furnishings and furniture (17th-18tth C.), Flemish tapestries and wall-hangings (*Wedding chamber* with canopied bed and 18th C. wall-hanging in embroidered silk).
16th-18th C. paintings on wood and canvas of the Italian and Flemish schools: Florentine works by A. del Sarto, Pontormo (*Portrait of Alessandro de' Medici*), Bronzino (*Portrait of Ferdinando I* and of *Don Garzia de' Medici*), G.B. Naldini, Cigoli, J. Ligozzi, J. Sustermans, F. Furini, J. Vignali, C. Dolci; Venetian works by J. Bassano, A. Schiavone, P. Veronese (*Peter the Hermit*), J. Tintoretto (*St. Mark freeing a slave*), S. Ricci; Bolognese works by G. Reni and G. Lanfranco; Sienese works by D. Beccafumi (*Scipio's temperance*) and Sodoma; Neapolitan works by S. Rosa and L. Giordano; also works by Morazzone, F. Barocci and G. Assereto. Niemack weaving workshop (in silk and other materials) complete with original loom and other tools.

Museo e territorio, by various authors, Lucca 1977

Museo Nazionale di Villa Guinigi

55100 Lucca
Via della Quarquonia
Tel. 0583/46033

Large

Winter, from 1st October to 30th April: weekdays 9 a.m.-sunset, Mondays and Sundays 9 a.m.-2 p.m.

Summer from 1st May to 30th September: weekdays 9 a.m.-7 p.m., Mondays, Sundays and public holidays 9 a.m.-2 p.m.

Entrance fee

Partially accessible

By arrangement

The museum is housed in the 15th C. home of Paolo Guinigi, presented to the Council in 1924 and subsequently passed to the nation in 1948. After being completely restored it was reopened to the public in 1968. The origins of the collection date back to the second half of the 19th C. and the suppression of religious organizations. Over the following years donations, bequests and acquisitions have added to the collection which today constitutes a real and true anthology of Luccan art. It also contains a fine collection of Etruscan and Roman archaeological exhibits, valuable paintings from the 13th-17th C., an important group of sculptures, carvings in wood, silver and fabrics. A section dedicated to Luccan ceramic production is currently being prepared.

Neo-eneolithic pottery. Bucchero pottery from tombs from the late 7th-early 6th C. B.C. Small northern Etruscan bronzes (5th C. B.C.). Attic pottery, goldsmiths' work, bronzes from Etruscan tombs in the Bientina area. Hellenistic period Ligurian grave-goods. Club-shaped funerary symbols. Architectural fragments; sculptures (monument of the imperial Constans, fragment of stele with curial saddle and fasces - 1st C. A.D. -, fragment of sarchophagus); mosaic depicting Triton and Nereid (2nd C. A.D.); inscriptions; Roman glass. Medieval clay and glass objects.
13th and 14th C. painting and sculpture, with works by B. Berlinghieri (*Crucifix*), Ugolino Lorenzetti (*Madonna and Child*), T. Gaddi, F. Traini, N. Pisano and school, D. Orlandi, (*Crucifix*), A. Puccinelli (*Marriage of St. Catherine*), Maestro del Bambino Vispo. 15th and 16th C. Tuscan painting with works by the Maestro di Borsigliana, Maestro dell'Immacolata Concezione, Maestro del Tondo Lathorp, Amico Aspertini (*Madonna and Child with Saints*), Zacchia the Elder, Fra' Bartolomeo (*Madonna 'della Misericordia'*, *The Lord with St. Mary Magdalen and St. Catherine*), Fra' Paolino, A. Lomi, R. Manetti, P. Paolini, D. Lombardi, G. Scaglia, P. Batoni (*Ecstasy of St. Catherine*).

Museo Nazionale di Villa Guinigi, by various authors, Lucca 1968

☞
The education department of the Museo di Palazzo Mansi (Lucca, Via Galli Tassi, tel: 0583/55570) provides by arrangement an educational service for schools with annual work programmes concerning the museum, the town and the surrounding area

Restoration workshop, open by prior arrangement

Exhibitions and conferences

Fra' Bartolomeo: The Lord with Mary Magdalen and St. Catherine

---

Museo dell'Opera del Duomo
55100 Lucca
Via dell'Arcivescovado
Tel. 0583/43096 (Opera del Duomo)

This soon to be opened museum will display treasures from the Cathedral comprising precious ecclesiastical silver, 15th-18th C. ornaments and hangings, illuminated choirbooks and paintings by artists from Lucca from the second half of the 16th C. It will be housed next to S. Martino in rooms owned by the Opera which are currently being restored.

Orto Botanico Lucchese
55100 Lucca
Via S. Micheletto, 5
Tel. 0583/41311-46665

Founded on the initiative of Maria Luisa di Borbone in 1820 the botanical garden is managed today by the Council in collaboration with the University of Pisa. It contains approximately three thousand species of plants mainly from the Mediterranean region. Of great interest are the collection of medicinal plants (approx. five hundred

Large

Winter, from 1st October to 31st March: weekdays 8.30 a.m.-12.30 p.m.

Summer, from 1st April to 30th September: all week 9 a.m.-noon

Closed on Mondays

Entrance fee

Accessible

By arrangement

Historical library open to consultation by prior arrangement

Exhibitions on the local flora, meetings, professional training courses, conferences

specimens), the collection of rare species from the Province of Lucca and the marsh plants from the humid areas of northern Tuscany. There is an historical library which can be consulted by arrangement with the administration.

Collections of heathers, water-plants, edible wild plants, cacti, aromatic and medicinal species.

P.E. Tomei, *L'Orto Botanico di Lucca*, in *Informatore Botanico Italiano*, VI, 1974, pp. 134-136

P.E. Tomei, *Quest'orto s'ha da fare*, in *Gardenia*, 43, 1987, pp. 100-105

Botanical garden

Antiquarium Civico di Massaciuccoli

55050 Massaciuccoli — Quiesa Massarosa (LU)
Via Pietro a Padule
Tel. 0584/93291 (Comune)

Opened in 1978 the museum displays material from various historical periods from excavations carried out since the 1950's in the area of Massaciuccoli and other sites in the municipality of Massarosa. Housed in a building constructed over the ruins of a Roman villa from the 2nd C. A.D. the small museum forms part of an interesting archaeological route which also takes in the thermal baths.

Small

By arrangement with the Council

Free

No access

Yes

Stone objects from the Middle and Upper Paleolithic periods from the Massaciuccoli lake. Fragments of Etruscan painted pottery. Fragments of architectural decoration, pottery, glass and coins from the Roman period recovered at the site of an historic complex linked to the name of the Venulei family. Collection of examples of Medieval and Renaissance ceramic.

Museo dei Puccini

55060 Celle dei Puccini —
Pescaglia (LU)
Via Meletori, 27
Tel. 0583/359154

Medium

By arrangement
Saturday and Sunday 3.30 p.m.-7 p.m.

Free

Partially accessible

By arrangement

This is the home of Giacomo Puccini's forefathers in the centre of the small hamlet. Opened in 1973 by the 'Lucchesi nel mondo' Society it contains furnishings, ornaments and various relics including photographs, letters and musical scores. It organizes annually concerts, exhibitions, conferences and music courses at various levels. The museum forms part of a wider Puccini itinerary taking in the Villa at Torre del Lago and his birthplace at Lucca, owned by the Puccini Foundation.

La Casa di Puccini a Celle, edited by I. Pini, R. Silva, Lucca 1973

Bedroom

Civico Museo Archeologico Versiliese

55045 Pietrasanta (LU)
Palazzo Moroni
Piazza Duomo
Tel. 0584/70541 (Comune)

Small

Tuesdays and Fridays 9 a.m.-12.30 p.m., Saturdays 3 p.m.-6 p.m.,
Sundays 9 a.m.-noon

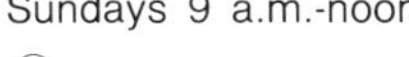

Free

Accessible

By arrangement

Exhibitions and conferences

Housed on the ground floor of the 16th C. Palazzo Moroni the museum contains archaeological material from Prehistory to the Roman period from chance discoveries and organized researches carried out in Versilia, in addition to a group of Medieval and Renaissance ceramics discovered at Pietrasanta. Opened by the Council in 1968 there is a programme of total redevelopment currently underway.

Prehistoric animal remains. Material from Bronze Age archaeological sites subsequently reoccupied during the Hellenistic period, as well as from Etruscan sites with ceramics and limestone funerary emblems in the form of clubs. Grave-goods from Ligurian box-tombs. Ceramics, metal objects and glass from Roman settlements and tombs and from early Medieval settlements. Selection of the Medieval and Renaissance ceramics found within the Sant'Agostino complex.

Museo dei Bozzetti

55045 Pietrasanta (LU)
Via Sant'Agostino, 1
Tel. 0584/791122 (Library)

Small

Winter, from 16th September to 14th June: Tuesday, Wednesday and Thursday 9 a.m.-noon / 2.30 p.m.-7 p.m.; Friday 2.30 p.m.-7 p.m. / 9 p.m.-11.30 p.m.; Saturday 2.30 p.m.-6 p.m.

Summer, from 15th June to 15th September: Tuesday, Wednesday and Thursday 9 a.m.-noon / 4 p.m.-8 p.m.; Friday 4 p.m.-8 p.m. / 9 p.m.-11.30 p.m.; Saturday 4 p.m.-8 p.m.

Free

Accessible

Yes

Annual exhibitions

Owned by the Council this museum opened in 1987 is situated in the historic complex of the former convent and church of Sant'Agostino also the seat of the Centro Culturale Luigi Russo. It displays around 200 sketches for sculptures produced in Versilia by Italian and foreign artists. The works are accompanied by explanatory panels. An archive of material on the works and artists is also available and can be consulted during opening hours.

Sketches by Italian artists (including P. Cascella, R. Gilardi, E. Gilioli, G. Guadagnucci, C. Nivola, G. Pomodoro, C.S. Signori) and foreign artists (including H.C. Adam, A. Bloc, F. Botero, Cesar, G. Fonseca, R. Ipousteguj, H. Jackson, J. Lipchitz, J. Miro, I. Noguchi, A. Penalba).

Il Passato e la Presenza, edited by J. Muhlendorph, Pietrasanta 1982

Il Museo dei Bozzetti, edited by J. Muhlendorph, Pietrasanta 1986

Casa Natale di Giosuè Carducci

55045 Valdicastello Carducci — Pietrasanta (LU)
Via Comunale
Tel. 0584/780541 (Comune)

Small

Winter, from 1st October to 31st May: all week 9.30 a.m.-12.30 p.m. / 3.30 p.m.-6.30 p.m.

Summer, from 1st June to 30th September: all week 9 a.m.-noon / 4 p.m.-7 p.m.

Closed on Mondays

This is the house where Giosuè Carducci was born in 1835. It contains documents, souvenirs and various relics. A permanent educational exhibition on the poet is currently under preparation.

Giosuè Carducci, bust

Free

No access

By arrangement

Mostra Didattica Archeologica

55016 Porcari (LU)
Via Roma, 28
Tel. 0583/298564 (Comune)

Small

On request to the library

Free

No access

Yes

Opened in 1981 the permanent exhibition consists in archaeological material from Prehistory to the Roman Age from surface sites in the Bientina area: stone implements from the Lower Paleolithic period to the Bronze Age; Villanovian pottery; Roman clay, metal and glass material.
It is housed in one room next to the local library. Educational activities are carried out for schools.

D. Cocchi Genick, P. Mencacci, M. Zecchini, *Storia di Porcari*, Porcari 1985

Centro Visitatori

Parco dell'Orecchiella
55048 San Romano in Garfagnana (LU)
Tel. 0583/619098

Small

Winter, by prior arrangement

Summer, from June to September: Saturday and Sunday 9 a.m.-1 p.m. / 3 p.m.-6 p.m.

Free

Accessible

Yes

Opened recently by the Ministry of Agriculture and Forestry the Centre provides material on aspects of the Parco dell'Orecchiella and displays specimens of plants and animals from the Serchio Valley. It serves as an ecological research and study centre and has a library and laboratory which can be visited on request.

G. Mirola, U. Poggi, G. Calzolari, *Il Parco Naturale dell'Orecchiella in Garfagnana*, Trento 1985

Civico Museo Preistorico e Archeologico «Alberto Carlo Blanc»

55049 Viareggio (LU)
Via Machiavelli, 2
Tel. 0584/961076

Small

Winter, from 1st September to 30th June: weekdays 8 a.m.-2 p.m.

Summer, from 1st July to 31st August: all week 6 p.m.-11 p.m.; closed on Mondays

Free

Accessible

By arrangement

Guided tours for schools by prior arrangement

Occasional exhibitions and conferences

The museum was founded in 1974 by the local Council to display Prehistoric relics from excavation sites in north-west Tuscany. Set up with educational aims in mind it includes a room with material on the origins of Man up until the earliest historical period, a section on the Middle Paleolithic period and Neanderthal Man with objects found in the sand-caves and grottoes around Massarosa. It also displays material from the Metal Age from excavations carried out by the museum at Candalla in the Municipality of Camaiore and from small tomb-caves in the municipality of Massarosa.

D. Cocchi Genick, R. Grifoni Cremonesi, *L'età dei Metalli nella Toscana nord-occidentale*, exhibition catalogue, Pisa 1985

I Neandertaliani, exhibition catalogue, by various authors, Viareggio 1986

D. Cocchi Genick, *Il riparo dell'ambra. Una successione stratigrafica dal Neolitico tardo al Bronzo finale*, Massarosa 1986

D. Cocchi Genick, *Il riparo del lauro di Candalla nel quadro del Bronzo medio iniziale dell'Italia centro-occidentale*, Massarosa 1987

Museo Villa Puccini

55048 Torre del Lago Puccini — Viareggio (LU)
Viale Puccini 264
Tel. 0584/341445

Small

From 1st October to 31st March: all week 9 a.m.-noon / 2.30 p.m.-5 p.m.; closed on Mondays

From 1st April to 30th June: all week 9 a.m.-noon / 2.30 p.m.-6 p.m.; closed on Mondays

Of all the sites connected with the composer Puccini in the territory of Lucca the Torre del Lago museum is without doubt one of the most important: it was here that Giacomo Puccini spent the last

Villa Puccini

From 1st July to 30th September: all week 9 a.m.-noon / 3 p.m.-7 p.m.

Entrance fee

Accessible

By arrangement

Guided tour

years of his life (1891-1921) and composed many works. The house converted into a museum displays documents, musical scores, letters, photographs, shotguns and various other relics. The composer's remains, along with those of his wife Elvira and son Tonio are preserved in the chapel.

Orto Botanico Pania di Corfino

55030 Villa Collemandina (LU)
Parco dell'Orecchiella
Tel. 0584/62994 (Comunità montana della Garfagnana)

Large

Permanently open

Free

No access

Yes

Guided tour on request

This botanical garden is situated at about 4500 ft. above sea level on a gentle slope on the western side of the group of mountains which carries the same name, below steep limestone cliffs. Founded in 1984 by the Comunità Montana della Garfagnana in collaboration with the University of Pisa the garden preserves and documents the flora of great naturalistic value on the Luccan Appennines, with particular attention to plant species in danger of extinction.

In the different sections can be found woodland plants, moorland plants, meadow plants, wasteland plants and mountain plants; there are internal routes with explanatory cards and panels on the plants which can be seen.

Museo di Storia Naturale della Lunigiana

54011 Aulla (MS)
Fortezza della Brunella
Tel. 0187/420374

Medium

On request

Founded by the Council the museum has been housed since 1984 at the Fortezza della Brunella. Still to be completed, it is intended to provide educational information on the most important natural environments of the Lunigiana area. At present three rooms are open to the public: the physical environment, the river and lake environment and the forest environment. A botanical garden has been laid out in the large park. The museum undertakes extensive research work and educational activities in the natural sciences: lessons on environmental awareness for schools and groups, specialized meetings for teachers, arrangement of nature trips in Lunigiana.

Free

No access

Yes

On request, guided tours of the museum and the Botanical Garden

Occasional conferences and exhibitions

Bollettino del Museo di storia naturale della Lunigiana, a periodical produced by the museum which comes out twice a year.

A. Farina, *Il Museo di storia naturale della Lunigiana*, Aulla 1981

Collezione di Sculture Romane

55033 Carrara (MS)
Accademia di Belle Arti
Via Roma, 1
Tel. 0585/71658 (Accademia)

At the Accademia di Belle Arti is housed a collection of Roman marble comprising statues, reliefs and inscriptions. The material which comes from the area of the Carrara quarries and from Luni is situated in one of the school's inner courtyards. It can be visited by prior arrangement.

Mostra marmo lunense, exhibition catalogue, by various authors, Carrara 1982

Museo Civico del Marmo

54033 Carrara (MS)
Viale XX Settembre
Località Stadio
Tel. 0585/71889-72269
(Comune)

The museum which was founded in 1982 has grown and envolved side by side with the research activities and the collection of material on the «marble culture» in the area of the Apuanian mountains and Versilia. An interdisciplinary institution it contains a range of diverse material. Of particular importance is the section dedicated to the archaeology of marble, the only museum in Italy to document quarry sites, working techniques and marbles from the Roman period. There is also an interesting 'marmoteca' displaying over 300 large scale samples of marble from Italy and abroad.

Large

Winter: on request

Summer, from 20th April to 31st October: weekdays 10 a.m.-1 p.m. / 3 p.m.-7 p.m.; closed on Sundays

Free

No access

By arrangement

Temporary exhibitions

Archaeology and history of the area: Roman sculptures, selection of marbles, quarrying tools, reliefs and photographs of the ancient Luni quarries.
Marmoteca: over 300 Italian and foreign marble samples.
Industrial archaeology: tools, machines, period photographs, original drawing, models.
Technical applications of marble.
Modern sculptures.

Mostra marmo lunense, by various authors, Carrara 1982

Museo del Territorio Alta Valle dell'Aulella

54014 Casola Lunigiana (MS)
Strada nazionale
Tel. 0585/90361

This essentially educational museum documents by means of a variety of material (artistic historical, archaeological, ethnographical and documentary) the history and culture of the Alta Valle dell'Aulella. Opened in 1981 at its present home, it is run by the Council and the Istituto Lunigianese dei Castelli.

Medium

Winter: weekdays 9 a.m.-1 p.m., Saturdays and Sundays 9 a.m.-1 p.m. / 2 p.m.-5 p.m.

Summer: weekdays 9 a.m.-1 p.m., Saturdays and Sundays 9 a.m.-1 p.m. / 4 p.m.-7 p.m.
Closed on Mondays

Free

No access

By arrangement

Guided tour of the museum, the town and the parish churches by prior arrangement

Animals remains, tools in stone and bone dating from between the Middle Paleolithic and the Eneolithic periods discovered in the 'Tana della Volpe' and the 'Tecchia di Equi Terme' from where comes also Medieval material. Fragments of Protohistorical pottery from Pieve San Lorenzo. Statue-stelae in stone from Reusa (5th-4th C. B.C.). Reconstruction of a Ligurian box-tomb.

Architectural fragments (capitals, fragments, baptismal fonts) from churches in the territory.

Plans of the area showing the main historical and architectural features (churches, castles, towns, plants and agricultural cultivations, roads).

Material on the tradition of the «maggio» singing (documents, photographs, lyric sheets).

Collection of religious art (silver, ecclesiastical ornaments, hangings and cloths, holy images from the 17th-19th C.).

Museo del Castello Malaspina

54100 Massa
Via del Forte, 15
Tel. 0585/44774

Small

Winter, from 1st October to 30th April: all week 9 a.m.-noon / 2 p.m.-5 p.m.
Summer, from 1st May to 30th September: all week 9 a.m.-noon / 4 p.m.-7 p.m.
Closed on Mondays

Opened in 1975 in a room of the castle by the Council and the Istituto Lunigiana dei Castelli the museum displays a small collection of archaeological material found in the area: Paleolithic and Neolithic objects; relics from the Bronze and Iron Ages and from the

Painted room

Entrance fee

No access

By arrangement

Guided tours by prior arrangement with the education and cultural department of the Council. Educational material available

Conferences on the Castles of Lunigiana and the territory organized annually by the Istituto Lunigianese dei Castelli

Roman period, late Medieval ceramics and fragments of architectural sculpture. The small museum is included in a visit to the Castle, an important construction rebuilt by the Malaspina family between the 15th and 16th C.

M.G. Armanini, G. Ricci, *Il Castello Malaspina di Massa. Guida storico-turistica*, Genoa 1983

Museo Etnologico delle Apuane

54100 Massa
Via Uliveti, 85
Tel. 0585/251330

Small

Winter, from 1st October to 31st March: all week 9 a.m.-noon / 4 p.m.-6 p.m.

Summer, from 1st April to 30th September: all week 9 a.m.-noon / 4 p.m.-7 p.m.

Closed on Mondays

Free

Accessible

By arrangement

Guided tours by appointment

Library and archive at the Centro Culturale Apuano (83 Via Uliveti, Massa)

Originally consisting of the Masnata collection of material on the pastoral agricultural culture of Lunigiana, the museum has grown considerably over the years. It today contains more than ten thousand items on local life and traditions not just from the territory of Massa Carrara but also from Versilia and the Garfagnana Valley. It is housed in three large sheds and is arranged thematically. It is run by a private association, the Movimento di Umanesimo Sociale, directed by Don Luigi Bonacoscia.

Various objects and material on country life and traditional trades arranged in the following sections: usages and customes; domestic arts and occupations; artisan arts and crafts; agriculture; rearing of animals; the home; lighting; heating; the shop (foodstuffs, meat, general goods); the travelling salesman; weights and measures; dress-making and wig making; printing; coffee making; clerks; iron products; marble and stone products; plaster products; means of transport; pedlars; industrial archaeology; miscellaneous; pottery; geology; collection; pictures and photographs; books and prints.

'Madonnaro' case

Museo Storico di Arte Sacra del Duomo

54100 Massa
Piazza Duomo, 1
Tel. 0585/42643

Opened in 1972 the museum is housed in rooms adjacent to the Cathedral.
It contains a fine collection of material from the Duomo comprising paintings, fittings and ecclesiastical ornaments. It also houses a library on local history, a parish archive and a photograph library which can be visited by prior appointment.

Medium

Paintings, sculptures (bronze *Crucifix* by F. Tacca; wooden *Crucifix* by F. Palma), church fittings and ornaments, goldsmiths' work (*Reliquary* in the form of statue with *Madonna and Child* by G. Vambré from 1685) and hangings (outstanding 17th C. *Planets*) from the 17th-20th C.

Winter: by arrangement

Summer, from 21st June to 21st September: all week 9 a.m.-noon / 4 p.m.-7 p.m.; closed on Mondays

Free

♿
No access

📷
By arrangement

Orto Botanico «Pietro Pellegrini»

Pian della Fioba — Massa
Tel. 0585/47801 (Comune)

In memory of Pietro Pellegrini, the author of interesting studies on plants in the Apuan area, the alpine garden (approx. 2820 ft. above sea level) stretches over an area of over 24 acres in a splendid panoramic position.
It contains almost all the indigenous plant species of the Apuan Mountains and there is a shelter-laboratory for educational projects; there are daily guided visits during the flowering season in Spring and Summer.
It is managed by the three Tuscan universities of Florence, Pisa and Siena in collaboration with the local council of Massa.

Large

D. Marchetti, G. Monti, E. Uzzo, *Guida all'Orto Botanico delle Alpi Apuane «Pietro Pellegrini»*, Pisa 1979

Winter: by arrangement

Summer, from 15th June to 15th September: 9 a.m.-noon / 3 p.m.-7 p.m.

Free

♿
No access

📷
Yes

Museo delle Statue-Stele Lunigianesi

54027 Pontremoli (MS)
Castello del Piagnaro
Tel. 0187/831439

Opened in 1975 by the local council and the Istituto Lunigianese dei Castelli the museum contains a substantial collection of stelae-statues from the Lunigiana area. Housed in the 15th C. Castello del Piagnaro it is arranged along educational lines. The museum also displays the Mario Fabbri archaeological collection comprising

Small

Winter, from 1st October to 31st May: all week 9 a.m.-noon / 2 p.m.-5 p.m.

Summer, from 1st June to 30th September: all week 9 a.m.-noon / 4 p.m.-7 p.m.

Closed on Mondays

Entrance fee

No access

By arrangement

Guided tours of the museum by arrangement with the management. Each room contains information on the material displayed

Small library and workshop for the restoration of stone and ceramics can be visited by arrangement

Conferences, lectures, meetings and temporary exhibitions

about a thousand stone objects from the Sahara dating from the Lower Paleolithic to the Eneolithic periods.

Systematic exhibition on the stelae-statues of Lunigiana dating from the Late Eneolithic period to the 2nd C. B.C. displaying originals and plaster casts and accompanied by information on the different types of monuments and where they are found. Reconstruction of an excavation site.

A.C. Ambrosi, *Il Museo delle statue-stele lunigianesi*, La Spezia 1975

Statue Stele «Minucciano III»

Museo Etnografico della Lunigiana

54028 Villafranca in Lunigiana (MS)
Via dei Mulini, 1
Tel. 0187/493417

The council-owned museum was founded in 1977 on the initiative of the Associazione Manfredo Giuliani which supports historical and ethnographical studies on Lunigiana. It displays pastoral and agricultural implements, craftsmen's tools, domestic objects, protective charms and religious objects from the area arranged thematically and chronologically. Of particular interest are the museum buildings which include the old water-mill building of the Villafranca community.

Winter: all week 9 a.m.-1 p.m. / 3 p.m.-6 p.m.

Summer: all week 9 a.m.-1 p.m. / 4 p.m.-7 p.m.

Closed on Mondays

Entrance fee

No access

By arrangement

Guided tours of the museum and lectures on anthropological themes on request. Research and study tours of the area

Book, photograph and tape library on oral traditions open to consultation during museum opening hours

Exhibitions, study meetings

The material which dates from the 18th C. to the post-war period is divided into the following sections:
hemp processing, weaving, woodworking, popular medicine, implements and vessels for food preparation, mill and milling techniques, chestnut and grain processing, processing of weaving material, weights and measures, milk processing.

Studi Lunigianesi, annual publication by the Associazione «Manfredo Giuliani»

Cultura popolare in Lunigiana. Vision de la Toscane, exhibition catalogue, by various authors, Florence 1983

Show-room

Museo di Storia Naturale e del Territorio

Centro interdipartimentale dell'Università di Pisa
56011 Calci (PI)
Certosa di Calci
Via Roma, 103
Tel. 050/937092

The museum's original collection was formed by Ferdinando I de' Medici in 1591. Expanded considerably over the years it was divided during the 19th C. into three distinct museums (zoology and comparative anatomy, geology and paleontology, mineralogy and petrography). In 1979 the collections were transferred and reunited at the Certosa di Calci in rooms presented to the University by the State. Currently under completion the 'new' natural history museum run by the University displays a rich collection of great historical and scientific value and undertakes extensive research and educational activities for schools at every level.

Large

Open only to schools and scholars by prior arrangement

Free

Accessible

History Gallery: several hundred items of great historical interest including the Gualtieri mollusc collection, four large dioramas by P. Savi and anatomical preparations by Richiardi.
Reptile Gallery: about one hundred specimens representing over half of the families in this class. Of great interest is the material on reptiles' respiratory apparatus.
Mammal Gallery: about 700 specimens covering all classes of mammal. Contemporary specimens are presented alongside fossilized remains and anatomical preparations. The Primate collection is of considerable interest.
Bird Gallery: about 800 specimens (still under preparation).

La Certosa di Pisa, by various authors, Pisa 1987

Educational activities for schools at every level

Museum library open on weekdays from 8 a.m.-1 p.m. Library of the Tuscan Natural Sciences Society open by prior arrangement (050/ 501457)

Thematic exhibitions and conferences on the natural sciences

Show-room

Museo Storico Artistico della Certosa di Calci

Certosa di Calci
56011 Calci (PI)
Tel. 050/938430

The state-owned 14th C. Certosa comprises a vast complex of buildings including a church, guest wing, cells and cloisters, largely rebuilt during the 17th C. In 1973 the Pisa Soprintendenza opened the buildings to the public: it subsequently (1986) fitted out five rooms with historical and artistic material from the priors' cells and other cells in the large cloister (paintings on wood, canvas and paper from the 16th-19th C. attributed to F. Traini, B. Poccetti, G. Vasari); the display of ecclesiastical vessels and fittings connected to the life of the charterhouse is also planned.

Medium

Winter, from 1st October to 30th April: weekdays 9 a.m.-4 p.m., Sundays and public holidays 9 a.m.-noon

Summer, from 1st May to 30th September: weekdays 9 a.m.-6 p.m., Sundays and public holidays 9 a.m.-1 p.m.

A. Manghi, *La Certosa di Pisa*, Pisa 1911

Entrance fee

No access

By arrangement

Archive and library open to consultation by prior arrangement with the Soprintendenza per i beni storico artistici di Pisa

Various cultural events: exhibitions, conferences and concerts

Certosa di Calci

Camposanto Monumentale

56100 Pisa
Piazza Duomo
Tel. 050/560547-561820 (Opera della Primaziale Pisana)

Large

Winter: all week 9 a.m.-4.30 p.m.

Summer: all week 8 a.m.-8 p.m.

Entrance fee

Accessible

By arrangement

Begun in 1278 to a design by Giovanni di Simone and intended to house the remains of prominent citizens it today represents one of the most important of Pisa's museum complexes. It contains a vast collection which has grown over the years and in particular since the early 19th C. when Carlo Lasinio turned the cemetery into a museum. It contains a fine collection of antiquities including Roman statues and architectural fragments, Medieval and Renaissance statues, stelae, gravestones and tombs; there is a very fine fresco cycle of the 14th and 15th C. restored following serious damage caused by the heavy bombing in 1944.

Attic stelae from the 4th C. A.D. Statues of figures in togas from the early Imperial period. Neo-Attik krater illustrate with Dionysian retinue. Roman urn and sarcophagi including one of the oldest examples of this type of monument, belonging to C. Bellicus Natalis Tebanianus. Sections of mosaic. Stone inscriptions. 14th and 15th C. detached frescoes by T. Gaddi, S. Aretino, A. Veneziano, A. Bonaiuti, Buonamico di Buffalmacco (*Triumph of Death*), Piero di Puccio, B. Gozzoli (*Stories from the Old Testament*). Medieval sculptures and sculptures from the 16th C. (B. Ammannati) and the 19th C. (L. Bartolini, G. Duprè).

Buonamico di Buffalmacco: Universal Judgement, detail

M. Bucci, *Affreschi e sinopie del Camposanto monumentale di Pisa*, Milan 1960

P.E. Arias, E. Cristiani, E. Gabba, *Camposanto monumentale di Pisa. Le antichità*, Pisa 1977

S. Settis, *Camposanto monumentale di Pisa. Le antichità*, II, Modena 1984

Collezioni Egittologiche dell'Università di Pisa

56100 Pisa
Palazzo Ricci
Via S. Maria, 8
Tel. 050/46074 (Dipartimento di storia antica, Sezione egittologia)

Opened in 1964 the collection which belongs to the Egyptology section of the Department of Ancient History of the University is housed on the ground floor of Palazzo Ricci. It consists of the Laura Birga Picozzi collection - about one hundred archaeological relics and ethnographical curiosities brought back by Ippolito Rosellini from Egypt and Nubia (1828-1829) - the Michela Schiff Giorgini collection comprising about five hundred items from excavations at Saleb and Sedeinga in the Sudan and a group of ostraka from Ossirinco. The collection is further enriched with valuable archives on excavations carried out in Egypt by the University of Pisa.

Small

By prior arrangement

Free

Accessible

No

Guided tours by prior arrangement

Archives, egyptology workshop and information workshop open to scholars by prior arrangement with the Department of Ancient History, Egyptology Section, 1 Via Galvani, Pisa

Picozzi Collection. Material mainly from the early period: amulets and scarabs in china, scarabs in green stone, ring stones, plates. Oil-lamps from the Roman period.
Schiff Giorgini Collection. Material from excavations carried out in the temple of Amenhofti III and in the Saleb necropoli and those at Sedeinga.
Prehistoric objects. Relics dating from the New Kingdom: Fragment of a statue and scarab commemorating Amenhofti; gilded bronze mirror; bowl in shaped soapstone. Material from the Low Age: door-jamb with relief decoration; table for offerings; pendants in semi-precious stones and gold; bronze statuette of Osiris; china amulets; rock-crystal baboon; bronze and silver rings. Glass goblet with polychrome decoration and Greek inscription (3rd C. A.D.).

M. Schiff Giorgini, *Saleb I*, Florence 1965

M. Schiff Giorgini, *Saleb II*, Florence 1971

Il Nilo sui lungarni, exhibition catalogue, by various authors, Pisa 1982

Atti del convegno Ippolito Rosellini. Passato e presente di una disciplina, by various authors, Pisa 1982

Collezioni Paletnologica e Paleontologica

56100 Pisa
Dipartimento di scienze archeologiche
Via Santa Maria, 53
Tel. 050/41347-41483

Housed at the Department of Archaeological Science the collection contains interesting palethnological and paleontological items.
The palethnological collection was formed during the last thirty years of the last century with material from excavations in the caves of the Apuan Alps and the Monte Pisano; it has grown over the years by exchanges and donations from other organizations.
The paleontological collection which was also founded at the end of the last century has grown considerably over the last twenty years and contains fossilized and contemporary animals from throughout

Italy. The collections can be visited by prior arrangement.

Stone objects from the Lower Paleolithic period to the Bronze and Iron Age. Neolithic, Eneolithic, Bronze and Iron Age pottery. Eneolithic metal objects. Objects in bone, dressed stone and wood. Ornaments in stone and shell.

Domus Galileana
56100 Pisa
Via S. Maria, 26
Tel. 050/23726

Small

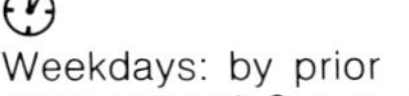
Weekdays: by prior arrangement 9 a.m.-noon

Free

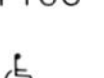
No access

By arrangement

This charitable organization was founded in 1941 as a study centre in Galilean science and the history of science; there is an extensive library, a collection of scientific instruments and the Pacinotti Fund containing electrology machines and prototypes of the dynamo. There is a very interesting «CEP» electronic calculator, a forerunner of the modern computer, produced in the Electronic Calculator Study Centre at the University of Pisa.

Physis, quarterly history of science magazine edited by the Domus Galileana

---

Domus Mazziniana
56100 Pisa
Via Mazzini, 71
Tel. 050/24174

Small

Weekdays 8.30 a.m.-12.30 p.m.

Free

No access

By arrangement

Guided tours by prior arrangement

Founded in 1952 the museum has its seat at the Rosselli Nathan house (built on the ruins of the original which was destroyed in 1943) where Mazzini spent the last years of his life.
There is a library specializing in the history of the Risorgimento, a very extensive archive and an exhibition of photographs, costumes, manuscripts and Mazzini relics.

Bollettino semestrale, a twice-yearly publication edited by the Domus Mazziniana

Catalogo degli autografi, documenti e cimeli, edited by A. Mancini, E. Michel, E. Tongiorgi, Pisa 1952

La Domus Mazziniana, edited by G. Adami, Pisa 1986

Gabinetto Disegni e Stampe

56100 Pisa
Dipartimento di storia delle arti dell'Università di Pisa
Via S. Cecilia, 24
Tel. 050/23793

Medium

By arrangement at the following times: 9 a.m.-1 p.m. / 3 p.m.-6 p.m.; closed on Saturday, Sunday and Monday

Free

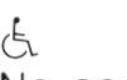
No access

By arrangement

The department's book and photograph library open by prior arrangement

Organization of temporary exhibitions

Founded in 1958 the museum has been housed since 1975 in Palazzo Agostini della Seta. It contains a large and valuable collection including the Timpanaro Donation, the museum's first collection, and extensive material on contemporary Italian graphic arts gathered mainly through donations. The museum has no permanent display but periodically organizes temporary exhibitions.

About 6500 drawings, prints and graphic works from the 16th-20th C.: the Timpanaro Collection comprising drawings and prints by Italian artists from 1920 to 1950 and 19th C. graphic works including an outstanding collection of engravings by Fattori.

Collection of contemporary graphic art with works from the 1950's on.

Test prints from plates preserved at the National Chalcography Centre in Rome.

M. Severini, *La Collezione Timpanaro*, Venice 1959

M. Severini, *Grafica italiana contemporanea*, 1 (A-B), Venice 1961

A.R. Masetti, *Grafica italiana contemporanea*, 2 (C-E), Milan 1965

Collezione Timpanaro. Grafica italiana del Novecento, exhibition catalogue, edited by D. Levi, Florence 1986

G. Fattori. *Incisioni nella Collezione Timpanaro*, catalogo della mostra, a cura di M.C. Bonagura, F. Fergonzi, D. Levi, R. Monti, Florence 1987

Gipsoteca

56100 Pisa
Palazzo Ricci
Via Santa Maria, 8
Tel. 050/23078 (Dipartimento di scienze archeologiche)

Small

Wednesdays 8.30 a.m.-12.30 p.m.

Free

Accessible

By arrangement

The Collection was founded at the end of the 19th C. on the initiative of the first professors of archaeology at Pisa University. It grew considerably over subsequent years until reaching its present size during the 1950's. It contains over a hundred pieces only some of which are on show which cover Greek, Etruscan and Roman production. With the transfer to the Palazzo Ricci in 1985 the University began a gradual programme of repair and restoration of the whole collection. As well as the Cast museum, the Archaeology Department also possesses an Antiquarium comprising more than 1500 original items of various types (Greek and Roman fragments of marble, terracottas and ceramics) and the «Pisa in Ancient Times» Documentation Centre containing items from discoveries and excavations in the territory of Pisa. The material from the two collections is currently undergoing research and reorganization.

Reproductions of small examples of Minoan plastic arts.
Great masterpieces of the art of statues, reproductions of Classical or Hellenistic Greek originals or Roman copies of these. Relief tiles reproducing part of the frieze of the Parthenon or of the breastwork of the temple to Athena Nike. Attic and Etruscan stelae. Reliefs and fragments. Bust-portrait section with Greek and Imperial Roman works.

The department's library and archive open to scholars by prior arrangement

Herbarium Horti Pisani

56100 Pisa
Via Luca Ghini, 5
Tel. 050/561795-560405

Housed at the Department of Botanical Sciences the Herbarium contains various collections of dried plants of great historical and scientific value, the oldest dating from the 18th C. A fungus collection, comprising one hundred and eleven wax models made by the Florentine wax-modeller and naturalist Luigi Calamai, is also open.

Weekdays: 8.30 a.m.-12.30 p.m. / 2.30 p.m.-5.30 p.m.; closed on Saturdays, Sundays and public holidays

Free

♿
Accessible

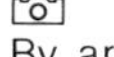
By arrangement

Guided tours by prior arrangement

The department's library and laboratory open by prior arrangement

General herbarium of cryptogams and phanerogams containing around 300,000 specimens including the collections by G. and P. Savi (area of Pisa and Florence). T. Caruel Herbarium (Italian flora). G. Arcangeli Herbarium (Tuscan flora). M. Guadagno Herbarium (Mediterranean flora). P. Pellegrini Herbarium (Flora of the Apuan and Friuli region). Also the C. Costa Reghini, F.A. Artaria,, E. Cittadella and N. Passerini herbariums with mainly Tuscan specimens. Moss collections by F.A. Artaria and A. Bottini.

G. Monti, C. Del Prete, *I Modelli ceroplastici dell'Istituto ed Orto botanico pisano: i funghi di Luigi Calamai*, in *Atti Società Toscana Scienze Naturali*, Series B, 85, 1978, pp. 217-232

C. Del Prete, G. Monti, *Collezioni dell'Herbarium Horti Pisani: le raccolte micologiche*, in *Rivista Micologia Italiana*, XIII, 1, 1984, pp. 83-87

L. Amadei, *Note sull'Herbarium Horti Pisani: l'origine delle collezioni*, in *Museologia scientifica*, IV, 1-2, 1987, pp. 119-129

Istituto e Museo di Anatomia e Istologia Patologica

56100 Pisa
Via Roma, 57
Tel. 050/561840-560368

This is an interesting collection of anatomical preparations coming from autopsies and operations which were brought together for educational purposes in the second half of the last century by the University of Pisa. Newly reorganized in 1970 it is housed in the Institute of Anatomy and Pathological Histology and can be visited by prior arrangement.

Show-room

Museo Anatomico Facoltà di Veterinaria

56100 Pisa
Viale delle Piagge, 2
Tel. 050/570715

The collection was started in 1800 by the first professor of Animal Anatomy at the University of Pisa for use by the students of the Faculty. Displayed in large rooms within the Department of Animal Anatomy and Physiology it contains anatomical animal parts of veterinarian interest preserved in various ways with explanations of biological details; of particular interest is the extensive material on the anatomy of the horse, on the reproductive apparatus of domestic animals and on the cardiovascular apparatus. It is open to scholars by prior arrangement.

Museo dell'Istituto di Anatomia Umana Normale

56100 Pisa
Via Roma, 55
Tel. 050/560071-560475

Founded for educational purposes during the second half of the 19th C. by the professors of the Faculty the museum is housed in the Institute of Human Anatomy. It contains anatomical preparations of various parts of the human body, a collection of Pre-Columbian Peruvian pots and anatomical diagrams by P. Mascagni. It is open to scholars by prior arrangement.

Museo Nazionale di San Matteo

56100 Pisa
Piazza San Matteo in Soarta, Lungarno Mediceo
Tel. 050/23750

Large

Weekdays 8.30 a.m.-7.30 p.m., Sundays and public holidays 8.30 a.m.-1.30 p.m.; closed on Mondays

Entrance fee

No access

By arrangement

☞
The education section at the Soprintendenza per i beni storico artistici di Pisa organizes annually for schools at every level research projects on groups of works from the museum, monuments in the town and areas of the town. Information sheets are available

Occasional exhibitions

Previously a municipal museum (1893) which then passed to the State, it was opened in 1949 at its present home in the 13th C. Benedictine monastery of San Matteo. Its origins go back to a group of paintings left to the Opera della Primaziale by the Canon Sebastiano Zucchetti in 1776. This first collection was expanded considerably by acquisitions and bequests in subsequent years. It contains a rich and varied collection with important groups of sculpture (particularly of the Pisan school from the Maestro Guglielmo to Biduino, Bonanno, Nicola and Giovanni Pisano and Andrea and Nino Pisano) and 12th-16th C. paintings of the Tuscan school including many precious paintings on wood on a gold ground. The museum undertakes extensive educational activities. Important restoration work on the building, redecoration of the rooms and rearrangement of the collections is currently in progress.

Archaeological material from excavations and donations: Etruscan marble cippus; male portrait bust from the Early Imperial period; sarcophagus 'del buon pastore', fragments of sarcophagus with Muses (3rd C. A.D.). Roman Corinthian and composite capitals.

Sculptures from the Middle Ages to the 19th C. of ecclesiastical and lay origin displayed in the separate section of the Royal Palace.

Collection of Medieval ceramics (decorative basins from church exteriors).

12th-16th C. detached frescoes and paintings on wood by Berlinghiero (*Cross*), Giunta Pisano (*Cross*), Maestro di San Martino, D. Orlandi, S. Martini (*Madonna and Child with Saints*), L. Memmo, F. Traini, Barnaba da Modena, A. Gaddi, A. Bonaiuti, S. Aretino, Antonio Veneziano, Masaccio (*St. Paul*), Gentile da Fabriano (*Madonna 'dell'Umiltà'*), Fra' Angelico, B. Gozzoli, D. del Ghirlandaio.

14th C. Pisan sculpture: works by N. and G. Pisano and by Tino da Camaino, and A. and N. Pisano (*Madonna 'del latte'*, *Pietà*). 15th C. sculpture in terracotta and bronze (Donatello, *Reliquary bust of St. Lussorius*).

Giunta Pisano: Cross

Sculptures in wood in the Pisan and Sienese styles from the 14th and 15th C. (A. Pisano, Agostino di Giovanni, Francesco di Valdambrino). Group of antique armour (late 15th to 17th C.) for use in the 'Gioco del Ponte'.

G. Berti, L. Tongiorgi, *I Bacini ceramici delle chiese pisane*, 1981

M. Burresi, *Restauri di sculture lignee nel Museo di S. Matteo*, Pisa 1984

R.P. Ciardi, A. Caleca, M. Burresi, *Il Polittico di Agnano e l'attività di Cecco di Pietro*, Pisa 1986

Museo dell'Opera Primaziale Pisana

56100 Pisa
Piazza Duomo, 17
Tel. 050/560547-561820

Opened in 1986 the museum is housed in a building which has seen various functional and structural alterations over the years; it was originally the seat of the Chapter before becoming a seminary, then a private residence, then the Pisa Academy of Fine Arts and finally a convent. It was acquired in 1979 by the Opera della Primaziale which undertook an extensive and comprehensive restoration programme to convert it to house the museum. The numerous works exhibited all come from the monumental buildings in the

Large

Winter: all week 9 a.m.-5 p.m.

Summer: all week 8 a.m.-7 p.m.

Entrance fee

Accessible

By arrangement

Book and photograph library and archive at the Opera Primaziale open from Monday to Saturday 9 a.m.-noon

Piazza dei Miracoli: in the ground floor rooms and under the arches of the cloister are the 12th-16th C. sculptures including masterpieces by Nicola and Giovanni Pisano, Tino di Camaino and Nino Pisano. One room is dedicated to the treasure of the Duomo; the 16th-19th C. church silver is preserved in the chapel. On the first floor are 16th-18th C. paintings and sculptures, Renaissance marquetry, Medieval illuminated choirbooks and scrolls, archiepiscopal vestments, an Egyptian, Etruscan and Roman archaeology collection formed in the early 19th C. by Carlo Lasinio and lastly the engravings by him and his son of the frescoes in the Cemetery. The great value of the work, the most modern display criteria and the care taken with the educational aspects make this one of the most important and impressive museums in the Region.

Fragments of Egyptian stelae.

Etruscan statue of a woman and cippi in marble. Volterran urns from the Morrona hypogeum. Portraits of *Caesar* and *Agrippa*; head of *Antinoo* reworked in the 15th C. Head of the *Borghese Ram*, of the *Diodalsas Aphrodite*, torso of the Sauroktonos Apollo. Roman urns. 12th-16th C. sculptures including *Griffin*, a rare Fatimidan work, *Christ lowered from the Cross* in polychrome wood by a Burgundian

Giovanni Pisano: Madonna and Child

artist, assembly of the works from the «tribute» by Rainaldo and Guglielmo from the facade of the Duomo; *busts* and *statues* from the exterior of the Baptistery by Nicola and Giovanni Pisano, the *Madonna 'del Colloquio'*, the *Madonna 'di Arrigo VII'*; *Altar-tomb of St. Ranieri*, *Arrigo VII group* and the *Councillors* by Tino di Camaino. Works by N. Pisano, A. Guardi, M. Civitali, Stagi, Tribolo, S. Corsini.

Church silver and ornaments including *Madonna* in ivory and *Crucifix* by Giovanni Pisano, the «Cintola» or «Belt» of the Duomo with enamelled plaques, precious stones and silver crosses, 12th-13th C. reliquaries from Limoges and 17th C. reliquaries, episcopal services including the one presented by the queen of France, Maria de' Medici, to Archbishop Bonciani; French goldsmiths' work (1616-17).

15th C. paintings on wood; 16th-18th C. paintings (B. Franco, O. Riminaldi, A. Lomi, G. and F. Melani, G.D. Ferretti) and sculptures in wood by G.B. Riminaldi.

Wooden marquetry and illuminated manuscripts; fragments of the wooden stalls from the Choir of the Duomo, liturgical texts including two Exultats from the 12th-13th C.

Cloths: 15th C. caparison, 16th-17th C. hangings, French 18th C. fabrics, Flemish lace, 19th C. vestments.

Il Museo dell'Opera del Duomo di Pisa, by various authors, Milan 1986

Museo delle Sinopie

56100 Pisa
Piazza del Duomo
Tel. 050/560547-561820

Large

Winter: all week 9 a.m.-1 p.m. / 3 p.m.-4.30 p.m.

Summer: all week 9 a.m.-1 p.m. / 3 p.m.-7 p.m.

Entrance fee

Accessible

By arrangement

Opened in 1979 on the occasion of the 700th anniversary of the foundation of the Memorial Cemetery, the museum displays an outstanding collection of sinopias which came to light during restoration work on the frescoes in the Cemetery which had been seriously damaged during the last war. It is housed in a 13th C. pavilion of the Ospedale di Santa Chiara which looks onto the Piazza dei Miracoli. It is an integral part of a museum itinerary of great artistic value taking in the Cemetery and the recently founded Museo dell'Opera Primaziale.

14th and 15th C. sinopias by Buffalmacco, F. Traini, T. Gaddi, A. Aretino, A. Veneziano, Piero di Puccio, B. Gozzoli.

A. Caleca, G. Nencini, G. Piancastelli, *Museo delle sinopie del Camposanto Monumentale*, Pisa 1979

Orto Botanico dell'Università di Pisa.

56100 Pisa
Via Luca Ghini, 5
Tel. 050/560045-561795-560405

Founded by the celebrated botanist Luca Ghini in 1543-44 it was transferred in 1591 to its present home. It covers an area of about 7.5 acres overlooked by antique historic buildings including the old seat of the Museum of Natural History (the 16th C. «Galleria»). It contains a large number of plants from various continents as well as

Large

Weekdays 8.30 a.m.-1 p.m. / 2 p.m.-5.30 p.m.; Saturday 8.30 a.m.-1 p.m.; closed on Sundays

Free

♿
Accessible

📷
Yes

☞
Areas set out for educational activities available by prior booking

Library and laboratories of the Department of Botanical Science at the University of Pisa open to visitors by prior arrangement

The Department's researches collected annually in the Acta Horti Pisani, published by the Department of Botanical Sciences at the University of Pisa

indigenous plants and plants grown for research purposes in pots and in the ground. Among the secular trees of great interest are the Ginkgo biloba and the Magnolia grandiflora planted in 1787. Managed by the University of Pisa it undertakes extensive scientific work and has an indoor educational area.

Plant species, both wild Italian species and exotic plants.

Officinal plants and numerous examples in pots of bulb plants from the Mediterranean basin.

In the glasshouses: cacti, euphorbiacae and thick-leaved plants from the main desert areas; examples of sugar cane and coffee plants. Tree essences (including South American *Auracarie*, *Taxodium* from Virginia, conifers from Northern Europe).

Of particular interest: two *Jubeaa chilensis* (from 1877), male and fermale *Cycas*, *Magnolia denudata* from China, *Quercus virginiana* (from 1829), *Magnolia grandiflora* (from 1787) and *Ginkgo biloba* (from 1787).

A. Chiarugi, *Le date di fondazione dei primi Orti botanici del mondo*, in *Nuovo Giornale Botanico Italiano*, 60, (4), 1953, pp. 785-839

G. Martinoli, *L'Orto botanico di Pisa*, in *Agricoltura*, 7, 1963, pp. 59-66

L. Tongiorgi Tomasi, *Il Giardino dei Semplici dello Studio pisano. Collezionismo, scienza e immagine tra Cinque e Seicento*, in *Livorno e Pisa, due città e un territorio nella politica dei Medici*, Pisa 1980, pp. 514-526

F. Garbari, *Nasce presso lo Studio pisano, nel XVI secolo, la botanica moderna*, in *Livorno e Pisa, due città e un territorio nella politica dei Medici*, Pisa 1980, pp. 527-533

L. Tongiorgi Tomasi, *Un 'Florilegio' pisano del XVII secolo*, in *Boll. St. Pisano*, 52, 1983, pp. 199-209

A.M. Pagni, *Le piante medicinali nella tradizione pisana*, in *Le piante officinali in provincia di Pisa. Possibilità di coltivazione e di commercializzazione*, Pisa 1986, pp. 109-127

Botanical garden

E. Coaro, *Dendroflora dell'Orto botanico pisano. Materiali per lo studio e la catalogazione del patrimonio vegetale dei Giardini Storici d'Italia*, in *Museologia scientifica* 4 (1-2), 1987, pp. 77-98

P.E. Tomei, E. Coaro, F. Garbari, *Il Catalogo di Dionisio Veglia, prefetto dell'Orto botanico di Pisa nel XVII secolo*, in *Museologia Scientifica* 4 (3-4), 1987

Museo Storico Enel

56044 Larderello —
Pomarance (PI)
Piazza De Larderel
Tel. 0588/673712 (ENEL)

Medium

By arrangement from 8 a.m.-5 p.m.

Free

Accessible

By arrangement

Guided tours on request

Founded in 1955 the museum owned by Enel is housed in the old manor-house belonging to the Larderel family. It contains material on the history of the industrial exploitation of the geothermal phenomenon of the fumaroles for the production of boric acid, begun at the end of the 18th C. by Francesco de Larderel. There is a collection of antique tools, machines, minerals and rocks from the area and extensive historical documentation and maps. The reorganization and enlargement of the collections is planned.

Historical and scientific objects and documents on the work of the Società Boracifera arranged in the following sections: the history of boric acid in industry, the history of drilling, collection of boracic rocks and minerals, lakes and fumaroles, the development of the exploitation of endogenous steam for the production of electrical energy, the history of the socio-economic organization of the local area.

Palazzo De Larderel

Collezione della Cassa di Risparmio di San Miniato

56027 San Miniato (PI)
Via IV Novembre, 45
Tel. 0571/4101 (Cassa di Risparmio)

In the bank's headquarters is housed a fine collection of 15th-17th C. paintings of the Tuscan school acquired by the bank and enlarged considerably over the last decade. It includes works by the Maestro di San Miniato, J. del Sellaio, G.B. Naldini, Empoli, Cigoli. The collection is open to scholars by prior arrangement.

P. Torriti, *Tesori d'arte antica a San Miniato*, Genoa 1979

Museo Diocesano di Arte Sacra

56027 San Miniato (PI)
Piazza del Duomo, 1
Tel. 0571/418071

Opened in 1966 the museum which is owned by the Bishop's See of San Miniato is housed in the fully restored old vestries of the Duomo. It contains an important group of 14th-18th C. works of the Tuscan school in addition to church fittings and ornaments from various churches in the diocese.

Medium

All week 9 a.m.-noon / 3 p.m.-6 p.m.

Entrance fee

Partially accessible

By arrangement

Frescoes, paintings on wood and canvas of the Tuscan school from the 14th-18th C. by D. Orlandi, the Maestro di San Miniato, Cenni di Francesco, Iacopo di Cione, Neri di Bicci, the Maestro di San Quirico and Giuditta, Rossello di Iacopo Franchi, G.B. Naldini, Empoli, L. Lippi and the Maestro di cultura fiamminga. Church fittings and ornaments from the 15th-18th C. 16th C. documents and illuminated manuscripts.

U. Lumini, L. Bertolini Campetti, D. Lotti, *Museo diocesano di San Miniato*, in *Bollettino dell'Accademia degli Euteletii*, 38, 1966

Museo della Zona del Cuoio

Centro di documentazione e informazione sull'archeologia industriale
56029 Santa Croce sull'Arno (PI)
Via Basili, 2
Tel. 0571/30853 (Comune)

Medium

Winter, from 16th September to 14th June: all week 3 p.m.-7 p.m.; closed on Mondays

Summer, from 15th June to 15th September: weekdays 3.30 p.m.-7.30 p.m.; closed on Saturdays and Sundays

Free

Partially accessible

By arrangement

Guided tours. Audiovisual material on the museum available

The museum was founded in 1982 by the Council of Santa Croce. Housed in the former «Imperial» tannery owned by the Pagni family which was originally used as a glue factory it documents the many aspects of the tanning industry. It undertakes extensive cultural and educational activities and has substantial archival material.

Material concerning the history of the territory and the town of Santa Croce sull'Arno and different aspects of the industrialization of the area.

Section on the history of the technology of leather production: audio-visual material on the production cycle, videos on the production stages in old factories. Tools, patterns and models.

Il Pappagallo giallo. La pelle nella moda, nelle arti minori, nell'industrial design (1900-1940), exhibition catalogue, edited by V. Bertini and F. Foggi, Florence 1986

Nel segno di Saturno - Origini e sviluppo dell'attività conciaria a Santa Croce sull'Arno, I and II, edited by F. Foggi, Florence 1985-1987

Show-room

Archival material available on microfilm. Small library. Audiovisual material on the tanning industry

Temporary exhibitions and conferences

Santa Croce sull'Arno: biografie di imprenditori, edited by G. Contini, Florence 1987

Museo d'Arte Sacra

56048 Volterra (PI)
Via Roma, 13
Tel. 0588/87654

Founded in 1936 by the Opera della Cattedrale di Volterra at the old episcopal palace the museum contains a collection of works of art from the Duomo and other churches in the diocese: important 14th-16th C. paintings on wood and canvas by Tuscan artists, 14th C. marble sculptures, ecclesiastical goldsmiths' work and vestments from the 14th-16th C., illuminated choirbooks and archaeological fragments.
It is currently closed to the public.

Museo Etrusco Guarnacci

56048 Volterra (PI)
Via Don Minzoni, 15
Tel. 0588/86347

Large

Winter, from 1st October to 15th March: all week 10 a.m.-2 p.m.

Summer, from 16th March to 15th October: all week 9.30 a.m.-1 p.m. / 3 p.m.-6.30 p.m.

Entrance fee

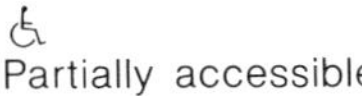
Partially accessible

By arrangement

Educational activities with schools consisting of guided visits and conferences on the museum's collections.
Audiovisual material available

Begun in 1732 with the donation of a collection of cinerary urns by the canon Pietro Franceschini, the museum acquired the main group of material in 1761 with the bequest by Monsignor Mario Guarnacci which brought to the museum a magnificent collection of archaeological material and his own library. It has grown over the years with further groups of material from excavations carried out in the Volterra archaeological area. Today is boasts an outstanding collection arranged over an area of over 1,600 sq. ft. of exhibition space organized in various sections. Of great interest is the Etruscan collection (containing over six hundred cinerary urns), one of the richest in Italy.

Stone tools from Eneolithic tombs. Villanovian grave goods (of particular note a bucchero *kyathos* with Etruscan inscription from Monteriggioni). Tomb sculpture in stone: stelae including the *Avile Tite stele*; statues of lions; bulb cippi and cippi with base decorated with ram's heads; tufa sarcophagus; *urns* in alabaster, tufa and terracotta dating from the 4th-1st C. B.C. decorated with bas-reliefs. Etrusco-Corinthian, Attic, red-figured Etruscan (from southern Etruria and the area of Volterra), black-painted (remarkable group from the «Malacena» factory) and red-painted pottery. Fragments of statues, votive statuettes, Hellenistic facing tiles in terracotta. Etruscan and Roman bronze remains: the series of statuettes includes some Archaic examples and the famous «Ombra della Sera»; also worthy of mention are the plaques, some of which with satyrs' heads, and the mirrors with engraved decoration. Jewellery (including the necklace and the fibulae from a tomb at Gesseri dating from the 7th C. B.C.). Objects in bone. Precious stones and cameos. Coins from Volterra and various other locations in ancient Italy, in particular Populonia. Glass including an Augustan ciborium in polychrome glass, cinerary urns. Etruscan and Latin funerary inscriptions, Roman stelae and urns. Portraits of *Augustus* and *Livia* from the Roman theatre, floor mosaics and painted plaster.

E. Fiumi, Volterra. *Il Museo etrusco e i monumenti antichi*, Pisa 1976

Museum library attached to the local library (Via Don Minzoni, Volterra)

Temporary exhibitions

E. Fiumi, *Storia e sviluppo del Museo Guarnacci di Volterra*, Florence 1977

Urne volterrane, 2, *Il Museo Guarnacci*, part 1, edited by M. Cristofani, Florence 1977; part 2, edited by G. Cateni, Florence 1986

G. Cateni, *Guida breve del Museo Guarnacci*, Pisa 1987

G. Cateni, *Il Museo Guarnacci di Volterra*, Pisa 1988 (in preparation)

Urn with the myth of Atheon

Pinacoteca e Museo Civico

56048 Volterra (PI)
Palazzo Minucci Solaini
Via dei Sarti, 1
Tel. 0588/87580

Large

Founded in 1905 by Corrado Ricci and originally housed in the old Palazzo dei Priori, the Picture Gallery was transferred in 1982 to Palazzo Minucci Solaini; to it has been added the Museo Civico comprising paintings, sculptures and other material from Organizations no longer in a position to guarantee their adequate preservation (hospitals, schools etc.).
Fine 14th-17th C. works by Florentine, Sienese and Volterran artists from the Council's collections and from charitable and ecclesiastical organizations are today preserved in the Palazzo, an unusual building attributed to Antonio da Sangallo the Elder.

12th-18th C. paintings on wood and canvas by Taddeo di Bartolo, Benvenuto di Giovanni, L. Signorelli, D. Ghirlandaio, Rosso Fioren-

Winter, from 15th September to 15th June: all week 9 a.m.-1 p.m.

Summer, from 16th June to 14th September: all week 9.30 a.m.-6.30 p.m.

Entrance fee

No access

By arrangement

Educational service for schools consisting in lectures on the historical and artistic heritage of Volterra and the surrounding area

Occasional conferences

tino (*Deposition* from 1521), Baldassarre Franceschini known as il Volterrano.
Medieval and Renaissance sculpures in tufa, marble and wood. Coin and medal collection with items from the 9th-19th C.: in particular coins from the territory of Volterra; medals by Pisanello and Matteo de' Pasti; 15th-17th C. Medicean collection.

E. Carli, *Volterra nel Medioevo e nel Rinascimento*, Pisa 1978

E. Carli, *La Pinacoteca di Volterra*, Pisa 1980

Momenti dell'arte a Volterra, exhibition catalogue, by various authors, Pisa 1981

Il Rosso Fiorentino, realtà e visione, by various authors, Siena 1985

F. Lessi, *La Pinacoteca e il Museo civico di Palazzo Minucci Solaini*, Milan 1986

Rosso Fiorentino: Deposition

Orto Botanico Forestale Abetone

51021 Abetone (PT)
Valle del Sestaione
Tel. 0573/60003 (Comando stazione forestale Abetone)

Opened in 1987 the museum was founded by an agreement between the national and regional governments, Tuscan universities and the Comunità Montana with the aim of recording and preserving the animal and plant species of the Tuscan and Emilian Appennines. Situated in the Alta Valle del Sestaione 4,280 ft. above sea level it covers an area of over 2.5 acres rich with beech, silver fir, red fir,

Large

Summer, from 1st June to 31st October: all week 9 a.m.-noon

Closed during the winter

Free

No access

Yes

Guided tours for groups by prior arrangement

alder, maple, sorb and birch. In a state-owned building in Fontana Vaccaia along the main road to Abetone a small natural history and forestry museum is being set up to accompany the Orto, and will be open to university students and professors.

Forest area (with large moss and lichen-coveres rocks), siliceous area for plants which live in sandstone soil, area for plants which live in limestone soil, stream and small lake for mountain marsh plants and animals.

Forest area, botanical garden

Museo Parrocchiale del Santissimo Crocifisso

51011 Borgo a Buggiano (PT)
Corso Indipendenza
Tel. 0572/32047

Small

By arrangement

Free

Accessible

By arrangement

Opened during the 1970's during the restoration work on the adjacent Santuario del SS. Crocifisso this small collection of religious art is housed at the parsonage.
Opened in 1982 it displays ecclesiastical ornaments and fittings and vestments from the 15th-19th C. (17th C. bronze *candlesticks*, 16th-19th C. *chalices*, 18th C. *reliquaries*).

Museo dell'Opera

51011 Buggiano (PT)
Piazza Pretorio, 3
Tel. 0572/32047

Of all the many small collections of religious art in the parish churches of the Valdinievole area the museum at Buggiano is one of the best-endowed and most interesting.
Opened in 1960 it displays fabrics, church silver and fittings from

Small

By arrangement

Free

♿
No access

By arrangement

the adjacent Romaneque parish church of the Madonna della Salute e di San Niccolao.

Church fittings and silver. Sculptures in wood. Vestments and cloth from the 16th-19th C.

Museo Etnologico della Montagna
51020 Rivoreta — Cutigliano (PT)
Via degli Scoiattoli
Tel. 0573/68383 (Comune)

Small

Winter, from 1st September to 14th July: Saturday and Sunday 9.30 a.m.-noon / 3 p.m.-5 p.m.

Summer, from 15th July to 31st August: all week 9.30 a.m-noon / 3.30 p.m.-5.30 p.m.

Free

♿
Accessible

📷
Yes

The collection was brought together by amateurs with the active participation of the local people and the Council. Opened in 1971 it displays domestic utensils and work tools illustrative of peasant and pastoral life in the Pistoian Appennine region.

The 19th and 20th C. material displayed is arranged in three sections: the home with domestic utensils, clothes and tools for spinning and weaving; the crafts, with tools and implements of the carpenter, blacksmith and shoe-maker; work in the fields, with implements for collecting chestnuts and bilberries and wood-cutters' tools.

S. Giannoni, *Un paese una storia un museo*, Cutigliano 1987

Show-room

Museo Civico
51036 Larciano (PT)
Piazza Castello
Tel. 0573/83002 (Comune)

Small

Opened in 1975 the museum is housed in the 12th C. Rocca di Larciano. It contains material from excavations carried out in the area and other regions of Italy by the Valdinievole archaeological group. It also displays a collection of Medieval and Renaissance ceramics found during restoration work on the Rocca which was carried out during the '70's by the Florence Soprintendenza per i beni architettonici e ambientali.

All week 8 a.m.-11 a.m. / 3 p.m.-5 p.m.

Free

No access

Yes

Activities for schools by prior arrangement

Prehistoric stone objects; bronze relics from the Iron Age. Pottery and bronze coins from the grave-goods of a Hellenistic period Ligurian tomb. Pottery and glass - including a particularly interesting fragment with engraved decoration - from Roman settlements in the area. Medieval and Renaissance pottery from the Rocca di Larciano. In the section given over to material from outside the local area are examples of Greek and Etruscan painted ceramics of various schools, impasto and bucchero pottery; examples of Medieval pottery from several areas in central and southern Ita y.

Quaderni di studio, periodical edited by the Council of Larciano and the Valdinievole archaeology society.

Museo di Casa Giusti

51015 Monsummano Terme (PT)
Viale Martini

Once the home of Giuseppe Giusti (1809-1850) the house, a typical 19th C. nobleman's home, was acquired by the nation in 1975 in order to found a museum dedicated to the poet. The comprehensive restoration and conversion work organized by the Soprintendenza per i beni architettonici e ambientali of the Provinces of Florence and Pistoia is currently under way. The architectural work and work on the interior distemper decoration is complete; currently under way is the arrangement of the museum exhibits: period furniture, ornaments and momentoes of the poet on the first floor and a section of his life and works on the top floor. There is also a well-equipped library and the 'Papers', part of which have been entrusted to the State Archives in Pistoia.

Casa Giusti. Decorazioni, documenti, restauri, by various authors, Monsummano Terme 1984

Museo del Santuario

51015 Monsummano Terme (PT)
Piazza Giuseppe Giusti, 38
Tel. 0572/51102

Founded in 1940 the museum is housed in rooms adjacent to the Santuario di Santa Maria della Fontenuova (17th C.). It displays religious ornaments and goldsmiths' work from the 17th C. and the present day and a valuable collection of ex votos connected with the cult of the Madonna to whom the Church is dedicated.

Small

By arrangement

Free

Accessible

By arrangement

Ecclesiastical goldsmiths' work, religious fittings and ex votos donated to the Madonna della Fontenuova between the 17th and 19th C. (ivory *Crucifix* attributed to Giambologna; *Royal Crown of the Madonna* in gold, enamel and precious stones from 1606 donated by the Grand Duke Ferdinando I; five pairs of early 17th silver *candlesticks* made in Florence.

C. Natali, *Il Santuario di Maria Santissima della Fontenuova Patrona della Diocesi di Pescia*, Monsummano Terme 1982

Raccolta dell'Accademia d'Arte «Dino Scalabrino»
51016 Montecatini Terme (PT)
Viale Diaz, 6
Tel. 0572/78211

The Academy of Art founded in 1963 and established as a charitable organization in 1972 houses and organizes annually exhibitions of work by contemporary artists. It contains a substantial collection of modern and contemporary painting, sculptures and graphic art (including works by P. Annigoni, G. Chini, V. Guidi, R. Guttuso, F. Messina, J. Mirò, O. Tamburi, J. Vivarelli). There is a section dedicated to Montecatini and the thermal baths and the prominent figures who have stayed in the town.
The collection can be visited by prior arrangement.

Museo della Propositura di San Pietro Apostolo
51010 Montecatini Alto — Montecatini Terme (PT)
Via Prataccio, 7
Tel. 0572/73727

The museum contains a collection of 12th-18th C. sculptures, paintings and church ornaments displayed in rooms in the parish building. It is currently closed to the public.

Gipsoteca Libero Andreotti
51017 Pescia (PT)
Via Sant'Apollonio, 2
Tel. 0572/478913 (Comune)

Opened in 1982 the museum comprises a permanent exhibition of casts (about 250 works including sketches and sculptures) by the Pescia sculptor Libero Andreotti (1875-1932) donated to Pescia Council by the artist's heirs. It is housed in part of the old Palazzo del Podestà («Palagio») which has been completely restored by the Soprintendenza per i beni architettonici e ambientali of Florence. The collection is temporarily closed to the public.

Un «Palagio» per la città, by various authors, Pescia 1982

Museo Civico Carlo Magnani
51017 Pescia (PT)
Piazza Santo Stefano, 1
Tel. 0572/478913 (Comune)

The museum founded in 1894 contains works from the area of Pescia brought together by acquisitions, donations by private citizens and loans from the Galleries of Florence. Housed in Palazzo Galeotti in rooms adjacent to the Municipal Library it displays 14th-19th C. paintings, some Etruscan remains, sculptures, prints and local relics from the Risorgimento period.

Medium

Monday, Wednesday and Saturday 9.30 a.m.-1.30 p.m., Friday 9.30 a.m.-1.30 p.m. / 4 p.m.-7 p.m.; closed on Tuesday, Thursday and Sunday

🚪
Free

No access

14th-20th C. paintings on wood of the Tuscan school including works by the Maestro della Santa Cecilia (*Madonna and Child*), Neri di Bicci and L. Monaco. Sculptures in stone from the 13th C. and in wood from the 13th and 14th C.

16th C. ceramics (Robbian wreath; apothecary jars).

Various objects and furnishings. Local Risorgimento relics (standards, documents, photographs, clothes). Works by the artist L. Norfini (19th C.) from Pescia.

G. Pacini Fund (musical scores, documents and relics from the 19th C.). J.C.L. Sismonde de Sismondi archive and library (open to consultation by prior arrangement).

Collection of antique prints.

By arrangement

Guided tours on request

Guida del Museo Civico di Pescia, Pescia 1968

Museo Civico di Scienze Naturali e Archeologia della Valdinievole

51017 Pescia (PT)
Piazza Obizzi, 9
Tel. 0572/478913

Medium

Weekdays 9 a.m.-1 p.m., Tuesday and Thursday 9 a.m.-1 p.m. / 3 p.m.-6 p.m.; closed on Sunday

Free

No access

By arrangement

Guided tours by appointment on Mondays, Wednesdays and Fridays 9 a.m.-1 p.m., Tuesday afternoons 3 p.m.-6 p.m.

Book and photograph library and laboratories open to the public by arrangement

International archaeology camps for schools organized annually; conferences, meetings and exhibitions

The museum was opened in 1976 by the Council and the local archaeology society. It contains minerals, fossils, interesting collections of Prehistoric material and Roman and medieval remains from various sources. It undertakes extensive educational and research activities. The transfer of the museum to another site is planned.

Introduction to Paleontology; invertebrate fossils, the evolution of life. Vertebrates: fishes, amphibians, reptiles, mammals, fossils of extinct and living plants.

Material on Human evolution, the climate and dwellings. Neolithic stone tools and pottery from Italy, Algeria and Jordan; Bronze Age arrow-heads from Afghanistan.

Ceramics (including a Villanovian bone-jar, Attic painted vases, bucchero and black-painted pottery) and glass from various sources. Etruscan grave-goods from Sovana. Roman and medieval relics, mainly clay, discovered in the area of Pescia. Egyptian china statuettes and amulets. Pottery and coins from Petra (Jordan).

Show-room

Museo del Parco di Pinocchio

51014 Collodi — Pescia (PT)
Parco di Pinocchio
Tel. 0572/429342
0572/476024 (Fondazione)

At the end of the Parco di Pinocchio itinerary the National «Carlo Collodi» Foundation has set up a permanent exhibition of preparatory studies, drawings, objects and wood engravings produced by Sigfrido Bartolini for a new edition of Pinocchio, published to mark the work's centenary. The educational exhibition opened in 1987 is housed in a new building designed by the architect Michelucci.

Small

All week: 8.30 a.m.-sunset

Entrance fee

♿
Accessible

By arrangement

Carlo Collodi. Le avventure di Pinocchio, illustrated with 309 woodcuts by Sigfrido Bartolini, introduction by L. Volpicelli, Florence 1983

Exhibition building

Museo della Cattedrale di San Zeno
51100 Pistoia
Palazzo dei Vescovi
Piazza del Duomo
Ingresso del museo: via Roma
Uffico Ente del Turismo
Tel. 0573/3691 (Cassa di Risparmio)

Small

Tuesday, Thursday and Friday guided tours at 10 a.m., 11.30 a.m., 3.30 p.m.
Group visits, book by telephone

Entrance fee

♿
Partially accessible

Previously housed in rooms adjoining the Duomo the museum was transferred to the 11th C. Palazzo dei Vescovi and reopened in 1986. It displays the treasure of the Cathedral comprising very fine ecclesiastical goldsmiths' work, illuminated choirbooks and altar-hangings displayed according to the most up-to-date standards of preservation and security. Set up with the collaboration of several organizations (the Cathedral Chapter, the local Cassa di Risparmio

Lorenzo Ghiberti and his studio: Reliquary of St. James

By arrangement

Guided tour

which owns the Palazzo and the relevant Authorities for the area) the museum adds a new and important element to the town's artistic panorama.

Medieval and Renaissance goldsmiths' work from the 13th-15th C. (*Chalice of St. Atto* by A. d'Ognabene from 1286; *Reliquary in the shape of arm of St. Zeno* by E. Bellandini from 1369; *Reliquary of St. James* from the studio of L. Ghiberti from 1407).

17th and 18th C. religious ornaments produced in Tuscany and Rome.

Also frescoes from the 14th C. (Giovanni di Bartolomeo Cristiani) and the 15th C. and sculptures from the 14th C. (pupil of Agostino di Giovanni, *The Virgin Mary* and *Male figure*, from the *Cenotaph of Cino da Pistoia* in the Duomo).
Altar-hangings and vestments section (exhibited in rotation for preservation reasons) (*'Casula di S. Atto'* in cloth and velvet embroidered with gold thread produced probably in Lucca in the 18th C.; *Chasuble* in gold cloth once belonging to Pope Clement IX Rospigliosi).

N. Rauty, *L'antico Palazzo dei Vescovi a Pistoia*, I vol., *Storia e Restauro*, Florence 1981

F. Falletti, E. Spalletti, *Museo della Cattedrale di S. Zeno*, Pistoia 1986

Museo Civico

51100 Pistoia
Palazzo comunale
Piazza del Duomo
Tel. 0573/3711

Large

Weekdays 9 a.m.-1 p.m. / 3 p.m.-7 p.m., Sundays and public holidays 9 a.m.-1 p.m.; closed on Mondays

Entrance fee

Accessible

By arrangement

Founded in 1922 and rearranged in 1956 in Palazzo Marchetti the museum was transferred in 1982 to the historic Town Hall. It contains important collections of art mainly from religious organizations in the area of Pistoia suppressed during the 19th C. It subsequently grew through donations, acquisitions and loans. The paintings on wood and canvas constitute the most substantial part of the collection and come from various periods: from Romanesque painting (the *'Pala di San Francesco'*) to the 19th C. works from the Puccini Collection. Arranged according to the most up-to-date museum standards it also has useful support material in the form of information sheets on the most important works. The museum also undertakes extensive educational and cultural activities.
Two Information Centres are an integral part of the museum. The first, dedicated to Marino Marini (opened in 1979), is housed in the ground floor rooms and will soon be transferred to Palazzo del Tau. The other, on Giovanni Michelucci, was opened in 1980; in addition to containing material on the architect's works it undertakes extensive consultation and information work.

13th-16th C. paintings on wood mainly of the Pistoiese and Florentine schools: works by a follower of B. Berlinghieri (*'Pala di San Francesco'*), by Lippo di Benivieni (*Lament over the dead Christ*), by the Maestro del 1310 (*Madonna and Child with Saints*), by Mariotto di Nardo, Lorenzo di Credi (*Holy Conversation*), Michele di Ridolfo del Ghirlandaio, Gerino da Pistoia (*Holy Conversation*) from 1509, Bernardino di Antonio Detti (*Madonna 'della Pergola'*), Fra' Paolino, G.B. Naldini, G. Pagani.

12th-19th C. sculptures in marble, wood, terracotta and plaster by

The museum's internal education section annually proposes activities for schools in the museum and on monuments in the town; guided tours for groups of adults by prior arrangement. Documentary material available

Book and photograph library open for consultation on weekdays from 8 a.m.-2 p.m.

Exhibitions, meetings and series of conferences planned annually

Francesco di Valdambrino (*Angel*), B. Buglioni (*Resurrection* in glazed terracotta), G.B. Foggini (*Bust of T. Puccini*).

17th-18th C. canvases by J. da Empoli, M. Rosselli, G. Gimignani (*Hero and Leander*), C. Bravo (*Apollo and Marsia*, *Hermione among the shepherds*), S. Coccapani, F. Paladini, A.D. Gabbiani, L. Crespi.

Objects of the minor arts from the 15th-19th C. (including *chalice* in gold and enamel by A. Braccini).

Puccini Collection: 14th-16th C. paintings on wood (Maestro di Francoforte); 17th-19th C. canvases by Cigoli, P. Dandini, L. Sabatelli, N. Monti, N.D. Boguet, E. Busi, A. Asioli, G. Bezzuoli; 19th C. furniture, ornaments and costumes.

Marino Marini Information Centre with sculptures in bronze (*Miracle*, *Pomona*), drawings, etchings and lithographs as well as a specialized library, videolibrary and photograph library.

Giovanni Michelucci Centre with drawings, sketches, tracings and architectural models.

Cultura dell'Ottocento a Pistoia. La Collezione Puccini, Catalogo del Museo Civico 1, by various authors, Florence 1977

C. Mazzi, C. Sisi, *La città e gli artisti. Pistoia tra Avanguardie e Novecento, Catalogo del Museo Civico 2*, Florence 1980

Pistoia: una città nello stato mediceo, exhibition catalogue, by various authors, Pistoia 1980

M.C. Mazzi, *Museo civico di Pistoia, Catalogo delle Collezioni 3*, Florence 1982

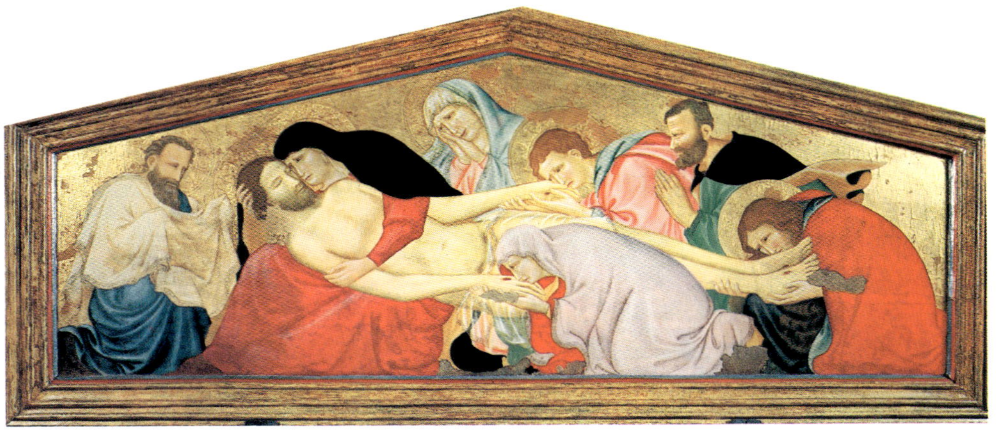

Lippo di Benivieni: Lament over the dead Christ

Percorso Archeologico Attrezzato

51100 Pistoia
Palazzo dei Vescovi
Piazza del Duomo
Ingresso del museo: Via Roma
Uffico Ente del Turismo
Tel. 0573/3691 (Cassa di Risparmio)

Opened in 1984 the museum is the fruit of extensive archaeological explorations carried out in the 11th C. Palazzo dei Vescovi owned by the Cassa di Risparmio. It comprises a real and true archaeological route through the excavation site within the Palazzo. It is set up according to up-to-date museum standards and has well fitted out stores containing the material not on display which can be consulted by prior arrangement.

Small

Tuesday, Thursday and Friday guided tours starting at 10 a.m., 11.30 a.m., and 3.30 p.m.
Telephone booking for group visits

Entrance fee

No access

By arrangement

Guided tour

Fully equipped depository open for consultation by arrangement

Etruscan funerary emblems from the Archaic period. Ceramics dating from the late Republican to the Imperial periods, clay and glass oil-lamps, personal ornaments, transport containers, building material. Early Medieval ceramics (an interesting group of jugs with engraved and painted decoration), from the late 14th-15th C. and from the late Renaissance. St. Edvige style drinking glasses of Egyptian manufacture (12th-13th C.); Islamic balsam-container and glass cup (12th-14th C.). Material from the Industrial Age (18th to mid-19th C.). Coin collection from the 2nd C. B.C. to the 19th C.

L'antico Palazzo dei Vescovi a Pistoia, 2 vols., part. 1, *Indagini archeologiche*, edited by G. Vannini, Florence 1985

L'antico Palazzo dei Vescovi a Pistoia, 2 vols., part. 2, *I documenti archeologici*, edited by G. Vannini, Florence 1987

Museo Ferrucciano

51025 Gavinana — San Marcello (PT)
Piazza Francesco Ferrucci
Tel. 0573/630439 (Biblioteca)

Founded in 1931 by the Council of San Marcello the museum is situated in the house on whose doorstep, according to tradition, Francesco Ferrucci was killed. Restored in 1957 it contains a varied collection of historical momentos and relics and a library of material on Ferrucci which can be visited by prior arrangement.

Small

Winter, from 1st September to 30th June: Thursday and Saturday 3 p.m.-5 p.m.

Summer, from 1st July to 31st August: weekdays 10 a.m.-noon / 5 p.m.-7 p.m., Sundays and public holidays 9.30 a.m.-12.30 p.m. / 4 p.m.-7 p.m.

Closed on Mondays

Entrance fee

No access

By arrangement

Collection of weapons and pieces of weapons (16th C.); 19th-20th C. drawings and prints; 17th C. Tuscan silver coins; 19th-20th C. commemorative medals. Ferrucci library and documents on F. Ferrucci. 19th C. historical paintings (M. D'Azeglio).

R. Chiarelli, *Il Museo Ferrucciano di Gavinana*, San Marcello 1957

Museo Amos Cassioli

53041 Asciano (SI)
Via Mameli
Tel. 0577/718745 (Comune)

The museum which is currently under preparation will contain over 250 works by Amos Cassioli (1832-1892) and by his son Giuseppe (1865-1942). The collection donated to the Council by the artist includes paintings on canvas, numerous sketches and drawings.

Museo Archeologico

53041 Asciano (SI)
Corso Matteotti
Tel. 0577/718745 (Comune)

Founded in 1959 the museum displays the material from a group of tombs in the nearby necropolis at Poggio Pinci. Housed in the former church of San Bernardino (14th C.) in the historic centre of the town it underwent a programme of complete restoration and rebuilding between 1979 and 1983. The transfer of the museum to another home is planned.

Small

Winter, from 1st September to 30th June: all week 10 a.m.-12.30 p.m.; closed on Mondays

Summer, from 1st July to 31st August: all week 10 a.m.-12.30 p.m.

Entrance fee

Accessible

By arrangement

Guided tour of the museum and the excavations by arrangement; educational activities arranged annually on aspects of the Etrusan civilization

Grave-goods from the necropolis at Poggio Pinci, dating from the 5th-1st C. B.C. comprising *Etruscan red-figured pottery* (cups from the Clusium Group, kraters from Vulci and Volterra from the studio of the Painter of Hesione and of the Painter of the Colonna Tuscanica), overpainted pottery (cups from the Sienese Workshop and from the Sokra Group) and black-painted pottery; also ordinary and sealed pottery from Arezzo, oil-lamps, bronze objects (including *engraved mirrors* with Minerva, the Dioscuri and a Lasa), jewellery, objects in bone. A series of travertine and tufa urns bearing inscriptions mentioning members of the Hepni family; sandstone urn with sculpted relief depicting a farewell scene.

E. Mangani, *Museo civico di Asciano. I materiali di Poggio Pinci*, Siena 1983

A. Ciacci, *Etruschi*, Siena s.d.

E. Mangani, *I centri archeologici della provincia di Siena*, Siena 1986

Museo d'Arte Sacra

53041 Asciano (SI)
Piazza Collegiata
Tel. 0577/718207

Opened in 1952 the museum is housed in the building which was formerly the seat of the Compagnia di Santa Croce. It contains an important and valuable collection of Sienese works of art from the Collegiate Church and from other churches in the territory.

Small

By arrangement

Free

No access

14th-15th C. paintings on wood of the Sienese school: works by A. Lorenzetti (*The Archangel St. Michael and two angels*), Barna, Piero di Giovanni d'Ambrogio, Giovanni di Paolo, by the Maestro dell'Osservanza (*Birth of the Virgin Mary*), Sano di Pietro, Taddeo di Bartolo, Matteo di Giovanni.
Polychrome wood sculptures by F. di Valambrino (*Heralding angel* and *The Virgin Mary*).

Ecclesiastical goldsmiths' work from the 14th C.

By arrangement

Several 14th C. detached frescoes will soon be returned to the Church of San Francesco from where they originally came.

Museo d'Arte Sacra della Val d'Arbia

53022 Buonconvento (SI)
Via Soccini, 17
Tel. 0577/806606 — 806788 (Comune)

Small

Tuesday and Thursdays 10 a.m.-noon, Saturdays 10 a.m.-noon / 4 p.m.-6 p.m., Sundays 9 a.m.-1 p.m.; closed on Mondays, Wednesdays and Fridays

Entrance fee

No access

By arrangement

The museum contains a fine collection of works of art, mainly paintings of the Sienese school and goldsmiths' work, from the territory of Buonconvento and from the Val d'Arbia. Opened in 1979 with the collaboration of the Soprintendenza per i beni artistici e storici of Siena it is housed in a building in the centro storico which also houses the local library. It is administered by a committee made up by the Council, the Bishop's See and the Soprintendenza.

14th-17th C. paintings of the Sienese school including works by the Maestro di Badia (*Madonna and Child* formerly attributed to Duccio di Buoninsegna), Luca di Tommè, Andrea di Bartolo, Stefano di Pietro, Matteo di Giovanni, Benvenuto di Giovanni, G. Cozzarelli, A. del Brescianino, R. Vanni, R. Manetti.
Also 14th-19th C. ecclesiastical goldsmiths' work and ornaments (*Incense-boat* dating from 1310-1320), sculptures in wood and marble (*Madonna and Child*, a bas-relief of the Florentine school from the second half of the 15th C.), 16th and 17th C. parchments.

S. Padovani, B. Santi, *Museo d'arte sacra della Val d'Arbia*, Genoa 1981

Matteo di Giovanni: Madonna and Child

Raccolta Permanente della Canapa

53022 Buonconvento (SI)
Piazzale Garibaldi, 14
Tel. 0577/806788 (Comune)

Small

By arrangement

Free

Accessible

Yes

The museum comprises material from two exhibitions «The Work of the Peasant» (1979) and «Bread in the life of the Peasant» (1982) organized in Buonconvento by the Council, the University of Siena and Cedlac (the Provincial Information Centre on Peasant Work). The collection which is of an educational nature consists in illustrated information panels, work implements and other objects connected with the production and processing of hemp and of bread. The material will be transferred to the Museum of Local Traditions currently being prepared by the Council.

Il mestiere del contadino, exhibition catalogue, by various authors, Siena 1979

Sulla condizione contadina, edited by Cedlac, Siena 1982

Sala d'Arte Antica

53042 Chianciano Terme (SI)
Via Solferino, 38
Tel. 0578/30378

Small

Weekdays 10 a.m.-12.30 p.m. / 4 p.m.-6.30 p.m.; Sundays and public holidays 10 a.m.-noon

Free

No access

By arrangement

Founded in 1945 the collection has been housed since 1966 in the St. John the Baptist parish building. It preserves works of particular historical and artistic interest by Florentine and Sienese masters from the adjacent cathedral and in part from churches and convents in Chianciano. It also displays a small group of ecclesiastical goldsmiths' work and hangings. A complete restoration and reorganization programme is planned.

15th-18th C. paintings on wood and canvas of the Florentine and Sienese schools (works by the Maestro di Chianciano, the Maestro di San Polo in Rosso, L. di Niccolò Gerini, D. Beccafumi). 14th-18th C. sculptures.

Church ornaments and goldsmiths' work, cloths, hangings and vestments from the 14th-19th C. Illuminated choirbooks from the 16th C.

Museo Archeologico Nazionale

53043 Chiusi (SI)
Via Porsenna
Tel. 0578/20177

Medium

This museum, one of the best-known on a national scale, contains an important collection of Etruscan remains and Greek and Roman works of art from excavations in the surrounding area and from donations (including the episcopal collection containing material from the François excavations, and the Paolozzi and Mieli Servadio collections). Founded in 1871 it is housed in a Neo-Classical building (built in 1902 to a design by the architect Partini) which has been rebuilt several times over the years. In 1963 the museum passed to State administration. A reorganization and expansion programme is currently in progress.

Weekdays 9 a.m.-2 p.m.; Sundays and public holidays 9 a.m.-1 p.m.

Entrance fee

Accessible

By arrangement

Restoration workshop

Prehistoric material from the territory of Chiusi. Villanovian clay material (of particular note a bone-jar lid with shaped handle and the *Paolozzi cinerary urn*); examples of Canopic vases including the *Dolciano Canopic vase* with embossed throne. Italo-geometric pottery; *Chiusine sculptures* in stone from the 6th-5th C. B.C. (female busts, lions, sphinxes; urns with relief decorations). Bucchero vases produced in Chiusi. Painted Greek pottery (of particular interest the series of *Attic vases*, some of which decorated with mythological subjects: Achilles and Ajax playing dice, Departure of Amphiarios, Penelope, Ajax and Cassandra etc.). Etruscan pottery from Vulci, Orvieto and Chiusi (black-figured vases by the Micali Painter, red-figured vases from the Vanth Group and the Clusium Group). Black-painted and achromatic pottery. Architectural terracottas dating from the Archaic to Hellenistic periods (outstanding antefixes with the head of Athena, of Heracles, in the shape of satyr's head and head of a maenad). Urns dating from the 4th-2nd C. B.C. Small ivory sheets decorated with bas-reliefs. Jewellery. Crockery and other domestic objects in bronze from the Classical and Hellenistic periods. Portrait head of *Augustus*. Statues of male figures in togas from a 1st C. A.D. tomb monument. Inscriptions. Longobardian grave-goods.

D. Levi, *Il Museo civico di Chiusi*, Rome 1935

A. Rastrelli, *Corpus Vasorum Antiquorum, Museo archeologico di Chiusi*, I, Rome 1980

A. Rastrelli, *Corpus Vasorum Antiquorum, Museo archeologico di Chiusi*, II, Rome 1981

A. Rastrelli, *Chiusi. La città e il museo*, Rome 1985

E. Mangani, *I centri archeologici della provincia di Siena*, Siena 1986

Urn of Larth Sentinates Caesa

Museo della Cattedrale
53043 Chiusi (SI)
Piazza del Duomo
Tel. 0578/226490

Large

Weekdays 9 a.m.-1 p.m.; Sundays and public holidays 9 a.m.-1 p.m. / 4 p.m.-7 p.m.

Entrance fee

Partially accessible

By arrangement

Guided tours by appointment

Annual conferences

Founded in 1932 by the Bishop of Chiusi Monsignor Giuseppe Conti in the Chapter House the museum was reopened in 1984 following a comprehensive restoration and rebuilding programme to enlarge the building and the collection displayed. It is housed in rooms adjacent to the Cathedral of San Secondiano. It contains religious works of art and ornaments from the Duomo, the Conservatorio di Santo Stefano, the Church of San Francesco and other churches in the diocese of Chiusi. It also displays a precious collection of books and Benedictine choirbooks from the Abbey of Monteoliveto Maggiore and archaeological remains found in the area and during the excavation work in the early Christian Cathedral (6th C.). The recent excavations in the Episcopal Gardens adjacent to the Cathedral have allowed the creation of a small but important archaeological park and the recovery of numerous Etruscan, Roman and Medieval remains, sections of the city walls (5th C. B.C.) and parts of a Roman building.

Archaeological remains (3rd C. B.C.-11th C.) from catacombs and from the ancient Basilica of S. Mustiola.

Ecclesiastical ornaments, silver and altar-hangings from the 15th-19th C. (15th C. ivory *casket*; 18th C. ivory *Crucifix*).

15th-17th C. paintings on wood and canvas (Girolamo di Benvenuto). Collection of Benedectine choirbooks from the 15th C. with miniatures by F. di Giorgio Martini, V. Mercati, L. da Verona, Sano di Pietro, G. da Cremona, B. Varnucci.

Antiquarium Etrusco «Ranuccio Bianchi Bandinelli»
53034 Colle Val d'Elsa (SI)
Piazza del Duomo
Tel. 0577/920015 (Comune)

Currently being rebuilt, the museum is temporarily closed to the public. The reopening is planned for 1989. Opened in 1976 and housed in the 14th C. Palazzo Pretorio it contains the Terrosi-Vagnoli collection acquired by the Council in 1971, subsequently enlarged with material from excavations carried out in the area and restored by the local archaeology society: of particular note a vase in bronze plate manufactured in Chiusi, a travertine stele in the Volterran style with Etruscan inscriptions, the late-Hellenistic ceramics from tombs in the area and the grave-goods, also from the Hellenistic period, from *the tomb of the Calisna Sepu*, discovered in the Casone necropolis near Monteriggioni.

Museo d'Arte Sacra
53034 Colle Val d'Elsa (SI)
Via Castello
Tel. 0577/920180 (Curia)

Comprising a fine collection of works from the Duomo and other churches in the Diocese the museum is housed in the Episcopal Curia. It contains 12th-17th C. paintings of the Tuscan school (*Madonna and Child with two Saints*, a triptych of the Sienese school from the end of the 14th C., *The Annuncation* by V. Salimbeni, *Deposition* by Cigoli) and precious ecclesiastical goldsmiths' work including the *Sant'Alberto's Chalice* from the 12th C. The museum is being reorganized and is currently closed to the public.

Museo Civico
53034 Colle Val d'Elsa (SI)
Via del Castello
Tel. 0577/920015 (Comune)

The museum administered by the Council contains 16th-17th C. paintings of the Sienese school. Founded in 1902 it is situated on the first floor of the 14th C. Palazzo dei Priori which was partially restored during the 1970's. On the ground floor is a permanent exhibition of photographs on the works of Arnolfo di Cambio. The museum is currently being reorganized and is temporarily closed to the public.

15th-16th C. paintings on wood and canvas including works by P. Fiorentino, G. Genga, R. Manetti, N. Tornioli, 16th and 17th C. statues in wood and marble (*Bust of U. Usimbardi*, by F. Palma). Various furniture and fittings (escutcheons, capitals etc).

E. Carli, *Arnolfo di Cambio. Guida alla mostra iconografica delle opere scultoree*, Florence 1982

Museo Civico e Diocesano

53024 Montalcinc (SI)
Via Ricasoli, 29
Tel. 0577/848135

Founded in 1958 by the joining of two existing collections, the municipal museum and the Episcopal Museum of Religious Art, it contains an outstanding collection representing Sienese art from the Middle Ages to the Renaissance. It also displays a small group of archaeological remains discovered during restoration work on the Town Hall and from chance dicoveries in the territory. Administered by the local Council in collaboration with the Bishop's See it

Medium

Winter, from 16th September to 30th June: all week 10 a.m.-noon / 3 p.m.-5 p.m.; closed on Mondays

Summer, from 1st July to 15th September; all week 9 a.m.-1 p.m. / 3 p.m.-7 p.m.

Entrance fee

Accessible

By arrangement

Heralding angel

is housed in part of the former seminary of Sant'Agostino (14th-15th C.). A plan is currently being prepared to comprehensively restructure the museum and to extend it to the adjacent Augustinian cloister.

12th-16th C. Sienese painting, with works by a follower of Duccio, Luca di Tommè, Bartolo di Fredi, Benvenuto di Giovanni, Sano di Pietro, Gerolamo di Benvenuto, G. Cozzarelli, Riccio, Sodoma.

14th-15th C. polychrome wood sculptures (Maestro Angelo, F. di Valdambrino, the Maestro del Crocifisso dei Disciplinati, Marrina). 15th and 16th C. sculpture in terracotta of the Sienese and Florentine schools (A. della Robbia and his studio).

Collection of religious material, with illuminated manuscripts (the *Sant'Antonino Bible* from the second half of the 12th C.), goldsmiths' work and fabrics from the 15th-18th C.

Stone tools dating from the Paleolithic period on; Prehistoric pottery and bone remains from the 'Buca di Sant'Antimo'. Travertine urns with inscriptions. Grave-goods including a plate in sealed ceramic and glass unguentarium. Medieval jugs in unglazed pottery and Archaic majolica with geometrical, plant and animal decoration.

E. Carli, *I musei di Montalcino*, Bologna 1972

Museo Naturalistico del Lago di Montepulciano

53045 Montepulciano (SI)
Località Tre Berte
Tel. 0578/716139

Small

By arrangement

Free

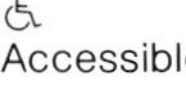
Accessible

Yes

By arrangement for school groups: guided tour of the museum and the lake area, lectures, audiovisual shows

Professional training courses for environmental workers

The museum contains material on the natural environment of the lake of Montepulciano. Owned by the Council it was founded in 1983 and entrusted to the management of the Natural Park Administration Co-operative Society. It is currently closed to the public for reorganization and expansion work; only a small section with some amphibian, reptile, fish and acquatic plant species is open. It carries out extensive educational activities for schools at every level.

M. Lambertini, *Ciclo annuale della comunità ornitologica del Lago di Montepulciano*, in Avocetta, 11, 1987

B. Granetti, *Le idrofite dei laghi di Montepulciano e Chiusi*, in *Studio sulle masse in movimento*, C.N.R., 1986

Exterior

Pinacoteca Crociani e Museo Civico

53045 Montepulciano (SI)
Via Ricci, 15
Tel. 0578/716935 (Biblioteca)

Medium

Winter, from 1st October to 31st March: all week 9 a.m.-1 p.m.; closed on Mondays

Summer, from 1st April to 30th September: all week 9 a.m.-1 p.m. / 4 p.m.-7 p.m; closed on Mondays and Tuesdays

Entrance fee

No access

By arrangement

Occasional exhibitions

The museum's original collection was donated to the Council in 1861 by Francesco Crociani. Opened in 1954 in the old Palazzo Neri Orselli it was then completely reorganized and reopened in 1984. It displays a remarkable collection of works including 13th-18th C. paintings of the Sienese and Tuscan schools, illuminated choir-books and Etruscan and Robbian relics. There is a very interesting section devoted to portraits (16th-18th C.).

14th-16th C. paintings on wood of the Tuscan school, by Luca di Tommè, Margaritone di Arezzo *(St. Francis)*, A. di Ceraiolo, R. del Garbo, Girolamo di Benvenuto *(Nativity scene)*, Pinturicchio (attrib.), Franciabigio (attrib.). Other paintings on canvas from the 17th and 18th C. by Cigoli, J. Sustermans, G.M. Crespi, Fra' Galgario.

Robbian terracotta: *St. John the Baptist*, fragment of a work by L. della Robbia and two altar-frontals by A. della Robbia.

15th C. illuminated manuscripts (not currently displayed).

Catalogo del Museo civico e Pinacoteca Crociani di Montepulciano, Montepulciano 1909

Luca di Tommè: Crucifixion

Museo d'Arte Sacra

53035 Montearioso — Monteriggioni (SI)
Seminario regionale Pio XII di Montearioso
Tel. 0577/50009

Small

Opened in 1980 the collection comprises a group of works on religious subjects from various parish churches of Siena. It is housed in the Seminario Regionale Pio XII di Montearioso. It is administered by the episcopal Commission for religious art.

13th-18th C. paintings on wood and frescoes in the Sienese style, including works by A. Lorenzetti *(Madonna 'del latte')*, the Maestro di Ovile, Vecchietta, D. Beccafumi and V. Salimbeni.

Ecclesiastical goldsmiths' work and fittings *(Reliquary of San Galgano*, 14th C. *Antiphonary*).
Etruscan vases.

Access reserved for scholars by prior arrangement with the Soprintendenza per i beni storico artistici and the archiepiscopal See of Siena

Free

No access

No

Ambrogio Lorenzetti: Madonna 'del Latte'

Museo Civico Archeologico
53016 Murlo (SI)
Tel. 0577/814213 (Comune)

The museum, whose preparation is in progress, will be housed in the old Episcopal Palace which is being totally converted to museum standards. It will display the relics from the Orientalist and Archaic buildings in Poggio Civitate excavated by Bryn Mawr College and Bowdoin College. The impressive complex in which two construction phases have been identified, dating from the end of the 7th C. B.C. and the first quarter of the 6th C. B.C., has revealed some remarkable material: particularly striking are the acroterium statues and the terracotta facing tiles. The museum will be divided into the following sections: historical and topographical concerning the territory, the history of the excavations and the various stages of construction of the Poggio Civitate complex; Orientalist and Archaic stages: personal ornaments, illustrated pottery, bucchero, domestic utensils; architectural decoration: acroteria of human figures, acroteria of animal figures, tiles from the frieze; conjectural reconstruction of the roof of the Archaic building. The opening is planned for 1988.

Case e palazzi d'Etruria, exhibition catalogue, edited by Simonetta Stopponi, Florence-Milan 1985, pp. 64-154

S. Bruni, S. Goggioli, N. Mannelli, *Guida del Museo di Murlo*, Florence 1988

Museo della Cattedrale di Pienza

53026 Pienza (SI)
Via Casello, 1
Tel. 0578/748549

Medium

Winter, from 1st November to 31st March: all week 10 a.m.-1 p.m. / 2 p.m.-4 p.m.

Summer, from 1st April to 31st October: all week 10 a.m.-1 p.m. / 4 p.m.-6 p.m.

Closed on Tuesdays

Entrance fee

No access

By arrangement

The museum contains a fine collection of vessels and vestments, ecclesiastical goldsmiths' work, hangings, tapestries and paintings of the Sienese school mainly from Pienza Cathedral and from other churches in the Diocese. The archaeological section containing mainly Etruscan relics found in the area has been closed to the public for several years. The museum is managed by the Opera della Cattedrale which is planning the transfer to the nearby Episcopal Palace.

Church ornaments and religious vestments from the 14th-15th C. including the *Cope of Pius II* with *Scenes from the life of the Virgin Mary* (14th C. English work), the *Reliquary Cross* by Goro di Neroccio from 1434 and illuminated choirbooks from the Cathedral.

15th and 16th C. Flemish tapestries.

14th and 15th C. paintings of the Sienese school by the Maestro dell'Osservanza, Bartolo di Fredi *(Madonna 'della Misericordia')*, Giovanni di Paolo and Vecchietta *(Madonna and Child with Saints)*.

Vecchietta: Madonna and Child with Saints

Museo Palazzo Piccolomini

53026 Pienza (SI)
Piazza Pio II, 2
Tel. 0578/748503 (Società di Esecutori di Pie Disposizioni)

Built for Pius II Piccolomini by Rossellino (1459-62) the palazzo was set up as a charitable institution by the last member of the family, the Conte Piccolimini della Triana. In 1963 it was entrusted to the Società Esecutori di Pie Disposizioni in Siena which still manages it today.
The piano nobile which still preserves the furnishings of a patrician residence with various pieces of furniture and fittings, relics of the family, the library (which can be consulted by prior arrangement) and the arms and armour room with various sets of period armour is open to the public.

Large

Winter, from 1st October to 31st March: all week 10 a.m.-1 p.m. / 3 p.m.-6 p.m.

Summer, from 1st April to 30th September: all week 10 a.m.-1 p.m. / 4 p.m.-7 p.m.

Closed on Mondays

Entrance fee

No access

By arrangement

Guided tours

Furniture (15th C. inlaid chest; 16th C. astylar crosses), fittings and family relics. Antique weapons, coins, rare books and incunabula. 15th-19th C. paintings and sculptures (Family portraits, *Portrait of Joanna of Austria* attributed to Bronzino; *Madonna and Child with Saints* by M. di Giovanni, stolen; *Female Bust* alabaster tondo by G. Cozzarelli; *Battles* by the artist known as the Burgundian). Etruscan remains.

Raccolta d'Arte Sacra

53038 Staggia-Poggibonsi (SI)
Piazza Grazzini, 4
Tel. 0577/930901

Opened in 1976 this small parish collection is housed in one room nextdoor to the Parish Church. It displays ecclesiastical goldsmiths' work and ornaments and some paintings including *Mary Magdalen* by Antonio del Pollaiolo.
It can be visited by prior arrangement with the parish priest or by contacting the chemist's at Staggia.

Museo d'Arte Sacra

53037 San Gimignano (SI)
Piazza Pecori, 1
Tel. 0577/940316 (Parish Office)

Founded in 1915 and reorganized during the 1970's, the museum owned by the Opera della Collegiata is housed in a parish building which also houses the Etruscan museum.
It contains works of art and other material from the Duomo, from suppressed convents and minor churches in the area of San Gimignano.

Small

Winter, from 1st October to 31st March: all week 9.30 a.m.-12.30 p.m. / 3.30 p.m.-5.30 p.m.; closed on Mondays

Architectural fragments (capitals, columns, tomb slabs) from the 12th-16th C.

Sculptures in wood, marble and terracotta by Goro di Gregorio, F. di Valdambrino *(the Abbot St. Anthony)*, G. da Maiano, B. da Maiano (*Bust of Onofrio di Pietro* from 1493), P. Torrigiano.

Summer, from 1st April to 30th September: all week 9 a.m.-12.30 p.m. / 3 p.m.-5.30 p.m.

Entrance fee

Partially accessible

By arrangement

Ornaments, goldsmiths' work and fabrics from the 14th-19th C. (*frontal* with golden doves from 1449 from the altar of Santa Fina).

14th C. illuminated choirbooks by Niccolò di Ser Sozzo, Lippo Vanni and others.

E. Carli, J. Vichi Imberciadori, *San Gimignano*, Milan 1987

Museo Etrusco

53037 San Gimignano (SI)
Piazza Pecori
Tel. 0577/940316 (Parish Office)
Tel. 0577/940340 (Comune)

The museum displays grave-goods from excavations carried out in the local area in addition to a collection, formed at the beginning of the century, of pottery, bronzes and urns from the Hellenistic period. Opened in 1977 it is housed in a parish building owned by the Opera del Duomo which also houses the separately administrated Museum of Religious Art.

Small

Winter from 1st October to 31st March: 9.30 a.m.-12.30 p.m. / 3.30 p.m.-5.30 p.m.; closed on Mondays

Summer, from 1st April to 30th September: all week 9 a.m.-12.30 p.m. / 3 p.m.-5.30 p.m.

Entrance fee

No access

By arrangement

Guided tours for schools organized by the Siena local Council

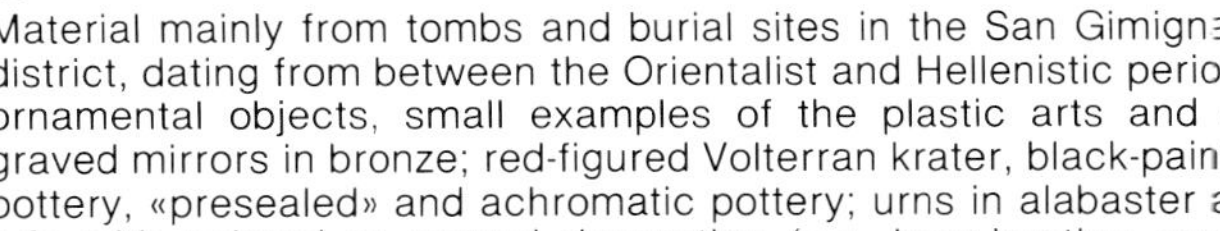

Material mainly from tombs and burial sites in the San Gimignano district, dating from between the Orientalist and Hellenistic periods: ornamental objects, small examples of the plastic arts and engraved mirrors in bronze; red-figured Volterran krater, black-painted pottery, «presealed» and achromatic pottery; urns in alabaster and tufa with painted or carved decoration (e.g. boar-hunting scene, Scylla). Amphoras, oil-lamps, glass, coins from the Roman period.

A. Ciacci, *Etruschi*, Siena n.d.

E. Carli, E. J. Vichi Imberciadori, *San Gimignano*, Milan 1987

Museo e Pinacoteca Civica

53037 San Gimignano (SI)
Piazza del Duomo
Tel. 0577/940340 (Comune)

The museum contains one of the most impressive and valuable collections in Tuscany of 13th-16th C. paintings of the Sienese and Florentine schools belonging to the old Museo Civico (founded in 1852) and to the Museo della Collegiata. It is housed in the Palazzo del Popolo which is also the seat of the Council. A comprehensive improvement programme is planned including a programme of restoration work and the creation of educational support apparatus.

Large

Winter, from 1st October to 31 March: all week 9.30 a.m.-12.30 p.m. / 2.30 p.m.-5.30 p.m.

Summer, from 1st April to 30th September: all week 9.30 a.m.-12.30 p.m. / 3.30 p.m.-6.30 p.m.

Closed on Mondays

Entrance fee

No access

By arrangement

Guided tours for schools by prior arrangement with the provincial council of Siena. Refresher courses for teachers arranged by the Società Storica della Valdelsa (San Gimignano section)

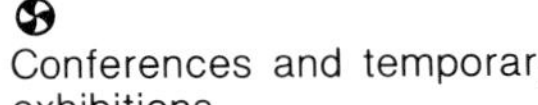
Conferences and temporary exhibitions

14th-16th C. architectural fragments. Furnishings and fittings from the 15th-16th C. (*bench-covers* attributed to Antonio and Bartolomeo da Colle). 14th-16th C. sculptures by Mariano d'Agnolo Romanelli *(Reliquary bust of St. Ursula)* and of the Tuscan school. 13th-16th C. paintings of the Sienese and Florentine schools including works by Coppo di Marcovaldo *(Cross with stories of the Passion)*, Guido da Siena *(Madonna and Child with angels and two worshippers)*, Memmo di Filippuccio, Niccolò di Ser Sozzo, Taddeo di Bartolo, P. Fiorentino, B. Gozzoli, Domenico di Michelino, Filippino Lippi (*The Virgin Mary and heralding Angel* from 1483), Pinturicchio (*Madonna in Glory and Saints Gregory and Benedict* from 1512).

Cycle of paintings by Memmo di Filippuccio in the Sala del Podestà. *Maestà* (1317) by Lippo Memmi in the Sala di Dante.

E. Carli, J. Vichi Imberciadori, *San Gimignano*, Milan 1987

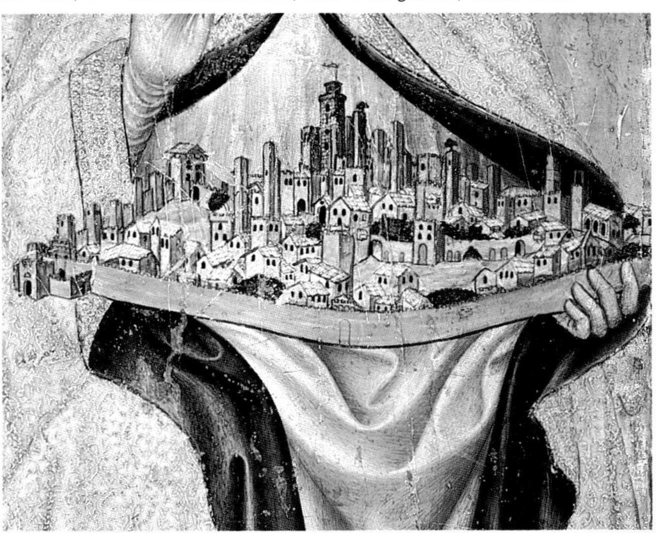

Taddeo di Bartolo: San Gimignano, detail

Spezieria di Santa Fina

53037 San Gimignano (SI)
Chiesa di San Lorenzo al Ponte
Tel. 0577/941269 (Library)

Summer, from 1st March to 30th November: 9.30 a.m.-12.30 p.m. / 3.30 p.m.-6.30 p.m.
Closed during the winter

Entrance fee

Accessible

This Council-owned museum contains a very fine and unusual collection of majolica and glass dating from the 15th-18th C. originally in the Apothecary of the old Spedale di Santa Fina in San Gimignano (founded in 1253). The collection is supplemented by some very interesting documentary material, the fruit of long and intensive research carried out by a team of experts. Opened in 1981 as a temporary exhibition («A pre-industrial pharmacy in Val d'Elsa») at the San Gimignano Museum it was subsequently transferred to the Church of San Lorenzo al Ponte and permanently opened to the public.

Una farmacia preindustriale in Valdelsa. La speziera e lo Spedale di Santa Fina nella città di San Gimignano secc. XIV-XVIII, exhibition catalogue, edited by G. Vannini, San Gimignano 1981

By arrangement

Sala d'Arte

53020 San Giovanni d'Asso (SI)
Piazza Vittorio Emanuele II
Tel. 0577/823110

Opened in 1981 in the chapel adjoining the Church of San Giovanni Battista the museum contains a small collection of 14th-17th C. paintings on wood and canvas and 16th-19th C. ecclesiastical ornaments and goldsmiths' work. It can be visited by prior arrangement.

Collezione Chigi-Saracini

Fondazione Accademia Musicale Chigiana
53100 Siena
Via di Città, 89
Tel. 0577/46152
Tel. 0577/294701 (Monte dei Paschi di Siena)

For its richness and comprehensiveness this can surely be considered one of the most important Italian and foreign collections; it contains fine 13th-17th C. paintings mainly by Sienese artists, a notable group of sculptures, archaeological remains, drawings, prints and fine pieces of furniture. It was started by the Sienese patrician Galgano Saracini between the end of the 18th C. and the early 19th C. with acquisitions largely carried out following the grand-ducal suppressions of religious communities. It is still today

Sassetta: Adoration of the Magi

Medium

Open to scholars by prior arrangement

Free

No access

No

Annual organization of exhibitions devoted to parts of the collection

housed in its original magnificent home, furnished and laid out in the style typical of late 18th C. picture galleries, enhanced with other objects of various types and styles. It was acquired in the 1950's by the Monte dei Paschi di Siena Bank with the aim of ensuring its survival and the possibilities for the public to enjoy it.

13th-17th C. Sienese painting: works by Sassetta *(Adoration of the Magi, St. Martin)*, Maestro dell'Osservanza, Sano di Pietro, Sodoma *(Adoration of the Child)*, Riccio, Brescianino *(Madonna and Child, St. Sebastian, Crucifixion with Saints)*, D. Beccafumi *(St. Anne, the Madonna and Child, Mystic Marriage, Madonna and Child)*, R. Manetti *(Pietà, Susanna in the bath, Concerto, Players)*, B. Mei *(Bethsabea, Judgement of Solomon)*. Also, from the 19th C., paintings by A. Cassioli and C. Maccari. Section of majolica (from Faenza, Deruta, Urbino, S. Quirico) and of terracotta sculpture by F. di Giorgio Martini, the Mazzuolis and G. L. Bernini.

M. Salmi, *Il Palazzo e la Collezione Chigi-Saracini*, Siena 1967

L. Bellosi, A. Angelini, *Sassetta e i pittori toscani tra XII-XV secolo*, Florence 1986

F. Bisogni, M. Ciampolini, *Bernardino Mei e la pittura barocca e Siena*, Florence 1987

Cripta delle Statue

53100 Siena
Scale di San Giovanni
Tel. 0577/283048 (Direzione dell'Opera della Metropolitana)

Opened to the public in June 1987 the Statue Crypt contains a large number of statues from the 13th-17th C. from the facade of the Duomo and 13th C. frescoes attributed to Guido da Siena. In the crypt are also displayed the *Storied Column* by Giovanni Pisano and his school, and the marble group by Giovanni d'Agostino from the side doorway of the new Duomo.

E. Carli, *Il Duomo di Siena*, Genoa 1979

Small

Summer, from 1st April to 31st October: all week 9.30 a.m.-1 p.m. / 3 p.m.-6 p.m.

Closed during the winter

Entrance fee

No access

By arrangement

Statue Crypt

Libreria Piccolomini

53100 Siena
Duomo di Siena
Piazza del Duomo
Tel. 0577/283048 (Opera della Metropolitana)

Medium

Winter, from 1st November to 14th March: all week 10 a.m.-1 p.m. / 2.30 p.m.-5 p.m.

Summer, from 15th March to 31st October: all week 9 a.m.-7.30 p.m.

Entrance fee

No access

By arrangement

This is a large rectangular room (reached from inside the Cathedral) commissioned by the Cardinal Francesco Piccolomini to house the precious library formerly belonging to his uncle Pius II. It is managed by the Museo dell'Opera.

In the centre of the room, marble group of the *Three Graces*, a Roman copy of a Greek original.

On the walls a cycle of frescoes by Pinturicchio with *Scenes from the life of Pius II* (1502-1509). Late 15th C. carved benches.

Illuminated manuscripts by Girolamo da Cremona, Liberale da Verona, Sano di Pietro, Benvenuto di Giovanni, G. Cozzarelli.

E. Carli, *Il Museo dell'Opera e Libreria Piccolomini*, Siena 1945

P. Misciatelli, *La Libreria Piccolomini del Duomo di Siena*, Siena 1968

Pinturicchio: Scenes from the life of Pius II

P. Scarpellini, *Pinturicchio. Libreria Piccolomini*, Milan 1968
M.G. Ciardi Duprè, *I corali del Duomo di Siena*, Milan 1972
E. Carli, *Il Duomo di Siena*, Genoa 1979

Museo dell'Accademia dei Fisiocritici, Zoologico, Geomineralogico e Paleontologico

53100 Siena
Piazza Sant'Agostino, 4
Tel. 0577/47002

The museum contains the most substantial group of the Sienese scientific collections. It is housed at the Accademia dei Fisiocritici (in the former monastery of the Camaldolites) an institution founded in 1691 by Pirro Maria Gabrielli of Siena. It comprises two distinct collections: a Geomineralogical Museum made up mainly of private donations with a rich collection of mineral, rock and fossil samples mainly from Siena and the surrounding region; a Zoological Museum founded in 1759 by G. Baldassarri, important for its collections of molluscs, birds, reptiles and animals from Maremma.

Medium

Weekdays 9 a.m.-1 p.m. / 3 p.m.-6 p.m., closed on Thursday afternoons, Saturdays and Sundays

Free

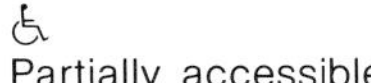
Partially accessible

By arrangement

Library open for consultation during the museum opening hours

Zoological section: with specimens of all the important classes of animals; birds (Ricasoli and Dei collection); a particularly interesting skeleton of *Balaenontera physalus*.

Geomineralogical section: minerals and rocks mainly from the regional territory; meteorite samples from the collection of the Academician A. Soldani (1974).

Paleontological section: Paleozoic, Mesozoic, Cenzoic and Neozoic fossils.

Collection of foraminiferous preparations of the Abbot A. Soldani.

Collection of over 1800 terracotta models of fungi from the first half of the 19th C. (Valenti-Serini).

Atti dell'Accademia delle Scienze di Siena detta dei Fisiocritici, published annually by the Academy

Museo Archeologico Nazionale

53100 Siena
Spedale di Santa Maria della Scala
Piazza Duomo

Founded in 1933 as a Council-owned Antiquarium and subsequently passed to the State and reorganized in 1941, the museum documents the evolution of civilization in the territory of Siena from the Prehistoric to Roman periods. The material has been expanded considerably by the acquisition of noble collections originally preserved at Castelluccio di Pienza (Mieli), Chiusi (Bonci Casuccini), Sarteano (Bargagli Petrucci) and Siena (Chigi Zondadari). It has been further supplemented by donations and smaller acquisitions, excavations and discoveries within the city (including at Campansi, Coroncina, Porta San Marco) and in the surrounding area (at Grotti, Guistrigona, Vescovado di Murlo, Monteriggioni, Castelnuovo Berardenga). The museum which is currently being transferred from its original home is temporarily closed to the public.

Pre- and Protohistoric antiquities from the province of Siena. Impasto pottery (bone-jars and cinerary urns, canopic vases — one

example is exhibited together with the rest of the grave-goods to which it belonged, found in a tomb in the area of Chiusi); bucchero; Attic pottery (of note, a *black-figured amphora*, from Monteriggioni decorated with a departure scene); Etrusco-Corinthian, red-figured and over-painted Etruscan pottery (a fine krater with decoration probably representing the death of Aegisthus); Apulian, Campanian, red-figured Italiot and black-painted pottery. Hellenistic and Imperial oil-lamps. Weapons, utensils and ornaments in metal (fine clasps with embossed decoration of wrestling scenes). Bronze statuettes from the Archaic to Roman periods. Funerary cippi from Chiusi. Urns from the tomb of the *Cumere* family and with inscriptions referring to members of the *Spiu* family. 1st C. A.D. stelae of the praetorian L. Avaenius Paser. Sarcophagus front with hunting scenes, 3rd-4th C. A.D. Etruscan antefixes in terracotta in the form of women's heads and lions; votive heads of southern production; antefixes in the form of Gorgon heads and sconces of Tarentine and Campanian production (6th-4th C. B.C.) and fragments of tiles from Campana from the Chigi collection. Jewellery, including a gold fibula from the Orientalist period and earrings from tombs in S. Colomba, Guistrigona, Vescovado di Murlo, Querceto di Caso e. Selection of coins from centres in northern Etruria and from Italic mints, Republican and Imperial coins. Egyptian china amulets, statuettes of divinities in basalt and in bronze.

A. Ciacci, *Etruschi*, E.P.T. (Provincial Board for the Promotion of Tourism), Siena s.d.

E. Mangani, *I centri archeologici della provincia di Siena*, Siena 1986

L. Cimino, *La collezione Mieli nel Museo archeologico di Siena*, Rome 1986

Museo Aurelio Castelli

53100 Siena
Basilica dell'Osservanza
Via Osservanza, 7
Tel. 0577/280250

Small

By arrangement

Free

Accessible

By arrangement

The museum is housed in the convent of the Observants adjacent to the Basilica (built between 1474 and 1490). Dedicated to the memory of the Franciscan Father Aurelio Castelli (1825-1880) it was opened in 1920 and subsequently rebuilt following serious damage suffered during the last war. It contains the works of art and church ornaments owned by the convent: sculptures, paintings, prints, hangings and a group of seventeen precious parchment manuscripts from the 15th C.

15th-18th C. paintings (*Universal Judgement*, detached fresco by Girolamo di Benvenuto). 17th and 18th C. prints.

14th and 15th C. sculptures in wood, marble and terracotta (fragment of wooden *Crucifix* by Lando di Pietro from 1337; *St. Anthony* and *St. Jerome* by G. Cozzarelli; cover from the *tomb of Niccolò Piccolomini* by a follower of A. Federighi from 1467).

16th-18th C. religious hangings.

Illuminated manuscripts, mainly 15th C., attributed to Frà Giovanni da Siena, Frà Iacopo di Filippo Torelli, Francesco di Giorgio Martini.

P.M. Bertagna, *L'Osservanza di Siena. Cenni storici e guida*, Siena s.d.

Museo Civico

53100 Siena
Piazza del Campo, 1
Tel. 0577/292263

Large

Winter from 1st November to 31st March: all week 9 a.m.-1.30 p.m.

Summer from 1st April to 31st October: weekdays 9.30 a.m.-7.30 p.m.,
Sundays and public holidays 9.30 a.m.-1.30 p.m.

Entrance fee

Accessible

By arrangement

Guided tours organized by the education section of the Soprintendenza per i beni artistici e storici di Siena (50577/41246)

Exhibitions, meetings and series of conferences

Housed in the magnificaent Palazzo Pubblico of Siena (14th C.) the museum is decorated with important series of frescoes of international reknown (such as the *Maestà* by Simone Martini and *Good and Bad Government* by Ambrogio Lorenzetti) produced between the 14th and 19th C. It contains various groups of works of art (goldsmiths' work; paintings, sculptures and ceramics) from various sources; these include works produced for the Palazzo or acquired by the Council, treasures from religious organizations suppressed during the 18th and 19th C. and donations (including the important Spannocchi collection). In the inner rooms of the courtyard of the Podestà the Picture Gallery has been newly set up with 13th-19th C. paintings. On the top floor, in the loggia overlooking Piazza del Mercato, are the original marble sculptures from the Fonte Gaia by Jacopo della Quercia.

14th-18th C. Sienese ceramics.

Italian and foreign paintings from the 16th-18th C. by Bamboccio, F. Napoletano, B. Strozzi, M. Preti, F. Curradi; 13th and 14th C. paintings on wood of the Sienese school by Guido da Siena, Niccolò

Ambrogio Lorenzetti: Good Government in the country, detail

di Ser Sozzo, Sano di Pietro, Matteo di Giovanni, Sodoma; also, again of the local school, works on canvas by Riccio, A. Casolani, F. Vanni, V. Salimbeni, R. Manetti,, S. Folli, G.N. Nasini.

14th and 15th C. sculpture in wood and marble (reliefs and figures from the *Fonte Gaia* by J. della Quercia from 1408; wooden *Choir* in the Chapel with carvings and inlays by Domenico di Niccolò dei Cori, from 1415-28).

12th-18th C. Sienese and French goldsmiths' work.

Series of frescoes in the rooms from the 14th-16th C. (*Maestà* by S. Martini from 1315; *Guidoriccio da Fogliano* traditionally attributed to S. Martini; *Good Government and Bad Government* by A. Lorenzetti; *Life and Exploits of Alexander II* by S. Aretino and Parri di Spinello; *Incidents of Civic Virtue* by D. Beccafumi; *Series of eminent people* and *Stories of the Virgin Mary* by Taddeo di Bartolo; *Figures of Saints and Blessed Souls* by Vecchietta, Sano di Pietro, Sodoma). 19th C. frescoes, paintings and sculptures.

Guida al Museo civico di Siena, edited by F. Bisogni and M. Ciampolini, Siena 1985

A. Cairola, *Il Palazzo pubblico di Siena*, Florence 1985

Museo dell'Opera della Metropolitana

53100 Siena
Piazza del Duomo, 8
Tel. 0577/283048

Large

Duccio: Maestà

This important museum founded in 1870 contains objects and works of art coming mainly from the Cathedral and Baptistery complex, the Oratorio dei Santi Giovannino e Gennaro and from the Oratorio di San Giovanni Battista della Morte, and acts as a supplement to a knowledge of the artistic and historical background of these buildings. Among the many groups of material displayed (sculptures, paintings, goldsmiths' work, illuminated manuscripts and hangings), international fame is brought by artists such as Giovanni Pisano, Pietro Lorenzetti, Jacopo della Quercia and Duccio di Buoninsegna (the celebrated *Maestà*). It is housed in rooms obtained by the closure of a part of the right aisle of the so-called «New Duomo» whose construction, begun in 1339, was suspended in 1348. It has been renovated and enlarged many times over the

Winter, from 1st November to 14th March: all week 9 a.m.-1.30 p.m.

Summer, from 15th March to 31st October: all week 9 a.m.-7.30 p.m.

Entrance fee

No access

By arrangement

Historical archive of the Opera della Metropolitana open to the public on Tuesdays, Wednesdays and Fridays from 10 a.m.-noon

centuries.From within the museum one can also reach the top of the Cathedral's façade from where there is a magnificant panoramic view of the city.

Sculptures by G. Pisano from the façade of the duomo (10 statues including *Maria di Mosé, Moses, Isaiah, David*, dating from 1284-1296). Sculptures in wood by G. Pisano (*Crucifix*), F. di Valdambrino, J. della Quercia.

12th-17th C. paintings of the Sienese school (Duccio di Buoninsegna, *Maestà*, and *Madonna 'di Crevole'*; P. Lorenzetti, *Birth of the Virgin Mary* from 1342; also works by A. Lorenzetti, G. di Paolo, Matteo di Giovanni, Sassetta, Sano di Pietro, Beccafumi, Sodoma, Pomarancio and others). Liturgical ornaments, goldsmiths' work and hangings and vestments from the 13th-19th C. (*Reliquary of the head of St. Galgano* in gilded silver, filigree and enamel, from the end of the 13th C.).

E. Carli, *Il Museo dell'Opera e Libreria Piccolomini*, Siena 1945

E. Carli, *Il Duomo di Siena*, Genoa 1979

Museo della Società di Esecutori di Pie Disposizioni

53100 Siena
Via Roma, 71
Tel. 0577/220400

The museum's original collection has been constantly expanded by bequests and donations to the Society, one of the oldest and most prestigious lay confraternities of Siena. Suppressed by Pietro Leopoldo in 1785, it was subsequently refounded and continued its work of charity, welfare and support and promotion of study and culture. Transferred in 1915 to its present home in Via Roma, the museum was opened in 1938 in rooms of the former convent of Santa Maria degli Angeli, known as 'del Santuccio'. It displays a fine collection of works spanning several centuries and constitutes an important step towards a knowledge of Sienese painting.

Girolamo di Benvenuto: St. Catherine of Siena leads the Pope to Rome

Small

By arrangement on weekdays from 9 a.m.-noon

Free

No access

By arrangement

13th-17th C. paintings of the Sienese school from the Company of Flagellants: works by an artist close to Duccio di Buoninsegra (*Cross* and *Triptych of the Passion*), Niccolò di Ser Sozzo, Andrea Vanni, Martino di Bartolomeo, Sano di Pietro, Girolamo di Benvenuto (semi-circular painting on wood depicting *St. Catherine of Siena leading the Pope to Rome*), G. Cozzarelli, Sodoma (*Holy Family with the Infant St. John*), R. Manetti (frescoes depicting *St. Cecilia* and *St. Agnes* from 1610).

Museo delle Tavolette Dipinte

53100 Siena
Archivio di Stato
Via Banchi di Sotto, 52
Tel. 0577/41271

Housed in rooms at the State Archive this collection, unique in the world, comprises the Biccherna and Gabella Tablets in painted wood, used as covers for the registers of the ancient magistracy of Siena.
The museum also contains important documents and illuminated manuscripts.

Small

Weekdays 9 a.m.-1 p.m.; closed on Sundays

Free

No access

No

Guided tour on request

Library and microfilm store open to scholars during the museum opening hours

107 Biccherna tablets by various artists including A. Lorenzetti, Sano di Pietro, Francesco di Giorgio Martini, Benvenuto di Giovanni, Neroccio di Bartolommeo, D. Beccafumi.

17th C. Sienese paintings including works by R. Manetti, B. Mei, F. Vanni.

Various documents from the State Archive.

Illuminated manuscripts.

Le Biccherne. Tavolette dipinte delle magistrature senesi, by various authors, Rome 1984

Biccherna Tablet, Francesco di Giorgio Martini: The Virgin Mary protects Siena during the earthquakes

Orto Botanico di Siena

53100 Siena
Dipartimento dell'Università di Siena
Via P.A. Mattioli, 4
Tel. 0577/298000

Large

Weekdays 8 a.m.-1 p.m. / 3 p.m.-5 p.m.; closed on Saturday afternoons and Sundays

Free

Accessible

Yes

Guided tours for schools by arrangement

The Department's library open for consultation by prior arrangement

Founded in 1784 by Biagio Bartalini on the site of an existing Giardino dei Semplici attached to the Spedale di Santa Maria della Scala, the garden was transferred in 1856 to its present site, adjacent to the Accademia dei Fisiocritici. The Orto stretches over an area of about five acres in a position which is particularly favourable for growing species with different climatic demands, from the dwarf palm (Chamaerops humils L.) to mountain plants (beech, Fagus sylvatica L. and Abies alba L.). The garden contains glasshouses and areas for rare plants, all in particularly suggestive settings. Annexed to the Orto is a herbarium with about fifty thousand specimens mainly from central-southern Tuscany.

«School section» with herbaceous plants and small shrubs.

Tree and shrub essences of wild species indigenous to southern Tuscany. Acquatic and hygrophilic plants. Fruit-bearing plants.

Hothouse: plants from equatorial climates such as Aracea, Bromeliacea, Ferns and Orchids. Glasshouse with a collection of succulent plants from hot and arid climates grown in soil; many varieties of Cactus and agave in the American section, and various types of Aloa and Euphorbia in the African section.

A. Nannizzi, *Piante grasse coltivate nell'Orto botanico di Siena*, in *Boll. del lab. ed O.B. di Siena*, Siena 3, II, 1900, pp. 70-76

A. Tassi, *L'Orto e il gabinetto botanico nell'anno 1903, in Boll. del lab. ed O.B. di Siena*, Siena I-IV, 1904, pp. 54-159

A. Tassi, *L'Orto e il gabinetto botanico nell'anno 1904*, in *Boll. del lab. ed O.B. di Siena*, Siena I-IV, 1905, pp. 112-118

A. Nannizzi, *Le piante officinali coltivate nell'Orto botanico della R. Università di Siena*, in *Atti della R. Acc. dei Fisiocr. di Siena* — Agr. sect., 4 (III), 1937, pp. 89-96

E. Maugini, *L'Orto Botanico di Siena*, in *Agricoltura*, 7, 1963

Pinacoteca Nazionale

53100 Siena
Via San Pietro, 29
Tel. 0577/281161

Large

Weekdays 8.30 a.m.-7 p.m., Sundays and public holidays 8.30 a.m.-1 p.m.; Closed on Mondays

Entrance fee

Accessible

By arrangement

Previously attached to the provincial Institute of Fine Arts of Siena the Gallery's origins go back to an initial group of paintings collected by the abbot Giuseppe Ciaccheri at the end of the 18th C. Expanded considerably by further groups of works from the religious suppressions, from donations, loans and acquisitions, the museum passed to the State in 1929 and was opened to the public in 1932. It boasts today a very fine collection, fundamental for a knowledge of Sienese art from the 13th-17th C., with masterpieces by all the leading artists. It is housed in the old Buonsignori and Brigidi Palazzos, with over 21,500 sq. ft. of exhibition space on three floors. In recent years it has been the subject of rebuilding and partial renovation work. There is an educational section.

12th-17th C. paintings of the Sienese school: works by Guido da Siena, Duccio di Buoninsegna (*Madonna 'dei Francescani'*), the Maestro di Badia a Isola, Ugolino di Nerio, Segna di Buonaventura, S. Martini (*Madonna and Child*), Lippo Memmi, P. Lorenzetti (the *'Carmine' altar-piece*), A. Lorenzetti (*Small Maestà, Annunciation*), Niccolò di Ser Sozzo, Bartolo di Fredi, Taddeo di Bartolo, Giovanni di Paolo (*Polyptych of St. Galgano, Madonna 'dell'Umiltà', Presentation at the Temple, Maestà*), Sassetta (fragments of the *'Art of wool-*

The education section of the Soprintendenza per i beni artistici e storici organizes occasional meetings for schools and the elderly on subjects chosen annually

Biennial exhibitions on specific themes relating to the restoration of works of art

making' altar-piece), Sano di Pietro, Francesco di Giorgio Martini, Vecchietta, Matteo di Giovanni, Neroccio di Bartolomeo Landi, Pacchiarotti, Riccio, Sodoma (*Deposition*), D. Beccafumi (*St. Catherine's stigmata, Birth of the Virgin Mary, Triptych of the Trinity, St. Michael drives out the rebel angels*), V. Salimbeni, B. Mei, R. Manetti.

14th-15th C. sculptures (J. della Quercia, *Annunciation*).

Spannocchi Collection with 16th and 18th C. paintings mainly of North European and Flemish schools. 16th-18th C. drawings (open to visits by prior arrangement).

C. Brandi, *La Regia Pinacoteca di Siena*, Rome 1933

E. Carli, *Guida alla Pinacoteca di Siena*, Milan 1958

P. Torriti, *La Pinacoteca Nazionale di Siena*, Genoa 1977-78

M. Torriti, *La Pinacoteca Nazionale di Siena*, Genoa 1987

Pietro Lorenzetti: Madonna and Child between St. Nicholas of Bari and the prophet Elijah

Duccio di Buoninsegna: Madonna 'dei Francescani'

Raccolta Bologna Buonsignori

53100 Siena
Via Roma, 50
Tel. 0577/220400 (Società di Esecutori di Pie Disposizioni)

This is a huge collection of furniture, arms and armour, porcelain, glass, bronzes and jewels donated by the Bologna Buonsignori family of Montepulciano to the Società di Esecutori di Pie Disposizioni. Opened to the public in 1983, the arrangement of the works faithfully preserves the character of a 19th C. private collection.

Small

By arrangement on weekdays from 9 a.m.-noon

Free

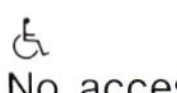
No access

By arrangement

Archaeological collection (pottery, small urns, votive material, bronzes from the Etruscan period).

15th-20th C. paintings on wood and canvas.

20th C. drawings.

Furniture.

Examples of the decorative arts: bronzes, ivories, silver, glass, goldsmiths' work, arms, coins and medals.

Italian and Eastern ceramics.

Raccolta della Sede Storica

53100 Siena
Monte dei Paschi di Siena
Piazza Salimbeni, 3
Tel. 0577/294701

Medium

By prior arrangement from Monday to Friday 8.30 a.m.-1 p.m. / 3 p.m.-5 p.m.

Free

No access

No

Guided tour by arrangement (tel. 0577/294798-204463)

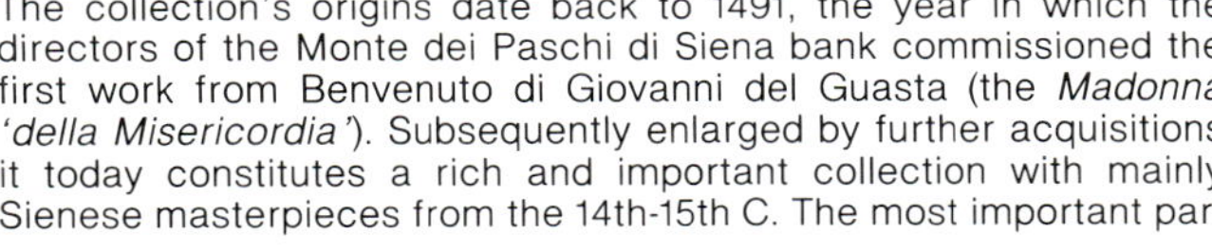
The collection's origins date back to 1491, the year in which the directors of the Monte dei Paschi di Siena bank commissioned the first work from Benvenuto di Giovanni del Guasta (the *Madonna 'della Misericordia'*). Subsequently enlarged by further acquisitions it today constitutes a rich and important collection with mainly Sienese masterpieces from the 14th-15th C. The most important part

Giovanni di Paolo: Madonna and Child

of the collection is housed within the bank, in the rooms of the former Church of San Donato (whose origins date back to 795) acquired by Monte dei Paschi in the early years of the 20th C. and renovated during the 1970's.

Collection of works (paintings and sculptures) by almost all of the Sienese school from the 14th-17th C.; the artists include the Maestro di Panzano, P. Lorenzetti (*Crucifixion*), Domenico di Niccolò dei Cori (*St. Francis*), Giovanni di Paolo, Sano di Pietro, Benvenuto di Giovanni, Sassetta (*St. Anthony the abbot*), A. Rossellino (*Madonna and Child with the Infant St. John*), D. Beccafumi (*St. Lucy*), Brescianino, L. Rustici (*Pietà*), Rustichino, V. Salimbeni, F. Vanni (*Joseph in Egypt*), R. Manetti (*St. Jerome comforted by the angels, Christ and Mary Magdalen*), B. Mei (*Elixir of love, the doctor Herosistratus discovers the cause of Antiochus's illness*).

Collection of 240 woodcuts by L. Viani.

Deposito Organizzato sul Lavoro Contadino

53018 Sovicille (SI)
Palazzo al Piano
Tel. 0577/345559-937008

Small

Friday, Saturday and Sunday by arrangement

Free

Accessible

By arrangement

Opened in 1984 on the initiative of Cedlac (the Provincial Information Centre on Peasant Work) the museum comprises material on the traditional agricultural implements and techniques in the territory of Siena. The display which is suitably supplemented by educational support material comprises a group of work tools and a visit to agricultural buildings, previously given over to particular types of work.

Transport workshop: material regarding the different means of transport (by hand, towing, animal power). Section devoted to domestic activities, furniture and objects of everyday use in the peasant's home. Section devoted to the annual agricultural cycle.

Old animal-driven oil-mill, complete with hand press, containers for the clarification of oil, the channelling of the liquids and the milling residue. Electrical oil-mill, complete apparatus for oil-milling.

G. Molteni, *Il deposito organizzato*, Siena 1984

G. Molteni, *Il vecchio frantoio*, Siena 1986

Museum index

Provincia di Arezzo

Provincia di Firenze

Provincia di Pistoia

Provincia di Siena

Provincia di Arezzo

Anghiari
Buses: BASCHETTI, CAT

Arezzo
FS: Arezzo station
Buses: BASCHETTI, CAT, FABBRI, LAZZI, LFI, SITA

Caprese Michelangelo
Buses: BASCHETTI, CAT, LFI

Castiglion Fiorentino
FS: Castiglion Fiorentino station
Buses: LFI

Cortona e Cortona/Farneta
FS: Cortona-Camucia station
Buses: LFI

Lucignano
FS: stazioni di Lucignano-Marciano and Monte San Savino station
Buses: LFI

Montevarchi
FS: Montevarchi station
Buses: CAT, FABBRI, LAZZI, LFI, MADDII, SITA

Poppi/Badia Prataglia e Poppi/Camaldoli
Buses: LFI

Sansepolcro
Ferrovia centrale Umbra: Sansepolcro station
Buses: BASCHETTI, CAT

Sestino
Buses: BASCHETTI, CAT

Stia/Porciano
Buses: LFI

Provincia di Firenze

Calenzano
FS: Calenzano station
Buses: ATAF, CAP, LAZZI, SITA

Carmignano/Artimino
Buses: CAP

Castelfiorentino
FS: Castelfiorentino station
Buses: SITA

Cerreto Guidi
Buses: COPIT, LAZZI

Certaldo
FS: Certaldo station
Buses: SITA, TRAIN

Empoli
FS: Empoli station
Buses: APT, COPIT, LAZZI, SEQUI, SITA

Fiesole
Buses: ATAF

Figline Valdarno
FS: Figline Valdarno station
Buses: ALA, CAT, LAZZI, MADDII, SITA

Firenze
FS: Firenze station

Buses: ALTERINI, ATAF, CAP, CAT, CLAP, COPIT, LAZZI, LFI, RAMA, TRAIN, SEQUI, SITA

Lastra a Signa
Buses: CAP, LAZZI, SEQUI

Montaione
Buses: RENIERI, SITA

Montelupo Fiorentino
FS: Montelupo Capraia station
Buses: LAZZI, SEQUI, SITA

Palazzuolo sul Senio
Buses: CAP

Poggio a Caiano
Buses: CAP, COPIT

Prato
FS: Prato station
Buses: CAP, LAZZI

Prato/Galceti
Buses: CAP

Rufina
Buses: MAGHERINI, SITA

Sesto Fiorentino
FS: Sesto Fiorentino station
Buses: ATAF, CAP, LAZZI, SITA

Vicchio
Buses: SITA

Vinci
Buses: COPIT

Provincia di Grosseto

FS: Grosseto station
Buses: RAMA, TRAIN

Manciano
Buses: RAMA

Massa Marittima
FS: Follonica station, bus service Follonica-Massa Marittima
Buses: ATM, GUERRINI, RAMA, TRAIN

Roccalbegna
Buses: RAMA, RICCHI

Scansano
Buses: RAMA

Provincia di Livorno

Castagneto Carducci
FS: Castagneto Carducci-Donoratico station
Buses: ATL, ATM

Castagneto Carducci-Bolgheri
Buses: ATL

Cecina/San Pietro in Palazzi
FS: Cecina station
Buses: ATL, ATM, APT

Livorno
FS: Livorno station
Buses: ATL, APT, LAZZI

Livorno/Montenero
FS: Livorno station
Buses: ATL

Marciana
FS: Piombino marittima station. From Piombino to Elba there are the following ferry services: TOREMAR, NAVARMA; from Livorno TOREMAR
Bus service on island: ATL

Portoferraio
FS: Piombino marittima station. From Piombino to Elba there are the following ferry services: TOREMAR, NAVARMA; from Livorno TOREMAR
Bus service on island: ATL

Rio Marina
FS: Piombino marittima station. From Piombino to Elba there are the following ferry services: TOREMAR, NAVARMA; from Livorno TOREMAR
Bus service on island: ATL

Rosignano Marittimo
FS: Rosignano station
Buses: ATL

Provincia di Lucca

Barga/Castelvecchio Pascoli
FS: Castelvecchio station
Buses: CLAP

Camaiore
Buses: LAZZI

Camporgiano
FS: Camporgiano station
Buses: CLAP

Castelnuovo Garfagnana
Buses: CLAP

Castiglione Garfagnana/San Pellegrino in Alpe
Buses: CLAP

Coreglia Antelminelli
FS: Coreglia-Ghivizzano station
Buses: CLAP

Lucca
FS: Lucca station
Buses: CLAP, DONATI, LAZZI

Massarosa/Quiesa
FS: Massarosa station
Buses: CLAP

Pescaglia/Celle dei Puccini
Buses: CLAP

Pietrasanta
FS: Pietrasanta station
Buses: CLAP

Pietrasanta/Valdicastello Carducci
Buses: CLAP

Porcari
FS: Porcari station
Buses: CLAP

Viareggio
FS: Viareggio station

Buses: LAZZI, CLAP

Viareggio/Torre del Lago Puccini
FS: Torre del Lago Puccini station
Buses: LAZZI, MASSEI

Provincia di Massa

Aulla
FS: Aulla station
Buses: CAT

Carrara
FS: Carrara station
Buses: CAT, LORENZINI

Casola Lunigiana
FS: Casola station
Buses: CAT

Massa
FS: Massa centro station
Buses: CAT

Pontremoli
FS: Pontremoli station
Buses: CAT

Villafranca in Lunigiana
FS: Villafranca-Bagnone station
Buses: CAT

Provincia di Pisa

Calci
Buses: APT

Pisa
FS: Pisa centrale station
Buses: APT, ATL, LAZZI, MASSEI, SBRANA

Pomarance/Larderello
Buses: APT

San Miniato
FS: S. Miniato-Fucecchio station
Buses: APT, RENIERI, SEQUI

Santa Croce sull'Arno
Buses: APT, SEQUI

Volterra
FS: Saline di Volterra station, Bus service Saline di Volterra-Volterra
Buses: APT, SITA, TRAIN

Provincia di Pistoia

Abetone
Buses: COPIT, LAZZI

Borgo a Buggiano
FS: Borgo a Buggiano station
Buses: LAZZI

Buggiano
Buses: LAZZI

Cutigliano/Rivoreta
Buses: COPIT

Larciano
Buses: LAZZI

Monsummano Terme
Buses: LAZZI

Montecatini Terme
FS: Montecatini Terme station
Buses: COPIT, LAZZI

Pescia
FS: Pescia station
Buses: CLAP, COPIT, LAZZI

Pescia/Collodi
FS: Pescia station
Buses: CLAP, COPIT

Pistoia
FS: Pistoia station
Buses: COPIT, LAZZI

San Marcello/Gavinana
Buses: COPIT, LAZZI

Provincia di Siena

Asciano
FS: Asciano station
Buses: TRAIN

Buonconvento
FS: Buonconvento station
Buses: RAMA, TRAIN

Chianciano Terme
FS: Chianciano Terme-Chiusi station
Buses: LFI

Chiusi
FS: Chiusi-Chianciano Terme station
Buses: LFI

Montalcino
FS: Montalcino-Torrenieri station
Buses: TRAIN

Montepulciano
FS: Montepulciano station
Buses: LFI, TRAIN

Monteriggioni
Buses: TRAIN

Pienza
Buses: TRAIN

Poggibonsi/Staggia
FS: S. Gimignano-Poggibonsi station
Buses: TRAIN

San Gimignano
FS: S. Gimignano-Poggibonsi station
Buses: TRAIN

San Giovanni D'ASSO
FS: San Giovanni D'Asso station
Buses: TRAIN

Siena
FS: Siena station
Buses: LFI, RAMA, SITA, TRAIN

Buses: adresses

ALA	52026 Piandiscò (AR) Tel. 055/960006
ALTERINI	Via G. Monaco 1 - 50065 Reggello (FI) Tel. 055/869015
APT	Via C. Maffi - 56100 Pisa Tel. 050/501038
ATAF	Viale dei Mille 115 - 50131 Firenze Tel. 055/56501
ATL	Via C. Mayer 16 - 57100 Livorno Tel. 0565/807096
ATM	Corso Italia 53 - 57025 Piombino Tel 0565/37440
BASCHETTI	Viale Vittorio Veneto 28 - 52037 Sansepolcro (AR) Tel. 0575/76045
CAP	Piazza Duomo 18 - 50047 Prato (FI) Tel. 0574/20203
CAT	Zona Industriale Trieste - 52037 Sansepolcro (AR) Tel. 0575/8550322
CAT	Via Giovan Pietro 2 - 54031 Avenza (MS) Tel. 0585/57551
CLAP	Corte Campana 12 - 55100 Lucca Tel. 0583/584991
COPIT	Piazza San Francesco - 51100 Pistoia Tel. 0573/21170
DONATI	Via Serchio 16 - 55027 Gallicano (LU) Tel. 0583/74028
FABBRI	Via V. Aretina - 52020 Laterina (AR) Tel. 0575/89169
FMF	58024 Massa Marittima (GR) Tel. 0566/902016
GUERRINI	Via Milano - 58027 Ribolla (GR) Tel. 0564/579210-579601
LAZZI	Via Mercadante 2 - 50144 Firenze Tel. 055/363041
LFI	Via G. Monaco 37 - 52100 Arezzo Tel. 0575/23687
LORENZINI	Via Larga 85 - 19034 Ortonovo (SP) Tel. 0187/66805
MAGHERINI	Via Garibaldi 22 - 50068 Rufina (FI) Tel. 055/839264
MASSEI	Via Vespucci 114 - 56100 Pisa Tel. 050/41123
RAMA	Via Buozzi 4 - 58100 Grosseto Tel. 0564/25380
RENIERI	Via Poggio alla Terra 6 - 50050 Montaione (FI) Tel. 0571/69607
RICCHI	58027 Ribolla (GR) Tel. 0564/579214
SBRANA	Via A. Pisano 45 - 56100 Pisa Tel. 050/530404
SEQUI	Via San Tommaso 9 - 56029 S. Croce sull'Arno (PI) Tel. 0571/479966
SITA	Viale Cadorna 105 - 50129 Firenze Tel. 055/278611
TRAIN	Strada Statale 73 Levante, 19 - Località Due Ponti - 53100 Siena Tel. 0577/221221

241

(MI) Autori Vari
GUIDA AI MUSEI DELLA
TOSCANA
Ed. Inglese
ELEMOND S.r.l. Milano

Stampato per conto della Electa Spa
dalla Fantonigrafica di Venezia